CRAFTING
TRUTH

CRAFTING TRUTH

Documentary Form and Meaning

LOUISE SPENCE

AND VINICIUS NAVARRO

RUTGERS UNIVERSITY PRESS
NEW BRUNSWICK, NEW JERSEY, AND LONDON

Third paperback printing, 2015

Library of Congress Cataloging-in-Publication Data

Spence, Louise.
Crafting truth : documentary form and meaning / Louise Spence and Vinicius Navarro.
p. cm.
Includes bibliographical references and index.
ISBN 978–0–8135–4902–6 (hardcover : alk. paper)—ISBN 978–0–8135–4903–3 (pbk. : alk. paper)
1. Documentary films—History and criticism. 2. Documentary films—Production and direction.
I. Navarro, Vinicius, 1967–II. Title.
PN1995.9.D6S5955 2010
070.1'8—dc22
2010008406

A British Cataloging-in-Publication record for this book is available from the British Library.

Para Afonso e Lourdes,
and for Regina and Milton,
our first teachers

CONTENTS

ACKNOWLEDGMENTS

Writing acknowledgements is a most pleasurable, yet difficult, task. The thanks we owe to the people who assisted, encouraged, and endured us during the five years we were working on this project are enormous. It is clear that this book was built on the wisdom and generosity of many people, especially Karen Backstein, Lemi Baruh, Melis Behlil, Julie Par Cadenhead, Dino Capone, Yunsun Chae, Michael Chanan, Elizabeth Corbett, Alfredo Dias D'Almeida, Martin Duncan, Jayne Fargnoli, Joseph Goldberg, Frances Grodzinsky, Ahmet Gürata, Roger Hallas, Roald Hoffmann, Jeffrey Howlett, John L. Jackson Jr., Lynne Jackson, Aslı Kotaman, Alisa Lebow, Michael Nitsche, Augusta Palmer, Robert Sklar, Qi Wang, and Mark Wyers.

We are especially grateful to Hardy Griffin, whose keen interest in our project and insightful reading of the manuscript are unsurpassed, Doğa Aytuna (Mac expert extraordinaire), who facilitated the photos, and Carl Lewis, who came to our rescue with his attentive ear for music.

And we must also thank a slew of film and video makers who loaned us works and answered questions, among them Kamal Aljafari, Magnus Bärtås, Alan Berliner, Jean Carlomusto, Kavery Dutta, Connie Field, Richard Fung, Louis Massiah, Abraham Ravett, Larissa Sansour, and Jalal Toufic, and a whole mess of librarians who helped us to find material we were looking for, especially Didem Önal and Sachi Spohn. Thanks as well to Videofilmes, Zeitgeist Films, Documentary

Educational Resources, and Magnolia Pictures for granting us access to some of their titles.

At Rutgers University Press, we are obliged to Leslie Mitchner and her staff for a sensitive handling of both our proposal and our manuscript.

A warm thanks to those who have gone before us, who have taught us, and who have inspired our interest in documentary, especially Bill Nichols, Michael Renov, Brian Winston, Paul Arthur, and Erik Barnouw. We are also grateful for funding support from Kadir Has University. And we thank the *Journal of Popular Culture* for permission to reprint sections of "Working Class Hero: Michael Moore's Authorial Voice and Persona" (43.2, Spring 2010).

As always, Louise Spence must thank David Curtis for years of moral support and for helping her find her way as a writer. Vinicius Navarro would like to thank La Frances Hui for her patience and support at various stages of this project.

And most of all, we are indebted to our students. Their enthusiasms and resistances have forced us to shape and reshape many of our theories and much of our language. Without them, these words would never have been written.

CRAFTING
TRUTH

Introduction

On the fifteenth of November, 1897, at the opening of the Empire Palace Theatre on Dame Street, citizens of Dublin were treated to a program of films that Alexandre Promio, an itinerant cameraman and promoter for the Lumière brothers' Cinématographe, took and developed just days before. Arriving in Ireland from Liverpool, Promio filmed the Belfast docks, the Belfast Fire Brigade, Castle Place, and Queen's Bridge. He traveled to Dublin by train and filmed various places, ten scenes in all, along the way. Once in Dublin, as was his habit, he used the device to film ordinary people in the streets, his intended audience, in the morning, inviting them to come and see themselves on screen the next day. In Dublin he shot the Carlisle Bridge, Sackville Street, and a display by the Dublin Fire Brigade in Saint Stephen's Green with cheering onlookers. Promio and other Lumière operators demonstrated the triple-purpose apparatus (capable of filming, developing, and projecting) in more than thirty present-day countries, taking films of Belfast and Dublin; the new beach in Schwerin, Germany; St. Petersburg and Moscow, including the coronation of Tsar Nikolai II in May 1896; the waterfalls in Avesta, Sweden; a tennis game on the grass courts of Saltsjöbaden, the seaside resort near Stockholm; footage taken from a gondola in Venice; views of Berlin, Amsterdam, Warsaw, New York City, Chicago, Mexico City, Constantinople, Bombay, Sydney, Jerusalem . . . and exhibiting them throughout the world. By the end of 1897, after two years of promoting the Cinématographe abroad, the Lumière catalogue had swollen to 750 films, the great majority of them nonfiction subjects (Leyda 17–23; National Library of Ireland; O'Brien 21–24).

This desire to capture lived reality on film has animated the spirit of cinema since its earliest years. Although the term *documentary* was not standard back then, recording actual occurrences was a common practice in the medium's beginning, when nonfictional films outnumbered fictional narratives. Nowadays, of course, we think of documentaries not as simple records of reality but as complex and sophisticated pieces, which may inform, provoke, and even entertain the audience.

But how can we characterize a "documentary"? What are its most prominent features? How does it differ from a fiction film? It has always been easier to recognize a documentary than to define the term. John Grierson, a Scottish filmmaker, producer, and theorist, famously described documentary as the "creative treatment of actuality." If we follow his thinking, documentary would be distinguished from fiction by the requirement that it work with the real—"actuality." Yet, as Dirk Eitzen points out, it is not always easy to determine *what* constitutes "actuality" (82). "Actuality" is infinite and can never be wholly represented. Any representation is a selective view of the world. All representations of actuality must choose which aspects to include and which to leave out. Decisions are made to emphasize one element and to downplay others, to assert some truths and to ignore others. First the documentary maker has to determine what actuality is worth exploring. Then there are other questions. Which aspects are considered important and which are considered unnecessary? Whose viewpoint on that actuality will we be getting? What means will be used to express that viewpoint? This book will be arguing that because there is no value-neutral treatment of actuality, it is important for viewers and scholars to analyze how a documentarian, to paraphrase Hayden White, translates knowing into telling (1).

Therefore, what is at issue is not so much "Is it true or untrue?" but rather "How is actuality treated in order to sanction the documentary's claims to be telling the truth?" And "How does the need to tell an effective story or make an argument encourage one kind of treatment over another?" Yes, documentaries direct us to the world. But they are also texts. And as texts, they are constructions—the documentary maker's construction of reality. It might be better to think of documentaries, as scholar Stella Bruzzi has noted, as a "negotiation between filmmaker and reality" (186).

This book looks at the means by which those "constructions" take shape, how documentaries help us make sense of the world. We examine both the overall structures of the films and their specific visual and aural aspects—what the images "tell" us, how they are put together, the significance of a particular sound track, and so on. We also discuss some of the common expectations surrounding nonfiction filmmaking, such as the desire for authentic and ethical representations, or, from the documentarian's point of view, the need to speak with authority about the world represented. How do documentaries proclaim themselves authentic? How can you responsibly represent someone whose culture is far removed from your own? What formal devices help secure the authority and credibility of nonfiction films?

To deal with the formal aspects of nonfiction filmmaking is, of course, to address the issue of documentary aesthetics. Central as it is to nonfiction cinema, this issue has often proved somewhat elusive, in part because of conventional assumptions regarding the role of documentary representation. We do not normally look for artistic virtuosity when we watch a documentary but focus instead on the subject matter. As John Corner has put it, "An apparent absence of style . . . constitutes at least part of the conventional grounds of trust and credibility" (96). This particular view of nonfiction filmmaking can easily obstruct the discussion of form in documentary, or at least relegate it to a somewhat marginal corner in nonfiction film scholarship.

Contrary to this argument, this book shows that there is no intrinsic conflict between aesthetics and nonfictional representation. In fact, what we get to know about the world is directly connected to the way that world appears on the screen. The book also proposes that there is no inherent divide between aesthetics and politics in nonfiction filmmaking. Following Michael Renov, we suggest that attention to "rhetorical device and formal strategy" does not assume "disregard for historical or ideological determinants" (19). Every time a documentary takes a stance or puts forward an argument about a particular subject matter, it does so through the formal procedures available to the filmmaker. Moreover, as we will have opportunity to show later on, aesthetic innovation in documentary often serves a clear political purpose as it introduces an unfamiliar or unconventional way of looking at the world. This overall approach to nonfiction filmmaking inspires and underlies each individual chapter in this book, starting with the discussion of how filmmakers strive to secure a sense of authenticity in their films.

The contingency and unreliability of "the real" and the profusion of imaginative works "based on a true story" cause us to be wary of such easy distinctions as "true" and "untrue." Still, with some exceptions (*The Blair Witch Project*, for example) and despite the fact that nonfiction comes in many varieties—from video news releases by commercial businesses, community organizing groups, and nongovernmental organizations, to entertaining feature-length films—we seem to know when we are watching a nonfiction work. And we bring some expectations to that experience. One of those expectations is that it be credible. We want to believe it accurately reflects the sociohistorical world—even when we know that it must be contrived. Whether it is the story of a public official's unfortunate indictment or of wild animals greedy for human prey, a documentary is presumed to be truthful (Eitzen 88). Our first chapter, "Authenticity," looks at how and why this is so. What textual factors kindle the presumption of truth? What social and cultural factors? The chapter introduces many of the themes of the book, such as the concept of representation, authenticity, and the relationship of the photographic image to sociohistorical reality. It also introduces some of the basic concepts of semiotics, the study of signs, as it relates to nonfiction film and video.

We certainly are not arguing that we *should* believe documentaries, or that they *do* tell the truth. Nor are we saying that they lie, or even that questions of perceptual or cognitive honesty are essential to our understanding of nonfiction. But it is important to examine the expectations that we bring to the documentary viewing experience. What do we want from and look forward to in a nonfiction work? What distinguishes the frames of reference that we bring to watching documentaries? As viewers, we are affected by documentaries' claims of truth but seldom notice it. Many spectators enter the theater with a naïve concept of "truth" and "reality." They see documentaries as innocent sources of information. But is truth or reality readily available, easily acquired, or undisputed? Or do documentaries construct their own "reality"? We are asking you to think more about how they urge us to believe these constructions.

When we watch a documentary, we are frequently drawing inferences from data, observations, or other evidence. Perhaps we need to ask ourselves, "How is it that we know what we know?" Sometimes a documentary's evidence seems so persuasive that we are unaware of the gaps in available information. Other times we seem to be asked to tolerate ambiguity and uncertainty. Documentaries have the power to impose a sense of order, purpose, and interconnectedness amidst the chaos of data, calling some "evidence" and relegating others to oblivion. Chapter 2 examines the notion of evidence and the aural and visual proof that documentaries offer to support their claims of truth.

The third chapter introduces the idea of authority. The notion of authority is relevant not only because it draws attention to the way documentaries make their truth claims but also because it ties those claims to a specific point of view. Anyone who speaks with authority does so from a particular perspective, and it is that perspective that tends to prevail when the documentary succeeds in convincing us of the truthfulness of its representations. This chapter maps out the ways documentaries speak to us, how they exert authority over their audiences, and how, in some cases, the documentary maker's authority can be decentered. It addresses questions such as: Where does the authority of a documentary come from? How does it help shape the world represented on screen? How can authority be shared? Some of these questions are difficult to pin down, but it is important to consider them carefully when we think about what documentary film and video makers do in order to make their "voices" heard.

Chapter 4 elaborates on the responsibilities that documentarians face. Documentary makers are not mere purveyors of evidence. Evidence only hints at the story. It doesn't tell it. It is up to the documentarian to examine the evidence critically and imaginatively. Since what emerges from this scrutiny can never be the absolute and total truth, the documentary maker faces many ethical concerns. Each decision has the possibility to affect the subject of the work, as well as the spectator. As Jerome Bruner asks, why is it that we consider how stories influence our lives *only* when we think we have been given the wrong story (9)? Even when we get "the right story," even when the film or video maker's vision of the truth coincides with our own, our lives can be influenced. Because making and viewing documentaries are social practices, a focus on ethics is a focus on the various conditions of production, representation, and reception.

These first four chapters constitute the first part of the book. It acquaints the reader with many of the basic theoretical issues that influence our understanding of documentary aesthetics.

The second part of the book, chapters 5 and 6, explains how documentaries build coherence. Documentary makers don't simply record life as they see it; they determinedly transform it with the conscious aim of giving it a structure and often a resonance that it lacks in reality. They take "facts" or available evidence and weave them into a coherent whole. Whether it is an argument, a dramatic narrative, or a looser associative form, such as a poetic meditation, that structure repairs the "directionlessness" (if you will pardon the inelegant term) of the uncontrolled sociohistorical world.

Documentaries repair not only the directionlessness of that world but also its apparent moral neutrality. Different aspects of the world are magnified or reduced, emphasized or diminished, newly examined, and reordered in order to maximize the effect on viewers. This process takes place primarily through the recording of historical reality and arrangement of the recorded materials. Chapter 5 examines the rhetorical power, logical coherence, and psychological effectiveness of a documentary's argument; chapter 6 concentrates on the dramatic and poetic aspects of a documentary's construction, as well as on how new digital media can expand the way we think about the structure of nonfiction works.

The third part of the book analyzes the micro-construction, exactly how sounds and images are recorded and put together, the formal design (both aural and visual) of the documentary. A different camera angle presents a different truth about the subject matter. How a film or video is edited can determine its pace, and the sequence in which the shots are arranged guides us in our understanding of the information. Music is capable of establishing a mood or affective associations. So, too, with the setting, its lighting, and décor. We could go on. These, and many others, are all important aspects of the "creative treatment" Grierson was talking about. In deciding how to depict the referential world, documentary makers have a wide range of formal choices. The final four chapters of the book look at those choices and how they affect the viewing experience.

We begin with the most cinematic: editing and camerawork. Chapter 7 explores editing. In early nonfiction films, each shot was a scene unto itself. But soon shots were combined. The way that one shot is joined to the next and the rhythm and order in which we experience them have significant impact on the way a spectator will understand the subject matter. Chapter 8 discusses the role of the camerawork in a documentary's assessment of the historical world. The camera does not simply record what passes before its lens. It helps give shape to that reality. A static shot, for instance, may enhance the formality or seriousness of the event recorded, while a fast moving camera can suggest a strong sense of immediacy. Because we see only what the camera sees, the camera forges a relationship between the spectator and that which is on the screen.

Chapter 9, "The Profilmic," turns in a more sustained manner to how performance and setting contribute to the production of meaning. When considering the grammar of representation and its significance, we often overlook the most obvious, that which we see so often in the social world. But that part of the referential world that is in front of the camera, whether posed as exposition or observation, is a vital component in the creative process.

Chapter 10 considers the many sounds that documentaries use. Images in themselves seldom have much explanatory power. Frequently sound, especially speech, but also music and noise, can help to tie down the meaning of those images. This concluding chapter of the book argues that sound, although not always as literal as the screen image, is an important part of a documentary's meaning-making system.

Many of the means that documentaries use to tell their stories and make their arguments will be familiar to contemporary audiences. Much of what now counts as nonfictional representation includes some form of stylization and artifice, as is the case, for instance, with reality television shows, where individual and collective experiences overlap with the theatricalization of ordinary life. Similarly, some forms of autobiographical discourse that circulate on the Internet make use of the observational fixed-frame long take and involve a high degree of often self-conscious performance. Other expository forms share stylistic features with, for example, television documentaries. All this suggests an interesting dialogue between documentary and other types of nonfiction, although sustained analysis of this dialogue exceeds the scope and contours of this book.

Throughout the book we will also be referring to exchanges between documentaries and fictional works. The boundaries between fact and fiction are often unraveled by the means a film or video employs. Filmmakers sometimes use nonfiction conventions in fiction films. The "News on the March" sequence in Orson Welles's *Citizen Kane* (1941), for example, appears indistinguishable from legitimate newsreel footage, except that Charles Foster Kane, the subject featured in the report, never really existed. What appears as a record of real events turns out to be little more than an ingenious fabrication. And, as we shall see, many of the techniques and forms of fiction film and television are employed by documentaries as well.

While they occasionally come up in our examples, we are not taking up mockumentaries. Nor are we focusing on actuality-based television entertainment programming or the recent TV genre of "docusoaps." Even if documentaries are entertaining, the implication of pleasurable learning seems stronger than in these other examples. Nor are we investigating films or television shows "based on" or "inspired by" a "true story." Or films that employ both fiction and documentary (such as Carlos Reygadas's *Battle in Heaven*, Michel Khleifi's *Canticle of the Stones*, or Márta Mészáros's diary films). All these other potentially rewarding projects plainly, albeit unfortunately, could not be part of our project here.

Finally, a word on our selection of documentaries: documentary is a historical phenomenon, a practice with a past. We are cognizant of that past, even though we don't survey it in this book. The sheer range and volume of documentary practice would offer a challenge for anyone who wishes to be comprehensive. We have aimed instead for some variety and have mostly chosen examples that vividly illustrate the points we wanted to make. Some of the works we discuss are associated with propaganda, others with muckraking, still others with more personal concerns such as motherhood or illness. Overall, the term documentary cinema, as we use it in this book, encompasses these various practices.

The year we give for each film or video is, to the best of our knowledge, the year of release, the dates they were first shown at a public screening. In some cases, Abbas Kiarostami's *ABC Africa*, for instance, the date may be a year or two before the work's general international release. When we write about a release in a specific venue, such as *The Bombing of Osage Avenue*'s appearance on public television, the date we give is of that debut.

Lastly, let us say that our selection of films is meant to be provocative rather than exhaustive. Many famous films, many popular films, many brilliant films, and many important films are missing. But if you would like to think more about the issues we raise in a chapter and want suggestions on films you might screen, we include an additional filmography at the end of each chapter. And whether you are a fan of documentaries, a scholar, or an aspiring documentary maker, we invite you to come up with more examples from your own viewing experiences. *Crafting Truth* was written not just for those well versed in film studies but also for those who have enjoyed documentaries in the past and want to understand more about them.

Works Cited and Further Reading

Bruner, Jerome. *Making Stories: Law, Literature, Life.* Cambridge, Mass.: Harvard University Press, 2002.

Bruzzi, Stella. *New Documentary.* 2nd ed. London: Routledge, 2006.

Corner, John. "Television, Documentary and the Category of the Aesthetic." *Screen* 44.1 (Spring 2003).

Eitzen, Dirk. "When Is a Documentary?: Documentary as a Mode of Reception." *Cinema Journal* 35.1 (Fall 1995).

Grierson, John. "The First Principles of Documentary." In *Grierson on Documentary*, ed. Forsyth Hardy. London: Collins, 1966.

Leyda, Jay. *Kino: A History of the Russian and Soviet Film.* New York: Macmillan, 1960.

National Library of Ireland. "The Angry Hedgehog." September 17, 2008. http://theangryhedgehog.com/2008/09/17/national-library-of-ireland-upcoming-events/.

O'Brien, Harvey. *The Real Ireland: The Evolution of Ireland in Documentary Film.* Manchester: Manchester University Press, 2004.

Renov, Michael. "Toward a Poetics of Documentary." In *Theorizing Documentary*, ed. Michael Renov. New York: Routledge, 1993.

White, Hayden. *The Content of the Form: Narrative Discourse and Historical Representation.* Baltimore: Johns Hopkins University Press, 1990.

PART ONE

General Concepts

1

Authenticity

We begin with an assertion: All representation is transformation. And that transformation is always partial—in both senses of the word. Stories are never lifted from life intact (they are constantly sifting out the superfluous), and we can never know something separate from our way of thinking. It is important to emphasize this early in our discussion because, as the title of this book suggests, some theorists, filmmakers, and spectators associate documentaries with "truth."

Because of the camera's ability to capture things as they happen, the photographic media are frequently considered to provide an authentic record of what was in front of the camera's lens when the scene was recorded, the "profilmic reality." Art critic John Berger, for example, in a 1968 essay, "Understanding a Photograph," describes the still photograph as an "automatic record" of things seen. "There is no transforming in photography. There is only decision, only focus" (181). And theorist Roland Barthes says in *Camera Lucida* that a photograph is "never distinguished from its referent (from what it represents)" (5).

With the discovery that silver halides were sensitive to light and the invention of the photographic process in the early nineteenth century, the innovation was visualized as a tool of scientific investigation, a means to register the action of light on chemically prepared surfaces. It was claimed that the camera would join the thermometer, barometer, hygrometer, and the telescope as the latest scientific instrument—a precision instrument for advancing knowledge (Winston, *Claiming the Real II* 133). By the 1870s still photography was already emerging as a tool for collecting scientific data about subjects in motion. Photographer Eadweard Muybridge constructed a special apparatus, a bank of twenty-four still cameras lined up horizontally twenty-one inches apart, in order to provide visual confirmation that a galloping horse at some point has all four hooves off the ground. Later, commissioned by the University of Pennsylvania, Muybridge recorded human locomotion in studies that were used for medical research. Étienne-Jules Marey, a French physiologist, devised the "chronophotographe," a camera that could record successive images of a subject in motion on a single surface. Physician Félix-Louis Regnault and his colleague Charles Comte used a chronophotographe to document West African villagers in an 1895 ethnographic exposition on the Champs de Mars in Paris.

This legacy, the idea of the scientific and pedagogical value of photographic images, was carried over to early cinema. One of the very first of the Lumière brothers' films recorded still photographers arriving at a scientific convention. And before their famous 1895 public showing of films at the Grand Café in Paris, the Lumières showed their films at scientific gatherings.

Certainly a documentary, which takes place over time, in which time can be manipulated, and which often includes a sound track, is not the same as a still photograph. Yet there is a residual sense of that ontological authority. Ethnographer and filmmaker Jean Rouch put it succinctly: "The camera eye is more perspicacious and more accurate than the human eye. The camera eye has an infallible memory" (quoted in Levin 135). We know what happened and how it happened because the camera was there to record it. The moving image recording media have the ability to preserve a time gone by. Like still photography, documentaries bear witness to a presence that is no longer there.

Consider, for instance, a very simple film, a view of a Wolpi snake dance taken in a single shot by a camera operator for the Edison Manufacturing Company in 1901. Shot on location in Arizona, the images were taken by a static camera positioned on a parapet looking down on the dancers. Unlike a painting, which organizes the pictorial field into a staged tableau, this film has the look of contingency, as if the world were a field of potential scenes and the filmmaker came across this one and caught it for us, registering it and preserving it forever. The inclusion of an audience in the image suggests that the scene was not created for the camera, that the subject preexisted the arrival of the filmmaker. And the dance would have taken place even if the camera had not been there. It was observed, not reconstructed, and the camera placement is "the best view possible of the action"

(Gunning 15). The camera was a witness to the occurrence—a sort of internal or surrogate audience. The filming and the dance coexisted at the same time and place, so there seems to be an "existential bond" between the representation and the event, that is, between the image and the sociohistorical world. All this contributes to the film's claims of truth. In any nonfiction film, "the real" is the one basic referent.

Although the Wolpi snake dance was shot at a time when the concept of documentary (as we know it today) did not yet exist, the Edison film—like many other examples of early cinema—already tells us something about why we are fascinated by documentaries. While documentaries and fiction films can share certain techniques, aesthetic qualities, and narrative structures, documentaries seem to depend less on the imagination of their makers than on the situations recorded by the filmmaking apparatus.

Most critics would agree that documentaries are *what they are* because they make particular claims about the sociohistorical world. As film scholar Carl Plantinga has put it, they "assert a belief that given objects, entities, states of affairs, events, or situations actually occur(red) or exist(ed) in the actual world as portrayed" (*Rhetoric and Representation in Nonfiction Film* 18). Whereas fiction films may allude to actual events, documentaries usually claim that those events did take place in such and such a way, and that the images and sounds on the screen are accurate and reliable. They speak about actualities and show us people who in some sense share—or once shared—the world we live in.

It is not surprising, therefore, that people tend to associate documentaries with truth. One of the reasons why we watch nonfiction films and videos is indeed to learn something about the world. And this would hardly be the case if we could not trust what we see and hear. At the same time, some documentaries suggest that there are different ways of presenting the truth about a particular event. Others openly dispute the idea that the world can ever be represented in a truthful and complete manner. And others go even further and question the very notion of truth as a philosophical concept. But most documentaries—if not all of them—have something to say about the world and, in one way or another, they want to be trusted by their audience. Nonfiction films and videos that have no concern for matters of truth and authenticity end up risking their own status as documentaries.

The tricky question, then, might be not whether documentaries are committed to telling the truth but what gives legitimacy to their truth claims—what makes a particular film or video worthy of our trust. The question can be more complicated than it seems because documentaries are not replicas of lived reality. They are, as we noted above, *representations*. The prefix "re" in the word "representation" implies an absence, presenting anew that which is no longer present. And whenever we present something anew, transformation is implied.

The Photographic Image and the Real

One of the basic aspects of the photographic media (compared, for example, with linguistic communication) is that they have iconic features; they resemble the sociohistorical world. A written account can evoke. But the photographic media are supposed to have such a strong resemblance that they can in fact show; they can demonstrate.

To this iconic aspect, we can add the physical dependence on the phenomenal world. A photograph only exists because light bounces off the scene in front of the lens and leaves an impression on the back of the camera. Therefore, we have not only an iconic resemblance but also an indexical relationship with the world, the trace of a presence that is no longer there but has left its imprint. Because the camera record certifies a presence, it is perceived to speak the truth—even if it is simply the truth that Grandpa really did attend that birthday party. This is one of the paradoxes of photography: although we know that photographic images can be tampered with or altered, we also believe them as records of events, a record of a particular moment in time. As Susan Sontag put it: "The picture may distort; but there is always a presumption that something exists, or did exist, which is like what's in the picture" (*On Photography* 5). Roland Barthes writes of having received a picture of himself that he did not remember being taken. He inspects everything in the photo to try to figure out where and when it was taken, but cannot. "And yet, *because it was a photograph* I could not deny that I had been *there* (even if I did not know *where*)" (85; emphasis in original). Neither writing nor painting can give us this certainty.

The terms "iconic" and "indexical" come from the writings of the late-nineteenth-century philosopher and semiotician Charles Sanders Peirce. Peirce used these terms to describe differing relationships or orders of meaning between the sign—a unit of signification—and that which it signifies. Icons, which have a relationship of similarity or close resemblance, offer the most direct communication. The desktop icon on a computer screen, for example, resembles the real object in such a way that we hardly need to explain what the picture means. Indexes, by contrast, might not look so similar to the object they refer us to. But they bear a relationship of causality or proximity to the object they represent. A cough or a sneeze would serve as indexical signs for a cold, just as footprints would indicate the trail followed by someone walking in the woods.

It is the iconic resemblance with the physical world, of course, that allows us to recognize and relate to the situations represented in a documentary. Yet when we look at nonfictional footage, we often expect more than an image that resembles the sociohistorical world. We expect a record of what was actually there. We expect documentaries to be indexically bound to the subject represented. The camera and its subject were there at the same time. As film critic André Bazin noted over half a century ago, the photographic image "shares, by virtue of the very process of its becoming, the being of the model of which it is the reproduction" (14).

We could extend this argument to the way documentaries use sound. The first nonfiction films had no recorded sound at all. And the term documentary itself was coined at a time when cinema was still silent. But sound technology introduced a new range of possibilities to documentary filmmakers. Just as the motion picture brought the photographic image one step closer to the world of lived experience, the sound track enhanced the similarity between the documentary film and the subject represented. Better yet, sound films could potentially preserve aural traces of the phenomenal world, thus reinforcing the sense of presence that is so compelling in documentaries. In part, we believe what we hear because of the microphone's ability to capture sounds as they occur in real life.

In Shirley Clarke's *Portrait of Jason* (1967), for example, the direct record of the protagonist's uninterrupted speech serves as a way of enforcing the integrity of the profilmic situation. The film uses lengthy takes in an effort to match screen time and actual experience. At different moments in the recording process, however, the camera runs out of film, and the cinematographer has to stop shooting and change magazines. Rather than interrupt the "scene," the filmmaker chooses to continue recording sound. While there is no image of the subject, we can still hear his voice over black leader. The image is abruptly cut; the sound is not. In different circumstances, the absence of visual record could imply that the subject before the camera is no longer there, or that the profilmic event itself has been disrupted. In *Portrait of Jason*, though, it produces the opposite effect, suggesting that life goes on even if the camera is not there to record it.

All this supports the notion that documentaries offer authentic representations of sociohistorical reality. Even if we know that those representations are incomplete, the closeness to the phenomenal world that is imparted seems to ground their truth claims.

This may be changing, of course, if documentaries rely more on digital simulations. Seeing Forrest Gump with President John F. Kennedy is clearly iconic, but not at all indexical. It resembles a real visit, but there was no concurrence of time and place. This kind of toying with history is fairly harmless, although not without meaning, in a fictional fantasy such as Forrest Gump (Robert Zemeckis, 1994). Yet in nonfiction film these manipulations can be more disorienting. One can think, for example, of a documentary created with stock sounds and images stored in a computer, or, better yet, made entirely of computer-generated images. While these images are becoming increasingly common in documentaries, they lack the kind of indexical bond with the world that we expect from photographic representations. Computer-generated images (CGI) are simulations, not "direct" records of lived reality.

Still, in appearance at least, these images can be virtually indistinguishable from photographic records, and that is one reason why they deserve further attention. The BBC documentary series *Walking with Dinosaurs* (1999), for instance, uses computer-generated images of prehistoric animals to (re)create the physical world as it might have existed millions of years ago. The makers of the series were not trying to fool the audience into believing that they could offer a photographic record of the actual creatures. But the strong photorealism of the images suggests that this kind of artifact could potentially replace the live action shots that we expect to see in a documentary. As new media theorist Lev Manovich has noted, "Filming physical reality is but one possibility" available for contemporary filmmakers (294).

Can we still talk about authenticity when the image, realistic as it may be, is not physically connected to a referent in the phenomenal world? Because of its relative autonomy from the physical world, digital imaging is likely to affect not only the making of documentaries but also the way we understand the relationship between representation and reality. Computer images remind us that documentaries are not mere traces of reality. They are conventionally accepted procedures that purport to offer credible representations of lived experience. By observing documentary conventions, filmmakers may claim legitimacy for the reality portrayed even if no photographic record is available. We will examine the conventional nature of documentary representations shortly. But first let's look at the way documentaries explore their indexical bond with the events represented.

The Real as Referent

In Robert Gardner's ethnographic film *Dead Birds* (1964), there is a sequence of an elaborate ritual for a child who died offscreen. We learn from the voiceover commentary that the boy was killed by an enemy tribe. The commentary covers over the missing sequence of the child's death. The death in *The Death of Mr. Lazarescu/Moartea domnului Lăzărescu* (Cristi Puiu, 2005), a Romanian fiction film shot in a documentary style, is announced in the title, but it happens after the two-and-a-half-hour film is over. But even if the character's death were shown on screen, we would assume that the performer who plays Mr. Lazarescu would survive his fictional death, that his demise is merely represented. The young boy's death in *Dead Birds*, on the other hand, was not confined to the realm of representation. Documentary space is of a different order than imaginary space, and our viewing experience is different as well. We bring extratextual cultural knowledge and judgment to documentary viewing. As film scholar Vivian Sobchack puts it, "There is an existential . . . bond between documentary space and the space inhabited by the viewer" (294). This is one of the reasons why certain documentary subjects are so difficult to watch.

We all know of films that have affected us so much that we wanted to flee the auditorium or classroom. *Silverlake Life: The View from Here* (1993) may be one of them. *Silverlake Life* is a video diary that chronicles the dying of the filmmaker and film teacher Tom Joslin from AIDS-related illnesses (edited after his death by one of his former students, Peter Friedman, and transferred to film for distribution). Like the event hidden from sight in Robert Gardner's film, this death was real; it existed beyond the realm of representation. Unlike what happens in *Dead Birds*, though, it is also visible on screen. *Silverlake Life* combines a relatively unadorned shooting style with a very personal approach to the documentary process, using both strategies as a means of authenticating the experiences represented in the film.

The documentary opens with an image of Mark Massi, Tom's lover of twenty-two years, lying in bed. The camera turns to the right and we see a monitor with a video valentine from Tom ("I love you Mark") and hear Mark's voiceover commentary, "What I remember most about Tom. . . ." The past tense is clearly established here. The precredit sequence continues with the camera on Mark as he talks of Tom's death: "It was very scary to look at him after he died. It's very strange to see a dead person staring." He recalls how he had tried to close Tom's eyelids properly, as they do in the movies, but they popped back open! "I apologized [to Tom] that life wasn't like in the movies." The opening of the film tells us what we will see: the death of Tom Joslin. Then we go back to witness it. What we see is what happened when the camera and microphone were recording, and much of it appears to be what would have happened even if the camera and microphone were not recording. (Indeed, it is clear that Tom would have died even if the film had not been made and there is nothing that we could have done to prevent it.)

In many documentaries, major information comes from the sound track via voiceover commentary or interviews. But in *Silverlake Life* much of the information also derives from changes in the physical appearance of both Tom and Mark, who is waging his own battle with AIDS. The primary mode appears more descriptive than interpretative, a rendering visible of the observable. Made with a video camera, usually handheld but sometimes on a stand when Tom is shooting himself, the documentary tends to efface "style" and "suspense," so that it appears that the sounds and images speak for themselves. What stands out is the indexical presence of the documentary subject, the impression that we are directly connected to what we see and hear. In *Silverlake Life*, this "presence" serves as an authenticating tool, a way of indicating to the spectator that the events on the screen did happen, and that they happened the way we see and hear them in the film.

This sense of immediacy is reinforced by the ordinariness of the actions included in the documentary. While the film's underlying subject is by no means trivial, there are several scenes that focus on simple tasks and uneventful situations. "You haven't told me where we are yet," Mark asks from offscreen. "We are at Hard Times Pizza," Tom answers, looking at the camera. The shot adds no significant information to the story that unfolds while we watch *Silverlake Life*. But it helps situate the viewer in relation to the subjects in the film. It marks the presence of the documentary's protagonists in a particular place, at a particular moment—the here and now of the shoot, which we are invited to revisit in the screening room.

More than a witness to a specific event, the recording apparatus is a sort of accomplice to the video makers, a tool that makes their presence available to the audience. Seeing health care providers, performing chores around their neighborhood (the Silverlake section of Los Angeles), visiting Tom's family in New Hampshire for Christmas, or enjoying a short vacation in the desert, the two men are at ease in front of the camera, frequently camping it up. "Here we are on our fabulous European ocean cruise," Mark says from behind the camera as he shoots Tom bundled up on a balcony behind their home. In this case, we cannot claim that what happened would have happened even if the camera had not been there. But neither should we assume that the camera "embellishes" the material it records. The opposite, in fact, seems to be true, as the recording apparatus becomes a channel through which Tom and Mark share their thoughts and emotions with the audience—or simply comment on their daily lives.

This complicity with the camera and its microphone seems particularly striking in a scene in which Tom is waiting for Mark in the car. At one point, Tom gazes down at the camera (which seems to be resting on the car's steering wheel) and expresses his frustration. He is exhausted after a visit to an herbalist and a few errands. His voice cracks; his anger is clear. Then, acting this out, he clenches his teeth and says, "You try to be helpful [and end up] getting screwed time and time again. I hate being a nice guy!" Both confiding in the camera—

1.1. "I hate being a nice guy!" From *Silverlake Life: The View from Here* (Tom Joslin and Peter Friedman, 1993).

and thus in his audience—and performing his irritation and resentment, he then, in a melodramatic gesture, turns his face away. Since there is no one else around, we can justly claim that Tom is talking to us, letting us know how he feels and how he wants us to perceive his frustration.

The moments when the camera is acknowledged become, then, another way of confirming the authenticity of what we see and hear. They ground the shooting process itself in real, lived experience. In some cases, it is in fact hard to separate the act of shooting from the incidents documented in *Silverlake Life*, the camera serving as a sort of catalyst for the situations represented in the film. Later in the documentary, as Tom's condition worsens, Mark uses the recording apparatus as a means of prompting him to talk about his health. "OK, tell the camera how you feel," he urges from behind the video camera.

Documentaries are frequently associated with the style of realism. In the realist mode of representation, the complex means by which the world is denoted are repressed. The means of representation are so naturalized that there appears to be an identity between sign and referent, a direct correlation between the text and the sociohistorical world. In *Silverlake Life*, this assumption is encouraged by the artlessness of the shots through which Tom and Mark document their daily lives—the illusion of presence that seems to overwhelm our knowledge of the representational process. As the examples above suggest, however, some of the documentary's most convincing shots are those in which we are aware of the shooting. Because the making of the video was part of Tom's and Mark's daily routines, we do not see the intervention of the camera as strange to their lives. Our awareness of the mediation broadens our knowledge of the world represented in the documentary. Not only do we have access to Mark's and Tom's everyday life, we also know something about how they interacted with the camera, how they felt about the video diary, how they wanted it to be perceived by the audience.

The image of Tom's corpse toward the end, even though we are expecting it, comes as a shock. Surely it is Mark's love and grief that are most moving; however, the image of the dead body, the transformation of that lively, feisty subject into an inanimate object, seems not only premature but an unjustifiable violation of

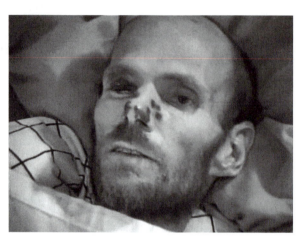

1.2. "Oooh! This is the first of July and Tommy's just died . . ." From *Silverlake Life: The View from Here* (Tom Joslin and Peter Friedman, 1993).

his life and our feelings. The dead body is too reminiscent of that man who has been onscreen for the past hour and a half. It is a token of his absence. This man has been. Vivian Sobchack notes that a corpse "engages our sympathy as an *object which is* an index of *a subject who was*" (288; emphasis in original). But this moment is not a freeze frame. The camera is once again where we have experienced it many times before, at Tom's bedside. Because the close shot of Tom's face is trembling, and we hear Mark's sobs, we know that Mark is behind the camera. So, in a way, we are watching Mark watching Tom's corpse, and the silence that we expect to accompany death is mediated by Mark's anguish. Mark's relation to Tom and to the death, the nature of his mourning, the way he inhabits his sadness, are clear and poignant. Although shot in Los Angeles, this is certainly not a Hollywood film.

This shot is also a powerful example of the way *Silverlake Life* entwines a first-person approach to documentary with the codes of realistic representation. The impact of Tom's death, conveyed by the close-up of his face, is magnified by Mark's reaction, registered through the unsteadiness of the frame. We do not see Mark, but his presence in the shot is unmistakable. Here the camera is not only the instrument but also the signifier that makes grief visible on screen. *Silverlake Life* brings us close to the experience of struggling with illness, of caring for those who are ill, and mourning the loss of a loved one. And because we see these experiences as grounded in the world we once shared with Mark and Tom, we find them touching. Video activist and archivist Catherine Saalfield describes the documentary as a "devastatingly real chronicle" (in Juhasz, *AIDS TV*

291). The "authenticity" of the sounds and images is an important part of the film's power.

Different Notions of Truth

We have established the appeal of truth. But what do we mean by truth? Defining truth is not an easy task. Philosophers have been talking about it since antiquity and have approached it from various perspectives. More importantly, the meaning and status of truth can vary from one sphere of human activity to another.

For both documentary filmmakers and spectators, truthfulness seems to involve an effort to establish an unequivocal correspondence between the representation and its referent. Although we know that nonfiction films can never be fully equated with the events they represent, we frequently expect some form of correlation between one and the other. In fact, knowing that the former cannot duplicate the latter only makes the question of correspondence more significant. We ask ourselves whether a certain documentary represents the world accurately. And if it fails to do so, we dismiss it as false, biased, or unreliable. Dirk Eitzen has written a carefully argued essay in which he notes that the question "Might it be lying?" can actually be what distinguishes nonfiction from fiction.

Seen this way, truth can be defined simply as agreement with the facts. We assume that a certain reality exists prior to the filmmaking process, and that the role of the documentarian is to honor that reality. Documentaries like *Silverlake Life*, which convey a strong sense of immediacy, are powerful in part because they make this correspondence seem direct and unproblematic.

In practice, though, truth can be a more complex matter. Agreement with the facts presumes that the facts themselves preexist the making of the film and that they are somehow accessible to the documentarian. But neither assumption is entirely correct. Inference can play an important part in the way a documentary makes its claims about the historical world, especially when there is no available evidence to support those claims. And there are cases in which the events recorded by the camera simply do not exist prior to the making of the film. Instead, they are part of the filming experience itself, as happens in *Silverlake Life* when Mark provokes Tom to talk about his worsening health condition. Here the question of whether the representation corresponds to the facts becomes inappropriate since one does not precede the other.

Matters of truth can get even more complicated when we consider the values involved in making and watching documentaries. Different people or different groups of people might look at the same event and see different things. As a result, what is perceived as truthful, either by the filmmaker or the audience, can also vary depending on who is looking at the facts, in what circumstances, and with what purposes. This is not the same as saying that all documentaries are biased. Neither is it arguing that all claims to truth are equally valid. But there might be different ideas of truth, different types of truth, which deserve further scrutiny.

Legal scholar Richard K. Sherwin distinguishes three kinds of truth: factual truth, a higher truth, and symbolic truth (49–50). Factual truth is observable truth. It is what we usually look for when we watch a documentary, since it presumes some form of agreement with the facts. In O. J. Simpson's highly publicized 1995 trial for the murder of his ex-wife, Nicole Brown Simpson, and her friend Ronald Goldman, a bloody glove found at the scene of the crime was introduced by the prosecution as evidence to establish the identity of the murderer, to establish factual truth. The question was whether or not it fit the man on trial.

But this is not the only truth that counts. There is also what Sherwin sees as a higher truth, a more abstract truth such as every individual has the right to due process. These principles supersede particular facts. For example, the bloody glove could not be considered evidence if it had been unlawfully obtained and violated an individual's rights.

And there is also a kind of truth that is more symbolic—national myths, archetypal stories, popular plot lines, and character types—our common knowledge and social values, that which we all know to be true, the conventional stories that we use to make sense of the world. In his defense of O. J. Simpson, attorney Johnnie Cochran told the jury to do the right thing and keep their eyes on the prize. These references to the Spike Lee film (1989) and the Public Broadcasting Service series on the civil rights movement (Henry Hampton, 1987–1990) told people that the issue is not the troublesome details of a glove that fits or not. The truth here is a long history that Cochran assumed the jurors knew about: the police do not treat black people well at all. These major truths—the shared knowledge we use to live our lives—can preempt the search for factual truths, and sometimes even those higher truths, the abstract principles that we all supposedly hold in common. These symbolic truths are also part of the way that we understand new material; they are part of the way we make sense of new information. We arrange this material into knowable stories—stories we can believe (Sherwin 24).

Let's return to *Silverlake Life* in the context of these three kinds of truth. There is a scene in the documentary in which Mark tells us that he has been asked to keep his shirt on while in a desert resort's pool so as not to "freak out" the other guests. Seated by the pool in a T-shirt and bathing suit, he explains the request and how he feels about it to us. Then we see Mark from the waist up, without his shirt, sitting on the edge of the hot tub. His torso is covered with Kaposi's sarcoma (KS) lesions, a sign of his deteriorating health. As he smiles, then turns his back to the camera, we hear Tom ask from offscreen, "What are you doing? Flashing me your KS?" Mark replies, "I'm being political."

The factual truth is that Mark's condition is worsening. The higher truth, the abstract principle American culture holds dear, that is activated in this scene is the dignity that should be accorded to all individuals. But the symbolic truth, which may be even stronger, is that in a culture where sexuality, pleasure, and the body are strictly regulated, gay men and AIDS are coded with morality and lurid metaphors. All kinds of feelings have contributed to making gay sex secret, mysterious, and horrifying—something to hide.

If we understand "truth" in its complexity, it helps us to see what kind of story is being told. Seen in this light, *Silverlake Life* may be making a political argument after all.

The Conventional Nature of
Documentary Representations

We can usually recognize a documentary when we see one, and that's because of conventional procedures and techniques that distinguish it from other types of films. Documentaries rely on specific codes, understandings, and expectations that are shared by a specific community—the makers and viewers of nonfiction films and videos. In fact, their claims to truth often depend on the effectiveness of these conventionalized codes and procedures. Like the documentary's iconic and indexical qualities, these conventions help establish the authenticity of nonfictional representations.

To understand how they function, we might once again find inspiration in the work of Charles Sanders Peirce. In addition to icons and indexes, Peirce's study of signs includes a category that presumes neither resemblance nor physical connection to the referential world. This type, the symbol, is a sign in which these relationships are arbitrary or conventionally established. This is the case with most written and spoken languages, as well as more figurative kinds of representation such as maps and charts. Symbols offer the least direct communication; it is by convention that we call a tree a "tree" and not a "blick." The words you are reading draw their meanings from conventions that are shared and accepted by users of the English language. (Even onomatopoeia is somewhat conventionalized. Roosters crow "cock-a-doodle-doo" in the United States, "cocorico" in France, "kiki-riki-kiiii" in Mexico, and "kukrookoo" in the Himalayas.) Such conventionalized visual analogies as maps and charts also have a symbolic relation to that which they represent.

Even photographic footage is often dealt with in conventional ways. Documentary interviews, for example, tend to follow well-established methods and predictable patterns, which reinforce the seriousness that is typical of the genre. The camera, in these cases, is normally static and self-effacing, positioned slightly to the right or left of its subject. The interviewees, in turn, speak in a somewhat formal tone but without addressing the audience directly. The result is a scene that looks sober and worthy of attention, and, at the same time, because we are used to seeing this in documentaries, authentic.

More generally, we can say that there is a conventional "contract" that binds nonfiction filmmakers to their audiences. Think for a minute about an interview with a college professor. We can hope that the spectators will pick up clues from her or his clothes, speech, and demeanor. Nothing in the image or sound, however, can assure the spectators that what they see and hear is not fake—that what we have is a scholar, and not, say, a professional actor posing as a scholar. What assures the viewer that the identity of the person interviewed is authentic is a sort of tacit agreement whereby documentarians are expected to earn the trust of the audience by offering truthful information about their subjects.

Breaking this agreement usually tests the limits of documentary representation. What happens, for instance, when public information is both compelling and untrustworthy? When a social document casts doubt on its own referentiality? When a documentary points us to the malleability of proof and truth? Ruth Ozeki Lounsbury's *Halving the Bones* (1995) does precisely this.

The film looks at three generations of women in the filmmaker's family. After her maternal grandmother, with whom she had little contact, died, Ruth Ozeki Lounsbury traveled to Japan for the funeral and came back with some of her grandmother's bones for her mother. She tells us the story of her mother's parents, Japanese immigrants in Hawaii at the beginning of the twentieth century. Based on her grandmother's autobiography and her grandfather's home movies, we see beautiful images of Hawaiian flora, a waterfall, and her grandmother as a young woman bathing in an idyllic setting. An accented voiceover commentary tells us what it was like arriving in Hilo, Hawaii, as a young bride to meet a husband whom she only knew through a photograph.

But then, twenty minutes into the seventy-minute film, as Ruth is finally going to deliver the bones to her mother in Connecticut, we get a surprising confession:

"Up until now, I haven't been 100% accurate. There are a couple of things that I made up. Like my grandmother's autobiography, for example. She never really wrote one, so I made it up from real family stories I heard from her and also from my other relatives. I did sort of the same thing with the home movies. I've seen a photo of my grandfather holding a movie camera, so I know he really made movies. But his cameras and films were all confiscated after Pearl Harbor." Using staged material is not uncommon in documentaries, as we shall see in a moment. But playing with the viewer's expectations puts at risk the "contract" between the filmmaker and the spectator. With Lounsbury's brazen acknowledgment of manipulation, certainties slip through our fingers.

Yet it would seem that the admission of wrongdoing makes us trust the rest of the film all the more. In *Halving the Bones*, the bond that ties documentarians to their audiences is broken by the filmmaker's mischief, but then seemingly reinstated by the confession. It is almost as if speaking the prohibition—a documentary that lies—inoculates the film against further transgressions. Also, the images that follow, images of her mother greeting her, the presentation of her grandmother's possessions and bones that Ruth brought back from Japan, seem to be sincere. Perhaps these later images seem so genuine because they are conventional talking heads, exactly what we expect to see in a nonfiction film. Toward the end of the film we see a silhouette of Ruth on a cliff in Hawaii, apparently heeding her mother's instructions, after her death, to throw both the mother's and the grandmother's bones into the ocean. How devilishly unexpected, then, to find out in the end credits that Ruth's mother is alive and well, living in Connecticut!

At one level the film does observe the conventions of documentary cinema: it uses voiceover commentary, interview setups, archival footage, and so on. At another, though, it upsets the overarching social contract that gives legitimacy to these procedures. But more importantly, it highlights the relevance of the agreement that makes us think of documentaries as credible sources of information—how a documentary proposes: "Believe me!"

Staging Truth

Filmmakers have fabricated sequences since the beginning of film exhibition. Reconstructing major events in the Boxer Rebellion in China was commonplace, as were reconstructions of the Spanish-American War. A U.S. film of the sinking of the battleship *Maine* in Havana harbor was made by blowing cigarette smoke over model ships in a bathtub. Jay Leyda tells of an 1898 film of the Dreyfus affair cobbled together from footage of "a French army parade led by a captain, [a street scene] in Paris showing a large building, a shot of a Finnish tug [boat] going out to meet a barge, and a scene of the Delta of the Nile." "With a little help from the commentator, and with a great deal of help from the audience's imagination," these scenes told the story of "Dreyfus before his arrest, the Palais de Justice where Dreyfus was court-martialed, Dreyfus being taken to the battleship, and Devil's Island where he was imprisoned" (23). And as documentary theorist Brian Winston points out, these news film re-creations were not even reconstructions of what the filmmakers had witnessed, but were based on journalistic accounts they read (*Lies, Damn Lies* 136).

Re-creation, however, does not necessarily mean falsification. It is sometimes a legitimately accepted procedure in nonfictional representation. In later chapters we discuss dramatic reenactments in Errol Morris's *The Thin Blue Line* (1988), as well as staging in Lin Tay-jou's *The Secret in the Satchel/Shubao li de mimi* (2007) and Mindy Faber's *Delirium* (1993). Here, let us look at *The Road to Guantánamo* (Michael Winterbottom and Mat Whitecross, 2006), which tells the story of three British Muslims, young men from Tipton, who traveled to Pakistan for a wedding, then crossed the border into Afghanistan in October 2001 as the U.S. military campaign in retaliation for the 9/11 attacks started. The three were captured in Afghanistan by the Northern Alliance forces, handed over to U.S. authorities, and later transferred to the American military prison in Guantánamo Bay, Cuba, where they were held for two years and eventually released without charges. *The Road to Guantánamo* uses interviews with the actual detainees after they were released, interspersed with occasional pieces of news footage. Most of what we see and hear, however, are re-creations of the events that led the young men from Pakistan to Guantánamo, enacted sequences that are clearly enacted and not meant to be misleading (what Winston calls "sincere and justifiable reconstruction" [*Claiming the Real II* 128]). The re-creations add dramatic intensity to the story. They also widen the gap between the actual events and what we watch in *The Road to Guantánamo*. But they do not impair the veracity of the film's truth claims.

While we know that this is not footage of the actual events, we still think of the reenactments as part of the story the film is trying to tell us. This disjunction may be similar to the reverberations in the spectator's experience of historical films that Jean-Louis Comolli writes about, in which a recognizable performer (such as Pierre Renoir) plays a well-known historical figure (such as Louis XVI). We never forget that Pierre Renoir is not Louis XVI, yet, at the same time, we want to believe in the truth of the representation. Perhaps there is a similar oscillation in our experience when we see these plainly enacted scenes. Because of this, the staged material can function as an extension or illustration of the testimonies documented by the filmmaker, a filmic rendition of events that are firmly grounded in lived reality.

The filmmaker Jean-Luc Godard once said, "Realism . . . is never exactly the same as reality, and in the cinema it is of necessity faked" (*Godard on Godard* 185). And filmmakers use specific cinematic means to fake it. Peter Watkins's filmed simulation of a nuclear attack on Great Britain, *The War Game* (1966), used cinematic means that made it look so much like news reporting that the British Broadcasting Corporation banned it from television. It looked too real. (The BBC said the film would be too horrifying to viewers.) There were many, of course, who debated if this was really the reason why the BBC suppressed the film or if it was the fact that the film destabilized civil authority. But for our purposes, we should consider what made the film appear so authentic and how this functioned in Watkins's strategy for effectiveness.

The War Game was based on extensive research on thermonuclear war, the North Atlantic Treaty Organization guidelines for intervention, British civil defense policies, the consequences of the atomic bombings in Japan, and the firestorms in Hamburg and Dresden during World War II, projected onto an imaginary incident in the future, an outbreak of war between NATO and Russia. This thoroughness was prompted by a perception of urgency and potentially imminent events: the escalation of the arms race threatened full-scale nuclear war. The film begins with a set of maps, then postulates a fictional crisis and provocations, and proceeds to show the effects and aftermath of the ensuing nuclear attack. The voiceover and the interviews with officials are loaded with facts on thermonuclear war and, quoting from the manual of the Home Office, information on evacuation, feeding, and

1.3. "Do you know what Strontium 90 is and what it does?" "No, I feel I don't." From *The War Game* (Peter Watkins, 1966).

shelter plans. Watkins used scripted interviews with nonprofessional actors playing both authorities and ordinary citizens. He also included unscripted interviews with locals playing people on the street. A performer playing a reporter asks some residents of Kent, members of the cast, "Do you know what Strontium 90 is?"

Person after person depicted gives an opinion, in a close shot with a puzzled look on his or her face, either thoughtfully admitting not to know, or offering a wildly incorrect answer. This combination of scripted and unscripted material coexists without undercutting the film's authority.

In a classical Hollywood fiction film, we see and hear only what is needed to further the narrative. The story is made manageable by the reduction of information. In philosopher Noël Carroll's words, "The flow of action approaches an ideal of uncluttered clarity" (180). In Hollywood films, even those based on a "true story," we do not see, for example, people taking out the garbage unless they are going to get mugged or kidnapped. The Hollywood fiction film is much more economical than daily life, where not all of later events are related to, or make sense in the context of, earlier events. In daily life, some actions—taking out the garbage, perhaps—seem to happen with little effect. And certainly some actions and events seem less clear, more cluttered, sometimes even fragmented.

But what about documentaries? The degree of control that documentary filmmakers have over profilmic events varies. Sometimes the sounds overlap and may not be fully audible. There may be some hesitations and stumbling over words. Occasionally someone walks between the camera and what it is shooting. Or there may be a lens flare. Documentaries are certainly more structured than daily life. But they may not seem as clear or uncluttered as a Hollywood narrative.

The War Game employs this lack of clarity as an aesthetic strategy for the sequences of the aftermath of the nuclear strike. The fantasy of the future is built with newsreel-like techniques. (It is shot with grainy black-and-white film stock, synchronized sound, available light, zooms, rapid panning, quickly changing focus, and an intrusive, participating reporter's handheld first-person camera.) Some of the dialogue is deliberately unintelligible. Performers were handed scripts complete with stammering and pauses. People look at the camera as they pass. Someone bumps into the camera operator and says, "Excuse me." At one point the camera is waved away by a soldier; at another it is given a gesture of defiance by a rioter. (The blocking was prearranged, as was the camera movement, but it comes across as spontaneous and unorganized.) The film uses this documentary mode (associated with truth and reality) to portray an unreal event.

Watkins also uses scripted interviews based on statements from authority figures about policies of the day: Civil Defense personnel, an Anglican bishop, a scientist, a doctor, and a psychiatrist. In contrast with the cluttered look of the futuristic scenario, the present-day interviews are shot with a straight-on look at the calm, complacent, well-groomed expert, nicely framed with his books, blackboard, and statistics, well-lit, well-miked, and the camera stable on a tripod.

Paradoxically, the present tense is rendered with the control one would expect in a Hollywood fiction film.

The War Game makes use of the future conditional tense, what might be (e.g., "It's more than possible that . . ." "Such scenes as these would be almost inevitable"). The future as Peter Watkins imagines it seems probable. What seem improbable are the current civil defense and military policies. The future conditional seems plausible and the present tense emerges as a strange flight of the imagination. It seems appropriate, then, that it was condemned for being too realistic, not for being untrue.

Falsification and Documentary

Bontoc Eulogy (Marlon Fuentes, 1995), an archival footage re-creation of the "Philippine" village at the 1904 St. Louis World's Fair, is also based on elaborate research. Words uttered by Markod, a fictional Bontoc warrior who is supposedly the narrator's grandfather, were originally an English transcription of an interview conducted with a Chief Famaoley while he was in a traveling show performing in Coney Island two years after the closing of the fair. Passages were selected from this document, translated back into old Bontoc, and read by a Bontoc elder, Fermina Bagwan, based in Southern California. Some of the archival footage comes from a faked film of the Spanish-American War, a reconstruction of the Battle of Manila Bay. In Fuentes's own words, *Bontoc Eulogy* "straddles fact and fiction, mixing imagination and interior dialogue with history" (in Juhasz and Lerner 116).

Watching *Bontoc Eulogy*, according to Fuentes, is like watching "an Indonesian shadow puppet performance (*wayang kulit*), where one can watch on either side of the screen. Watching the puppeteer's side shows the movements of the craftsperson." Watching from the other side, it is easier to become involved in the story (118). *Bontoc Eulogy* presents the narrator's search for evidence of his "grandfather's" history and Markod's first-person reflections on the tragedy of his ordeal. But at times, the narrator's voice and Markod's voice become interchangeable. Fuentes has said that he wanted the film's seams and sutures to show. He wanted viewers to realize that they were viewing an "optical illusion." And he wanted them to be aware of their process of perception "at the very moment of perception," what he calls the "bidirectionality of the act of observing" (118–119). For Marlon Fuentes, authenticity can be anti-illusionist. The filmmaker intends to engage the viewer with the process of storytelling.

Other forms of falsification can be more insidious, misleading the audience both about the events represented and the nature of their filmic representation. Rather than allow "the seams and sutures to show," these films mimic the conventions of documentary cinema in such a way that we can hardly tell fictional from nonfictional material. This is the case with *David Holzman's Diary*, a 1968 fiction film by Jim McBride. Although staged, *David Holzman's Diary* scrupulously copies the sound and camerawork of a direct cinema diary. The film portrays a young man, David Holzman, in July 1967, having just been declared A1 (draftable), making a 16mm film that he believes will tell him some truth about his life. Like *The War Game*, the film uses a specific means of representation in an attempt to make it seem more realistic. Because it looks unrehearsed, because much of it is awkwardly framed and unevenly lit, and because all the sound is direct and some of the musings are mumbled, we associate it with lived reality.

At the beginning of the film, David Holzman (played by Kit Carson) directly addresses the camera and introduces us to his equipment. Quoting Godard, he rhapsodizes on its ability to evoke "truth 24 times a second." The film is an ode to his Nagra portable tape recorder, unrivaled at the time for its ability to document sound under local conditions, and to his Éclair camera, with its ability to shoot for long durations and in low luminosity, unshackled by lights, tripods, and cables, and hence more mobile and flexible—as if these attributes of cinematic technology could induce people into uttering a truth that they would not reveal in ordinary situations; as if this unobtrusive, lightweight portable equipment could show us aspects of actuality that otherwise would have been obscured from view.

1.4. "The noted French wit Jean-Luc Godard said, 'What is film? Film is truth 24 times a second.'" From *David Holzman's Diary* (Jim McBride, 1968).

David Holzman's flight of fancy, his attempt to faithfully preserve "the real" on celluloid, suggests a higher aspiration, a self-indulgent, sentimental effort to transcend his life via this equipment. Yet, as several scholars have noted, technology grows out of a particular ideology. The image-making technologies that Holzman celebrated grew out of, as visual anthropologist Jay Ruby once said of all Western image-making technologies, "a profound need to have an irrefutable witness—to control reality by capturing it on film" (219). Imagine how much "purer," unfettered and easier, this must seem with the new compact digital cameras!

It is not until the credit sequence at the end of the film that audience members are cued that the film is a fictional enactment. Discovering that the film is a fabrication, we understand the text to be a lie. *David Holzman's Diary* playfully suspends the contract that binds documentary filmmakers to their audiences, but the abrogation of that contract has consequences. After all, we process fiction and nonfiction differently. The existence or absence of the sociohistorical referent, the real world and characters that exist in it, fundamentally alters our mode of reading the text and changes our position toward it. Unlike *The Road to Guantánamo* or *The War Game, David Holzman's Diary* uses staged material not to render visible an experience that is unavailable for the camera but to upset our faith in documentary representation and the presumptions that are often associated with non-fiction cinema.

If Kit Carson and Jim McBride saw *David Holzman's Diary* as, in Brian Winston's words, a "slap against the new documentary's truth-telling pretensions" (*Claiming the Real II* 202), Marlon Fuentes must see his film as striking a blow at ethnographic and historical films, films that offer smoothed-over surfaces and embedded truth claims that purport to be unambiguous and consistent, and where all the actions and evidence serve the anthropologist's or historian's argument. Fuentes respects gaps and ellipses, as well as the fragility and fallibility of memory, which "are just as important as the materials we have in our hands. If they are missing for certain reasons, whether by accident or force of omission, perhaps these irregularities force us to reflect on the nature and origins of our own situation" (120).

Markers of Authenticity in Fiction Films

Some of the major reasons why we take *David Holzman's Diary* to be nonfiction are the direct address to the camera, the wandering narrative, the visual and aural disorder (muddy sound and blurred focus), and the compulsive use of dates to describe that day's shooting (even when it is clear that some of the footage was taken on days too cold to be July in New York City). These are formal conventions that normally function as markers of authenticity. They tell the spectators that what they are watching is a documentary, a nonfictional representation of the sociohistorical world.

Other fiction filmmakers, too, are aware of the conventional character of documentary discourse and have used similar markers of authenticity to enhance the realism of their narratives. *The Death of Mr. Lazarescu*'s long takes, flat lighting, and handheld camera all contribute to its documentary look and to the moral outrage that the film aims to rouse about the character's treatment by the public health system. *The Battle of Algiers* (Gillo Pontecorvo, 1966), a fictional reconstruction of some events in the Algerian war for independence, uses no documentary footage but gives the impression that we are watching historical events as they occurred in real life. The action seems unscripted and spontaneous, and the camerawork conveys a sense of immediacy that is easily associated with documentary filmmaking. Even more interestingly, the Cuban film *The Other Francisco/El otro Francisco* (Sergio Giral, 1975) contrasts documentary and fictional conventions to represent different aspects of Cuban society in the nineteenth century. It uses a documentary shooting style (a handheld, whirling camera) to throw us into the action of a slave rebellion and a more melodramatic style (with a stable camera on a tripod) in the scenes that depict the slave owners.

These days we think of handheld camera, obscured views, and overlapping sound as markers of documentary truth. And a general "messiness" (the word is Todd Gitlin's), unbalanced compositions, and an aesthetic of visual and aural clutter are easily read as signifiers of immediacy, instantaneity, and authenticity. They seem to evoke the unpredictability of experience. Yet these different markers, and realism as a style, have changed over time. Voiceovers were particularly popular after World War II; *T-Men* (Anthony Mann, 1947), *Boomerang* (Elia Kazan, 1947), and *Naked City* (Jules Dassin, 1948) are fiction films that come to mind. But today, their commentaries seem contrived. Look at an episode of the television show *Dragnet* (1952–1959), with its travelogue opening and voiceover commentary. Then compare it with the opening of another TV police procedural, *Hill Street Blues* (1981–1987), with its quick pacing, nervous camera, overpopulated cast list, multiple storylines, lack of resolutions, and overall density of sound and image. As documentary scholar Bill Nichols points out, the "comfortably accepted realism of one generation seems like artifice to the next. New strategies must constantly be fabricated to re-present 'things as they are'" ("The Voice of Documentary" 17).

These fiction films and television shows employ the conventions of documentary filming and sound recording (as they were practiced in their day) to play off the spectator's expectations of a documentary's authenticity. "Documentary" has become a style or an aesthetic that evokes "the real." But when we go to see a documentary, we generally know beforehand that it is not fiction. And we make certain assumptions about authenticity based on that. Hence Eitzen's "Might It Be Lying?" But we must not forget that when documentaries assert "This happened," they do so through formal cinematic conventions. We explore these in more depth in the rest of the book.

Additional Filmography

One Way or Another/De cierta manera (Sara Gómez, 1974/77)

Killer of Sheep (Charles Burnett, 1977)

The Learning Path (Loretta Todd, 1991)

Imagining Indians (Victor Masayesva Jr., 1992)

The Blair Witch Project (Daniel Myrick and Eduardo Sánchez, 1999)

The 3 Rooms of Melancholia/Melancholian 3 huonetta (Pirjo Honkasalo, 2004)

Death of a President (Gabriel Range, 2006)

Lakshmi and Me (Nishtha Jain, 2007)

Works Cited and Further Reading

Aristotle. *Introductory Readings.* Trans. Terence Irwin and Gail Fine. Indianapolis: Hackett, 1996.

Barthes, Roland. *Camera Lucida: Reflections on Photography.* New York: Hill and Wang, 1981.

Bazin, André. "The Ontology of the Photographic Image." In *What Is Cinema?,* vol. 1. Trans. Hugh Gray. Berkeley: University of California Press, 1967.

Berger, John. "Understanding a Photograph." In *The Look of Things.* New York: Viking, 1974.

Carroll, Noël. *Mystifying Movies: Fads and Fallacies of Contemporary Film Theory.* New York: Columbia University Press, 1988.

Carson, L. M. Kit. *David Holzman's Diary: A Screenplay by L. M. Kit Carson, from a Film by Jim McBride.* New York: Farrar, Straus and Giroux, 1970.

Clifford, James. "Introduction: Partial Truths." In *Writing Culture: The Poetics and Politics of Ethnography,* ed. James Clifford and George E. Marcus. Berkeley: University of California Press, 1986.

Comolli, Jean-Louis. "Historical Fiction: A Body Too Much." *Screen* 19.2 (Summer 1978).

Eitzen, Dirk. "When Is a Documentary?: Documentary as a Mode of Reception." *Cinema Journal* 35.1 (Fall 1995).

Fuentes, Marlon. "Extracts from an Imaginary Interview: Questions and

Answers about *Bontoc Eulogy.*" In *F is for Phony: Fake Documentaries and Truth's Undoing,* ed. Alexandra Juhasz and Jesse Lerner. Minneapolis: University of Minnesota Press, 2006.

Gardner, Robert. *The Impulse to Preserve: Reflections of a Filmmaker.* New York: Other Press, 2006.

Gitlin, Todd. "*Hill Street Blues:* Make it Look 'Messy.'" In *Inside Prime Time.* New York: Pantheon Books, 1983.

Godard, Jean-Luc. *Godard on Godard.* Ed. Jean Narboni and Tom Milne. New York: Viking, 1972.

Gunning, Tom. "Before Documentary: Early Nonfiction Films and the 'View' Aesthetic." In *Uncharted Territory: Essays on Early Nonfiction Film,* ed. Daan Hertogs and Nico de Klerk. Amsterdam: Stichting Nederlands Filmmuseum, 1997.

Juhasz, Alexandra. *AIDS TV: Identity, Community, and Alternative Video.* Durham, N.C.: Duke University Press, 1995.

Juhasz, Alexandra, and Jesse Lerner, eds. *F Is for Phony: Fake Documentaries and Truth's Undoing.* Minneapolis: University of Minnesota Press, 2006.

Levin, G. Roy. *Documentary Explorations: Fifteen Interviews with Filmmakers.* Garden City, N.Y.: Doubleday, 1971.

Leyda, Jay. *Kino: A History of the Russian and Soviet Film.* New York: Collier, 1960.

Manovich, Lev. *The Language of New Media.* Cambridge, Mass.: MIT Press, 2001.

Nichols, Bill. *Ideology and the Image: Social Representation in the Cinema and Other Media.* Bloomington: Indiana University Press, 1981.

———. *Representing Reality: Issues and Concepts in Documentary.* Bloomington: Indiana University Press, 1991.

———. *Introduction to Documentary.* Bloomington: Indiana University Press, 2001.

———. "The Voice of Documentary." In *New Challenges for Documentary,* 2nd ed., ed. Alan Rosenthal and John Corner. Manchester: Manchester University Press, 2005.

Peirce, Charles Sanders. "Logic as Semiotic: The Theory of Signs." In *Philosophical Writings,* ed. Justus Buchler. New York: Dover, 1955.

Plantinga, Carl. *Rhetoric and Representation in Nonfiction Film.* Cambridge: Cambridge University Press, 1997.

———. "What a Documentary Is, After All." *Journal of Aesthetics and Art Criticism* 63.2 (Spring 2005).

Rony, Fatimah Tobing. *The Third Eye: Race, Cinema, and Ethnographic Spectacle.* Durham, N.C.: Duke University Press, 1996.

Rosenthal, Alan. "The War Game: An Interview with Peter Watkins." In *New Challenges for Documentary*, 2nd ed., ed. Alan Rosenthal and John Corner. Manchester: Manchester University Press, 2005.

Ruby, Jay. "The Ethics of Image Making." In *New Challenges for Documentary*, 2nd ed., ed. Alan Rosenthal and John Corner. Manchester: Manchester University Press, 2005.

Sherwin, Richard K. *When Law Goes Pop: The Vanishing Line Between Law and Popular Culture.* Chicago: University of Chicago Press, 2000.

Sobchack, Vivian. "Inscribing Ethical Space: Ten Propositions on Death, Representations, and Documentary." *Quarterly Review of Film Studies* 9.4 (1984).

Sontag, Susan. *On Photography.* New York: Anchor Books, 1977.

———. *Regarding the Pain of Others.* New York: Farrar, Straus and Giroux, 2004.

Vogel, Amos. "Grim Death." *Film Comment* 16.2 (March-April 1980).

Watkins, Peter. "Watkins Discusses His Suppressed Nuclear Film, THE WAR GAME, with James Blue and Michael Gill." *Film Comment* 3.4 (1965).

Winston, Brian. *Claiming the Real II: Documentary: Grierson and Beyond.* London: British Film Institute; New York: Palgrave Macmillan, 2008.

———. *Lies, Damn Lies and Documentaries.* London: British Film Institute, 2000.

2

Evidence

Documentary films and videos do not simply represent sociohistorical experience; they have to convince us that what we see on screen did happen. How do they do this? What kinds of evidence do they use to persuade us to accept them as truthful and accurate? Why do we believe this evidence? These are easy and important questions to pose but tough ones to answer.

Jehane Noujaim's 2004 documentary *Control Room* offers a powerful attempt to engage these questions. It looks at the way the American-led invasion of Iraq was represented by al-Jazeera, the Qatar-based satellite channel. The war itself serves as the underlying context of the documentary. But the real subject of the film is the media battle that was fought alongside the military conflict. In March 2003, just before the war started, the filmmakers began following television reporters and producers from al-Jazeera. As the military campaign unfolds on the screen, we see the journalists working and watch their reactions to the bombing of Iraq. *Control Room* makes us think about the way the news media handle information, how evidence is used by media producers, and what consequences their choices may have. It asks us to compare factual information presented by the Arab news channel with material gathered by Western TV channels. Watching the film, we realize that "evidence" of the same event can have significantly different meanings when seen from dissimilar sides of the political spectrum.

Noujaim's documentary, too, involves an effort to gather and present evidence, and it, too, uses that evidence to support a particular point of view, a more positive opinion of al-Jazeera than Western audiences might have expected in 2004.

Control Room questions managers, producers, and reporters (including in-depth interviews with senior producer Samir Khader and correspondent Hassan Ibrahim) about what al-Jazeera's journalistic goals are. We also see and hear correspondents from major U.S. news outlets, a member of the U.S. State Department, and even a U.S. marine spokesperson expressing respect for al-Jazeera. But most importantly, we see and hear some of al-Jazeera's footage from the war, much of which contradicts the information we get from press conferences with U.S. Secretary of Defense Donald Rumsfeld and General Vincent Brooks. For instance, Noujaim shows us images of hospitalized bloodied children inserted in the middle of a speech in which Rumsfeld states that "al-Jazeera has a pattern of playing propaganda over and over and over again. . . . When there is a bomb that goes down, they grab some children and women and pretend that the bomb hit women and children. . . . We are dealing with people who are perfectly willing to lie to the world to attempt to further their case." The sequence asks us to question what we may have come to take for granted: the information conveyed by top U.S. officials in charge of the war. It also asks us to question why some evidence does not appear in the U.S. media, and if that omission is not taking a position on the war.

Some of the most potent evidence is the photographic substantiation of an event that the filmmakers could not have anticipated. The morning of April 8, U.S. missiles fired on the Baghdad office of al-Jazeera, killing a correspondent, Tarek Ayyoub, on the rooftop of the building. We hear Samir Khader explaining that he had received a call from Baghdad saying that there was air fire near their office. Next we see Ayyoub with a helmet on his head, dressed in a bulletproof vest, huddled by the sandbagged perimeter of the roof. Soon we hear and see a plane flying nose down, in attack formation, followed by missiles falling from the fuselage into the sky. A CNN correspondent reports on the day's events: the strike against al-Jazeera, one against Abu Dhabi Television, and a shot fired at the Palestine Hotel where many journalists were housed. Later that day, at a press conference, we hear Ayyoub's wife via telephone, emotionally telling the audience, "My husband died trying to bring the truth to the world," entreating them to give an honest account of the incident. And we see the tears of the journalists assembled.

Whether they present a well-reasoned argument or offer enduring complexities over which to puzzle, all documentaries take "facts" or "actuality" and weave them into a coherent whole. The difference between a point of view that is questionable or tendentious and one that is credibly documented is frequently the effectiveness of the available evidence and the way it is presented to the audience. Evidence, as we see in this chapter, helps authenticate the reality represented. If films such as *Control Room* are able to exert substantial influence, it is because they garner persuasive evidence and arrange it in a convincing manner.

As Aristotle taught us, the work of persuasion involves both the art of rhetorical inventiveness and the use of resources that are "there at the outset," such as witnesses, written records, and so on (*Rhetoric* 7). Evidence gives credibility to a particular argument or assertion. It offers ground for belief. Fingerprints, for example, can be used as evidence of someone's identity. A signed contract might serve as proof that a commercial transaction was agreed upon. And love letters might be called upon to verify an illicit relationship. Each example seems meaningful on its own. In practice, however, evidence hardly ever appears by itself and never has much significance until it is used for a particular purpose.

This pursuit of credibility makes documentaries close to legal discourses. In their most conventional forms, legal discourses assume that we can prove the truthfulness of a particular assertion based on the availability of credible evidence. Traditional documentaries follow a similar pattern. They seek out evidence to justify their claims. But documentaries deal with evidence in ways that are both more accessible and more complicated. Think of how Jehane Noujaim took photographic images of injured children and edited them into Donald Rumsfeld's speech in order to criticize his account of al-Jazeera's "misinformation." Through the power of the visual record and the magic of editing, she opposed two conflicting realities and managed to discredit what we hear from the secretary of defense.

Evidence and the Photographic Image

Every time we aim the camera, we are deciding that some things should and some things should not appear in our picture. George Stoney and Jim Brown show how political this can be in *"Man of Aran": How the Myth Was Made* (1978), when they turn their camera and disclose the lush, fertile fields owned by large landholders that Robert Flaherty ignored in 1932–33 when he shot his romantic story of the inhospitable, rocky terrain that the impoverished Aran islanders struggle to plant. Even the footage from an apparently neutral and apolitical bank surveillance camera, which we often think of as pure record or unadulterated truth, is taken with a camera that is aimed in a certain direction and eliminates what is above, below, and behind the camera.

Despite these limitations, however, the photographic image has been historically considered evidential. Already in the second half of the nineteenth century, still photography was being used as a criminological tool. By the 1860s, the photographic documentation of prisoners was common. In the first ten years of collecting, the Identification Bureau of the Paris police archived more than 100,000. The Paris police also used photographs of communards at the barricades to make arrests. Similarly, medical authorities at the time turned to photography as a means of recording and documenting their patients. The Royal Society of Medicine in Great Britain holds prints from an album entitled *Portraits of Insanity* taken by Dr. Hugh Welch Diamond of some of the female inmates of his asylum in Surrey in the mid-1850s. And the nineteenth-century French neurologist Jean-Martin Charcot opened a Photographic Department at the Salpêtrière asylum in an effort to make manifest the hysteria in his patients. Photography was also used to verify paranormal phenomena and to provide empirical evidence of a spiritual realm—that which even the eye cannot see. As photography historian John Tagg has demonstrated, this coupling of evidence and photography was not neutral or given, but was bound up with the emergence of new disciplinary institutions and new practices of surveillance and recordkeeping (5). The use of the camera as a tool of precision and measurement was also related to the notion of the photographic image as a direct transcription of the real. The photograph, according to photographer and critic Allan Sekula, "operated as the *image* of scientific truth" (40). To reiterate the semiotic terms employed in the last chapter, the signifier seemed so transparent that the referent appeared to present itself. Elements of production such as framing were frequently discussed as professional procedures and as measures taken to guarantee accuracy.

We mention these nineteenth-century uses of the camera not as technological precursors to cinema but as an introduction to the idea of the photographic image as proof. Photos functioned as tools to analytically record life and sources of visual evidence. When film and video were introduced as recording devices, this role was enhanced by the incorporation of movement and sound to the visual record. Those early uses of photographic images, however, already anticipated our faith in documentary evidence. In fact, this fascination with the ability to photographically record events occurring over time permeates most of the history of nonfiction film and video. The footage of Rodney King's beating at the hands of Los Angeles policemen in 1991 is a good example. And soon after, the Black Planet Productions collective amassed many more amateur videos of police brutality around the country.

At issue, however, is not simply the reliability of the film or video but, as we suggested earlier, their status as representations. We all know that photographs and videos can be retouched or digitally processed to make a double chin disappear, to hide an embarrassing detail from a particular scene, or to make the sky in Los Angeles appear blue. We also know that computer-generated images are now increasingly common in documentaries. "The camera's capacity to capture the real [has not been] erased," but contemporary image-making technologies require "a far greater sophistication on the part of the audience" (Winston 9). This, however, is not new. Manipulating photographs in order to make a point was already a familiar practice in the nineteenth century. And it continues. O. J. Simpson's mug shot was darkened on the cover of a national magazine. More modern technology has made it possible to digitally suture someone else's lips into the only known film footage of Hank Williams singing so that he appears to be crooning "Tears in My Beer" instead of "Hey, Good Looking" (Winston 8). We know that we can't always trust what we see and hear, and, in order to establish the credibility of a documentary, we cannot "rely solely," in Brian Winston's words, "on some innate quality of the image" (9). That's why it is important to understand the different types of evidence available to documentarians, the ways film and video makers use evidence in their documentaries, and the ways viewers process the evidence so that they feel that they are justified in believing it.

Uses of Evidence

As we saw in *Control Room*, when it appears in a documentary, evidence has already been interpreted by the documentarian and arranged in a particular way; its impact is usually the result of this kind of arrangement. In other words, the relevance of even the most established facts may vary with the use they are put to. It is how evidence is used in the flow of information that gives it cogency.

Let's look briefly at *Night and Fog/Nuit et brouillard* (Alain Resnais, 1955). The film alternates black and white archival photographs and some moving images of World War II Nazi extermination camps with color tracking shots of the camps in the present day, images of emptiness and loneliness, images of almost lyrical beauty. Throughout the film, this juxtaposition of archival footage and contemporary shots helps give meaning to the evidential material by suggesting that we compare the past with the present, or by inviting us to examine the present in light of historical events. *Night and Fog* uses a voiceover commentary that also contributes to this dialogue between past and present. The commentary, written by poet Jean Cayrol, himself a survivor of the camps, interrogates the beauty of the color footage and questions if we have learned anything from those death camps. Written after the revelations of French use of torture during the Algerian war for independence, the film's commentary ends in the present tense: "Nine million dead haunt this landscape. . . . Who among us is on the lookout from this strange tower to warn of new executioners. . . . We who want to believe it happened but once, in one country; we who refuse to look around us; we who do not hear the endless cry." The voiceover commentary and the very structure of the film, the alternation of past with present, the alternation of evidence of unspeakable devastation with evidence of material remains, asks viewers to question how they should relate to contemporary quandaries. When we ask ourselves

2.1. "Then who is responsible?" From *Night and Fog/Nuit et brouillard* (Alain Resnais, 1955).

how we know what we know, we need to take into account those sounds and images. It is not only the commentary that persuades and engages us, but also the way the evidence is structured in the film.

Returning to the bank surveillance camera, what do we make of this raw footage? It takes on meaning when it becomes part of a story, part of an interpretation, or part of an argument. But is the story about inadequate security? Or robbery as the last resort of the downtrodden? Even the most untainted footage can be used for different scenarios, as we know from the video of Rodney King's beating by members of the Los Angeles Police Department. Ironically, "incontrovertible" evidence can be inconclusive. It can be used to tell many different stories. Only rarely is archival footage seen by itself, as the prosaic example of the bank surveillance camera or the more notorious footage of President John F. Kennedy's assassination indicates. Still, here as well, the archival evidence continues to call for interpretation; it asks for a "narrative" that will help us make sense of what we see and hear.

This is what the makers of *Point of Order* (1963) had in mind when they put together their documentary about the 1954 Army-McCarthy hearings. Drawing from 188 hours of footage from the CBS coverage of the events, Emile De Antonio and Daniel Talbot compiled a ninety-seven-minute film that portrays one of the most controversial political figures in American history, Joseph McCarthy, the junior U.S. senator from Wisconsin. The hearings, which were broadcast live from April to June of 1954, involved charges that the senator had sought privileges for one of his assistants, Private G. David Schine. McCarthy counter-attacked, saying that his accusers were trying to prevent investigation of communist infiltration in the U.S. Army. *Point of Order* is made up entirely of this archival material. But the filmmakers arranged the footage in a specific way, thus inviting us to interpret it from their perspective. While the film does give us an overall idea of what the hearings were about, it ends up privileging the dramatic story of McCarthy's fall, serving as an indictment of the senator and the political views he embraced. With no voiceover commentary—except for a brief initial introduction over black leader—*Point of Order* goes beyond the original footage, adding a particular slant to events that were well known at the time and demanding that we make a clear distinction between the 1954 television kinescopes and the 1963 documentary.

Some other films combine existing footage with material shot specifically for the documentary, creating a sort of "conversation" between various kinds of evidence. They juxtapose archival footage to witness testimonies, for example, and allow us to weigh one type of evidence against the other. Or they rely on different media: photographs, sound recordings, newspaper clippings, or the like. In these examples, too, the use of factual material exists in conjunction with an effort to present evidence in a compelling manner. We explore the way documentaries arrange evidence to build up arguments in chapter 5. For now, we look at how diverse types of evidence may affect our documentary experiences.

Different Types of Evidence

One inspiring example of the way different kinds of evidence can be used in documentary cinema is *The Life and Times of Rosie the Riveter* (Connie Field, 1980), a film about women's experiences in the workforce during World War II. In this film, the testimony of five women who worked in war industries is interwoven with the "facts" in wartime government newsreels and shorts. Two types of evidence are used here: firsthand testimony of those who worked in the defense plants and archival footage compiled by the filmmaker. As they appear in the documentary, these different materials contradict each other. The testimonies of the women interviewed do not correspond, in content or style of delivery, with the official version of their story presented in the newsreels and shorts. Instead, their memories lead us into a world that seems to have been overlooked or deliberately omitted.

Connie Field's film uses this discrepancy in order to validate a history that had until then received scant or insufficient attention.

In the United States, the late 1960s and 1970s were marked by a serious scrutiny of the assumptions and methods of mainstream history writing, and a re-evaluation of the contributions of marginalized peoples to history. There was a general move among progressives to rethink the way that history had been written and understood and to reconsider the values and criteria that have gone into it. This reevaluation was influenced by the Black Power and the Women's Liberation movements. One area of focus was the acknowledgment that blacks and women have been makers of history even though they had been left out of standardized historical narratives.

In order to explore experience in all its diversity and complexity, these liberation movements set out to uncover, identify, and interpret the reality missing from the historical record. By documenting the lives of those omitted or overlooked in most accounts of the past, they brought unseen experiences out of the shadows and rendered significant what had hitherto been neglected. One of the means used was oral histories of "ordinary" people—people who have not generally been thought of as movers and shakers. These experiences produced a wealth of new evidence previously ignored and drew attention to dimensions of life and activities usually deemed unworthy of mention.

In *The Life and Times of Rosie the Riveter*, common experiences of working-class women are recognized as evidence and given credibility because, once contrasted to the slick and bombastic newsreels, they provide an alternative account of the past. As heard through the film's interviews, these experiences constitute the bedrock of data on which our understanding of the subject is built. That these witnesses are women, and three of the five are African American women, suggests that history (or her/story) can contain multiple perspectives, indeed differing perspectives.

Personal history interviews can be valuable not only because they tell us about events that do not usually get into written records but also because they tell us of the meanings that those events have to the people who recount them. Interviews looking back on people's lives can explore unknown events or new aspects of known events. But perhaps even more important, they are vital sources of the speaker's subjective feelings, beliefs, and values. Such interviews can reveal not just what people did but what they wanted to do, what they believed they were doing, what they feel about having done it. As historian Alessandro Portelli has pointed out, subjectivity is as much a part of history as the more visible facts (100). What someone believes or believes happened, and what they felt about it, are indeed important. They may tell us quite a bit about imagination, needs, hopes, and aspirations. "Errors" can be very revealing. Faulty memory may tell us how people wished they had lived their lives. And self-promotion may tell us a great deal about one's desires.

Since it is inevitable that we know something and describe it through our own system of feelings, beliefs, and values, such interviews should be seen as evidence of those feelings, beliefs, and values—as well as a means of opening new possibilities for exploring how individuals connect with larger-scale historical processes. If we simply see memory as an impressionistic source that needs to be confirmed by scholars and independent sources, we neglect to recognize how indispensable the evidence of memory is, as historian Michael Frisch points out, for observing those pesky moral, political, and emotional questions of contemporary consciousness that complicate the study of history.

Two distinct, albeit related, issues come to mind when we look at the way *The Life and Times of Rosie the Riveter* treats the women's testimonies. The first has to do with the fact that documentarians might—and often do—privilege one type of evidence over others. Some materials seem more worthy of attention and are therefore called upon to give us a sense of the way things "really" are. In the case of *Rosie the Riveter*, it is the recounting of firsthand experience that makes the film believable. The other issue relates to the way the various pieces of evidence "talk" to each other, how they are situated within the overall design of the documentary. Oftentimes, it is this specific arrangement that determines what kind of evidence should be considered relevant and worthy of attention. The testimonies in the film stand out precisely because they are made to contradict the archival footage.

"Facts" are all around us all the time. Faced with the chaos of information, someone must decide that a person's memory of an event or some aspect of sociohistorical reality might be relevant to an argument or to a story and declare it evidence. Everything that happens is not equally worthy of being included in a particular story. When we declare some experiences "evidence," others, by implication, are deemed "irrelevant." Facts become evidence in response to particular questions or as needed by a particular argument or mode of storytelling. As Bill Nichols explains, facts, events, and testimony convert to evidence when taken up by the documentary's interpretive discourses ("The Question of Evidence" 31).

This attitude toward facts and history sees the past—or even the present—as a series of somewhat random occurrences that are given a retroactive coherence by the history writer, documentarian, or storyteller. Some facts are presented and others are withheld. And the decisions about what to include are calculated and tactical. Facts may seem to have a natural organization once the documentary maker has chosen a subject and a story. But it is important to remember that it is the documentarian's job to fashion that organization.

For a film that puts so much emphasis on the way evidence is used in non-fictional representations, however, *Rosie the Riveter* says remarkably little about evidence itself and its relationship with lived reality. Instead, it seems content to substitute one type of evidential material for another. As a polemical thesis, *The Life and Times of Rosie the Riveter* respects archival documents as period "facts," even while they are contradicted by the more multifaceted evidence of women's experience. The film offers a new version of "Rosie," a new truth, contrary to the one suggested in the wartime propaganda. (It is implied, of course, that this new Rosie is representative of others.) The film seems to assume that the facts of experience are logically self-evident and speak for themselves. But do they? Or do they speak through the individual subjectivities of the women interviewed and then, ultimately, through the eyes, ears, and opinions of Connie Field, director-producer-coeditor? It is she who makes the experience accessible to all—and it is she who determines the salience of certain things and not others. As she put it in a symposium, "Although *Rosie* was not scripted, it was carefully planned before shooting. I outlined the history, all the issues. The women I had chosen for the film—five of them—I had interviewed quite extensively before filming, and then, in filming, I asked specific questions which would elicit certain stories I knew they could talk about" (in Zheutlin 157).

Other films go beyond the revisionist impulse that motivates Field's project, offering a more radical challenge to normative history and an even greater enlargement of the picture. Documentaries such as *The Ties That Bind* (Su Friedrich, 1984), *Handsworth Songs* (John Akomfrah, 1986), and *Delirium* (Mindy Faber, 1993), discussed below, presume that history can contain irreconcilable perspectives, none of which is complete or completely "true." They make us reflect not only on the legitimacy of documentary evidence but also on the way cinema—and other forms of nonfictional representation—uses memory and experience to create personal and historical narratives. After all, just as framing always involves excluding, remembering also always involves forgetfulness.

Su Friedrich's *The Ties That Bind* (1984) treats evidence both as partial (in both senses of the word partial) and contingent. In this film Friedrich interviews her mother about her life in Germany during the rise of Hitler, during World War II, during the American occupation after the war, and, later, after settling in the

United States, participating in antiwar protests and demonstrations. Importantly, she not only asks her mother questions but also responds and reacts. Rather than seeming detached and supposedly impartial, the filmmaker is clearly part of the picture—as the daughter of the woman who tells her history, as someone who instigates the stories that her mother tells, as the person who ponders, assesses, and appraises the evidence (her mother's testimony), and as the person responsible for choosing the images, arranging them, and combining them with the sounds. The interdependence of the filmmaker and her subject, on the one hand, and the act of interpretation, on the other, are palpable. In fact, the hand of interpretation is evident throughout the documentary (the filmmaker's hand, literally, as a frequent image in the film, and figuratively, as the person responsible for making the film), so we cannot ignore Friedrich's role as interpreter of, and as contributor to, her mother's story.

Testimony is always conditioned by circumstances: personal history and material life, for instance, and the organization of power and control over the social relations in the filmmaking process. In *The Ties That Bind*, Su Friedrich exposes many of those conditions by including moments that other filmmakers might have omitted. At one point in the film, we hear the mother sobbing over black leader, after discussing the mistreatment of old people during the occupation and imagining what would have happened to her parents had they still been alive. At another, she is playing the piano and chides her daughter for recording her music. Friedrich also uses intertitles scratched into the film's emulsion to tell us about her own motivations, to pose questions for her mother to answer, and to convey her incredulity. Appearing slowly, word by word, as if to mimic her thought process, these titles talk back to the testimony, weighing and evaluating it, even questioning its veracity. We

2.2. Su Friedrich comments on her mother's testimony in *The Ties That Bind* (Su Friedrich, 1984).

hear, for example, her mother's voice insisting, over images of barbed wire and concentration camps: "It was the main leaders of the countries that knew. But the people did *not* know. And I will say this to the end of my day, we did *not* know the Jews were gassed or killed. They were put into concentration camps; that is all we knew." Then a title asks: "So you did know about the camps?" The voice continues: "We, our family, knew of one camp and that was Dachau. And at Dachau, according to the investigation, only at the very end of the war were there killings." The titles return with vehemence, in capitals and larger than usual: "NO." Then they read: "from 1933 to 1945, 30,000 people were either shot, killed in medical experiments, or worked to death." The image that follows is the most conventionally framed shot in the film, a five-second portrait of her mother from the waist up, a two-thirds profile leaning on her fist in silence.

By allowing her mother to tell her story from her memories (and by including footage of dubious accuracy), *The Ties That Bind* acknowledges recollections as subjective and sees memories, like values and beliefs, as conditioned by circumstances, points of view, and ways of thinking. That is, testimony provides data for analysis, not a simple conclusion. The point is not that her mother's life is fraught with ambiguities and contradictions, but the evidence of her life is. The openness of this film's representation and the titles invite us to reappraise what that evidence entails in terms of how the witness has experienced her reality, psychically as well as politically. The film doesn't promise completeness—it doesn't smooth over inconsistency, incoherences, or loose ends. *The Ties That Bind* never wraps up.

Compared to a film like *The Life and Times of Rosie the Riveter*, Friedrich's documentary seems rather unconventional. It treats witness testimony with a wariness that is absent from Connie Field's work, revealing the filmmaker's own intervention in the process through which evidence is solicited, gathered, and made available to the audience. Field's documentary, by contrast, allows us no insight into this process. Connie Field auditioned seven hundred Rosies over the phone. Two hundred were audiotaped in person, thirty-five were videotaped, and only five were selected to appear in the film. The filmmaker also edited and abridged the interviews according to her needs. Those that she selected had stories that expressed Field's point of view about what was typical of the times (Zheutlin 160).

This does not mean that Field's project is less worthy than Friedrich's—or that the truth claims in *Rosie the Riveter* are less legitimate. Given the choice between presenting straightforward testimonies and questioning their motivations on the screen, most filmmakers would probably opt for the former. What *The Ties That Bind* offers us, though, is a chance to look beyond the referential value of the material presented on the screen. We have access not only to the mother's memories but also to the way the filmmaker approached the material, from framing to editing. Throughout the film, we learn something about the filmmaking process itself and, by extension, about documentary cinema in general.

Evidence as Subject Matter

Several documentaries made in the last three decades take a similarly self-critical approach to the way evidence is used by nonfiction film and video makers, historians, reporters, and even lawyers. While their main subject might be external to the process of representation—racial disturbances, for example—the problems they examine often involve the authenticity of the evidential material itself. What types of evidence should be considered acceptable in a documentary film or video? What are the consequences of including or omitting a particular piece of evidence? And what interests do these choices serve? These questions are familiar to most, if not all, documentary makers, but we do not necessarily expect to see them included in the films themselves. When this happens, evidence becomes a documentary subject in its own right, a topic worthy of attention.

Several of these documentaries expose what they see as fraudulent or biased interpretations of evidential material. Some suggest that the management of information is a privilege of government and corporate public relations and are happy to counter the "official evidence" with independent judgments. Others acknowledge the impossibility of so-called objective reporting to get at anything close to the truth. It is not simply that documentary makers are driven by their own ideology; they often feel that the longer form gives them leeway to analyze, explain, and put things into contexts, helping to guide viewers through the tide of information.

Handsworth Songs (1986), a British documentary by the Black Audio Film Collective, exemplifies this approach to nonfiction filmmaking by contrasting different types of evidential material and interrogating the traditional goals of nonfictional representation. While the underlying theme in the film is the 1985 racial disturbances in Handsworth, Birmingham, *Handsworth Songs* also makes us think about the way the media handle information, what they do with existing evidence, and what consequences their choices may have. More interestingly, even though the film uses criticism of mainstream journalism as a structuring device, it does not merely present a new version of the racial disturbances. Rather, *Handsworth Songs* "challenge[s] the assumption that you can ever tell it like it is," as director John Akomfrah put it (Fusco, "An Interview with Black Audio Film Collective" 50–53). Instead of "correcting" television news reports or filling in the holes they willingly leave empty, *Handsworth Songs* took as its agenda "to re-open the questions."

Regardless of the fact that more white people than blacks were arrested in earlier unrest, a popular image grew of a black threat with the black male youth as the archetypal instigator. By the time of the 1985 disturbances in Handsworth, there was an already established, limited aural and visual vocabulary about blacks in Britain—what Coco Fusco calls a "riot iconography." And the image of the antagonisms between black male youth and the police was a consistent and primary factor in the formation of this riot iconography ("A Black Avant-Garde" 10–18). *Handsworth Songs* undercuts this iconography and unseats the authenticity of this evidence by bringing forward the experiences of black families and black male youth. Besides images of the disturbances (TV footage shot from behind the protection of police lines, as well as footage shot from the point of view of those being born down upon by the troops), we are introduced to evidence of happier times: wedding photos, archival footage of interracial dances, of settlers arriving on ships, and of toddlers in multiracial childcare. But the film presents this new evidence without direct explanation, not as if it were monolithic, timeless, unitary, or fixed evidence but as part of a dialogue, a lyrical, intimate struggle between different voices.

The contrast between these different types of evidential material is rendered obvious at various moments in the film. An old newsreel of a labor unionist assuring viewers that West Indian workers want social integration is followed by an overturned car on fire. Footage from the 1950s of Luther Thomas, a bus driver trainee, kissing his wife goodbye is juxtaposed to a traveling shot of the destruction of shops and businesses. And the death of an Afro-Caribbean woman (described in a radio interview with her daughter over an image of a cold, gray housing project) as a result of a police raid on her home precedes an excerpt from a vintage documentary showing fresh-faced young women at work in a factory and a folk song about fine young women on the sound track. In each of these examples, the "new" evidence coexists and competes with the images of violence, although it never really disputes the fact of the disturbances.

This thought-provoking use of evidential material also differs from the view of colonial history proposed by accredited sources. *Handsworth Songs* shows, for instance, an excerpt from an unadorned address by Prime Minister Margaret Thatcher, sitting calmly in a wing chair, stating, "People are really rather afraid that this country might be rather swamped by people of a different culture. And you know, the British character has done so much for democracy, for law, and done so much throughout the world. But if there is any fear that it might be swamped, people are going to react and be rather hostile. . . . The moment the minority threatens to become a big one, people get frightened." Thatcher's statement seems shocking not solely because of its moral shallowness but also because it lacks credibility. As the history of the riots shows, the complex reality of British society in the

1980s cannot be subsumed under the idea of a cultural threat to what she calls the "British character." Thatcher's comments reflect the blind patriotism of a nation besieged and reinforce long established prejudices against cultural diversity, the same prejudices that are discredited by the documentary's use of different types of evidential material. Not accidentally, *Handsworth Songs* follows the television address with slowed down footage of nearly a dozen police chasing, capturing, and subduing a lone dreadlocked young man.

Handsworth Songs confronts the problems of trying to re-present the complex and sometimes contradictory meanings and experiences of diaspora culture and identity—the culture and identity of peoples far from their homeland, often living in an environment that no longer welcomes them. It is both a reflection on racial disturbances and an indictment of the inadequacy of television news and other dominant institutions to represent racial violence. By exposing evidence as conditional and often precariously constructed, the film renders doubtful as well the values that keep the mainstream media in power as the provider of information. If the evidence on television aims toward definitive understandings of the events, the evidence in *Handsworth Songs* destabilizes not only those understandings but also what "Britishness" meant as a national and cultural identity in the mid-1980s.

In *Handsworth Songs*, there is some archival footage of Lord Kitchener, the calypso king, singing "London Is the Place for Me" to reporters, from the ship's deck upon his arrival in England. As it is used in *Handsworth Songs*, this sequence seems clearly ironic. After seeing so much violence, it is not possible to take this footage at face value. The same footage is used in an American film celebrating calypso, *One Hand Don't Clap* (Kavery Dutta, 1989). In this case, though, the meaning and effects of the evidential material are without irony. In *One Hand Don't Clap*, the footage follows an interview with Lord Kitchener talking about how he grew to enjoy London and became accustomed to the cold. There is not a hint of either hostility or thwarted dreams. The same footage thus operates as evidence in two separate films, but is employed for different purposes and takes on different meanings in each case. The dissonance between the said and the unsaid invites skepticism in *Handsworth Songs*. In *One Hand Don't Clap*, the context and consequences of the choice of evidence, its social and political aims, do not invite the same epistemological dialogue with the viewer. The footage speaks with little ambiguity.

Documentaries that examine the nature and function of evidence do more than simply represent a particular aspect of the sociohistorical world. They serve as critical texts as well. Like *Handsworth Songs*, they offer insight into problems that are commonly discussed by film critics but not necessarily addressed by documentary filmmakers. In their own way, they contribute to debates that find resonance in books like the one you are reading. At their most ambitious, these films tend to implicate their own strategies of representation in their critique of the documentary process, drawing attention to their particular interests and exposing the nature of their intervention in the world of lived experience. Rather than simply criticize someone else's work, the filmmakers here show what lies behind their efforts to gather and present evidence in a coherent and persuasive manner.

Evidence and Reflexivity

Film scholars have used the adjective *reflexive* to characterize this type of documentary, suggesting that the finished work reflects upon its own "constructedness." A reflexive documentary lets us know how it was made and what was involved in its making, turning the process by which the documentary produces meaning into part of the film. While the "outside world" continues to be a relevant subject, the way that subject is transposed to the screen can be just as important. Reflexive documentaries trouble the relationship between the film and what it represents, rendering opaque what other works might have tried to present as transparent. Since much of the credibility of nonfiction films depends on the authority of their evidential sources, these documentaries can draw considerable attention to the way evidence is made available to the audience.

At the center of most reflexive documentaries is thus the awareness, foregrounded in the work itself, that nonfictional representations are artificial constructs, not natural or unchangeable revelations. They are the result of a laborious process that involves particular material and technological conditions, institutional obligations, and specific interests. Any one of these factors can potentially determine the way evidence is gathered and presented to the audience, or influence the decision to omit or reveal a particular piece of information. While other films might suppress knowledge of this artificial quality, providing access only to a finished product that conceals its history, reflexive documentaries invite us to look at this process from the inside. Perhaps for this reason, reflexive documentaries have earned the reputation of being intellectually demanding and mistrustful of nonfictional representation in general. Seen from a different perspective, though, documentaries that are self-referential can also be compelling, thoughtful, and stimulating.

This is the case with Errol Morris's *The Thin Blue Line* (1988), which can be described as a reflexive documentary precisely because of the way it deals with its evidential material. While the filmmaker himself is never present on the screen—and the filmmaking process remains hidden "backstage"—the struggle over the legitimacy of evidentiary sources is a central topic in the film. *The Thin Blue Line* exposes a series of faults in the trial of Randall Adams, a man convicted of murdering a Dallas police officer in November 1976, roughly one decade before the shooting of the documentary. Much of the film revolves around the effort to show the uncertainty of the evidence that put Adams on death row—the doubtful testimonies by witnesses, the questionable interests of the prosecution, and so on. Parallel to this effort is Morris's reflexive approach to his own film: how it deals with conflicting evidence, what it can do to denounce the oversights in Adams's trial, and how it can represent an event that took place years earlier. *The Thin Blue Line* combines a critique of the judicial system with an assessment of the difficulties and impasses that surround the documentary itself.

Morris's task seems particularly interesting because there was no visual record of the crime and only the most conventional secondary material (mug shots, newspaper articles, road signs, maps, court drawings). Nor were there reliable witnesses. Adams's accuser, a young man named David Harris, who was allegedly in the car with Adams at the moment of the shooting, was himself involved in a series of crimes and was incarcerated at the time the film was made. Other witnesses failed to provide a convincing account of the event or, even worse, offered conflicting or contradictory testimonies. Morris illustrates the various accounts of the murder with reenactments that correspond to what the witnesses claimed to have seen. But because the testimonies do not necessarily coincide with each other, we end up watching different versions of the same event, the discrepancies underscoring the uncertainty of the case. Additionally, the highly stylized reenactments, drenched in cold film-noirish light and accompanied by Philip Glass's languid, repetitive score, detract attention from the crime, as if to suggest that everything had been reduced to images that could no longer point toward any consequential revelation.

To our surprise, however, *The Thin Blue Line* does offer a final statement about the Randall Adams case. At the end of the film, Morris rewards our thirst for credible evidence by

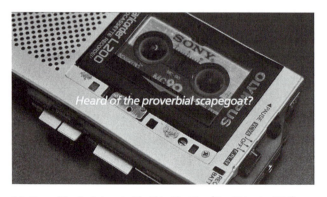

2.3. One of the final shots in *The Thin Blue Line* (Errol Morris, 1988).

disclosing a piece of information that had been withheld until then. The closing shots of *The Thin Blue Line* show a tape recorder playing a confession in which Harris, the accuser, all but admits that he, not Adams, committed the crime. First we hear him say that he is sure Adams was innocent. When the filmmaker asks him how he can be sure, Harris replies: "'Cause I'm the one that knows." Lacking visual material to go with the confession, Morris leaves the camera on the tape recorder, cutting to closer shots of the tape as Harris reveals his secret. The last image in the sequence is an extreme close-up of the recorder, whose size on the screen matches the importance of Harris's declaration.

As film scholar Linda Williams has noted, the effort to establish some form of truth while simultaneously interrogating the nature and use of documentary evidence is probably the most provocative quality in Morris's film (62–67). By drawing attention to his own manipulative strategies—the stylized reenactments and the juxtaposition of contradictory statements, for example—Morris reminds us of the distance that separates the mediating process from the actual event. Yet, despite this suspicion, he also seems to believe that documentary filmmakers have an obligation to confront lies and falsehood. And his efforts were not without consequences. One year after the film opened, Adams was released from jail.

Because they address problems that pertain to the filmmaking process, reflexive documentaries like *The Thin Blue Line* often appear more honest, and therefore more credible, than many other films. As anthropologist Jay Ruby has argued, these works connect product, process, and producer, offering insight into the *hows* and *whys* of nonfiction cinema. "Being reflexive means that the producer deliberately and intentionally reveals to his audience the underlying epistemological assumptions that caused him to formulate a set of questions in a particular way, to seek answers to those questions in a particular way, and finally to present his findings in a particular way" (35). This equation between reflexivity and credibility, however, can also be misleading, not to say deceptive. Reflexive strategies can tell us something about the making of a documentary and its intervention in the world of lived experience. But there is no guarantee that they will provide a reliable or satisfactory account of sociohistorical reality. Even if a documentary does expose the choices and motivations that underlie the production process, nothing can assure us that this reflexive impulse is not in itself an attempt to manipulate the audience. As our discussion of *David Holzman's Diary* demonstrates, there is no simple correlation between sincerity and reflexivity. Indeed, at the end of the film, we find out that *David Holzman's Diary* is not even a documentary.

Similarly, we should be cautious about rushing to equate reflexivity and progressive thinking. There is a venerable tradition that relates reflexive strate-gies to liberal and leftist politics, as well as to avant-garde aesthetics. The idea in this case is that by exposing the means through which documentary films—or fictional representations, for that matter—reconstruct reality, we can encourage a critical attitude on the part of the spectator. Reflexive strategies confront and demystify the cinematic illusions that enable filmmakers, writers, and artists to conceal their particular biases. But these assumptions, too, need to be assessed carefully, or discussed on a case-by-case basis. Film scholar Robert Stam astutely notes that reflexivity "does not come equipped with an *a priori* political valence" (153). While some reflexive documentaries do call upon us to scrutinize the pro-cess of representation, others might simply veer toward narcissism, obscuring whatever progressive value they might have had. To stick with a familiar example, it is this narcissistic attitude that is satirized in *David Holzman's Diary*, in which the filmmaker appears enamored both of himself and the filmmaking apparatus.

What reflexive documentaries can offer, however, is an opportunity for dia-logue between filmmakers and their audiences. By foregrounding their "construct-edness," they allow the documentarian to address the spectator more directly and make it easier for the audience to respond to the filmmaker's provocations. "The reflexive mode of representation gives emphasis to the encounter between the filmmaker and the viewer" (Nichols, *Representing Reality* 60). A similar "conver-sational dynamic" seems to exist between the filmmaking process and evidence from lived experience. What stands out in a reflexive documentary is not the al-leged autonomy that separates one from the other but their interdependence. The act of representation is incorporated into the sociohistorical world and vice-versa. Perhaps for this reason, reflexive strategies are more common in documentaries that combine individual and collective experiences with personal and political aspirations. By overlapping the filmmaking process with the world of lived experi-ence, the documentarian personifies the act of filming with evidence from his or her concrete situation.

Mindy Faber's *Delirium*, a 1993 video that looks at the history of female hyste-ria, is one of those works that use reflexive strategies to connect the personal and the political. The documentary is an autobiographical piece in which the artist looks at her mother's psychiatric history and comments on how it affected her own personality. However, as soon as we start watching *Delirium*, we realize that the mother's story is only part of Faber's project. It serves as a catalyst to a more ambitious discussion that also includes the experiences of other women and the ways madness has been represented in both popular culture and medical literature.

Faber combines individual memory and collective history, asking us to look at her mother's troubles not only as a medical condition but as a social problem as well, a consequence of female domesticity and passivity in a male-dominated society. Importantly, she does this by interrogating the so-called evidence of mental illness. And by doing so, she also invites us to wonder about what is implied in traditional uses of evidential material by documentary film and video makers.

What allows Faber to entertain this ambitious project is her reflexive intervention in the "scenes" recorded by the camera. Faber's presence in the video is obvious from the very beginning. Already in the first minutes of *Delirium*, we hear her voice, speaking in the first-person singular, over a set of family photographs that evoke memories of a deceptively normal childhood. "Two years after I was born," she comments, "my mom had a traumatic nervous breakdown. I never really knew exactly what had happened. But while I was growing up, it was always there." Slowly, *Delirium* lets us into a world of repressed anger, fear, and frustration, from which the mother emerges as emotionally and mentally unstable. Rather than reinforce this impression, though, Faber tries to undo received notions of female hysteria. She insists, for example, that the mother's illness was directly related to the imprisonment of domestic life, the constraints that normally come with traditional gender roles: "Is hysteria truly mental illness, or is it simply a sane reaction for having been born female and powerless in an oppressive world?" Faber's argument lacks the kind of evidence that we associate with scientific discourse. Yet it does not fail to convince us because we see it as growing out of lived reality. By bringing together life and art, Faber ends up granting to the second the evidential authority that we normally attribute to the first.

One of the video's intriguing aspects is the use of movie excerpts, both medical footage and fictional material, as representations of women's mental illness. As noted at the outset of this chapter, female hysteria has been visually documented since the nineteenth century. Fictional cinema, too, has contributed its share of images to our collective understanding of the subject. In her video, Faber uses both types of material, suggesting a sort of incongruous—but highly provocative—parallel between fictional and nonfictional representations. Like the fictional selections, the nonfiction footage conforms to preconceived ideas about women's mental instability. These are the very ideas that Faber tries to dispute in her work. *Delirium* never goes as far as saying that there are no differences between fictional and nonfictional representations. But it makes us question the motives behind the use of evidential material by Charcot in the nineteenth century as well as by documentarians.

At one point in the video, the mother, who has already discussed her own feelings about her breakdown in a closely framed interview, voices historical explanations of madness: "The uterus is the controlling organ of the female body" and "They used to think that if a woman used her brain too much, she wouldn't be able to have babies." Then, in a more ambiguous tone: "It's true. It's really true." Later, dressed up as a medical doctor in glasses, white coat, and tie, Patricia Jane Faber speaks what certainly seems to be scripted dialogue, but what is probably not untrue, questioning some of the motives behind Freud's work.

This playfulness, of course, is not inconsequential. By using her mother as both informant and actor, Faber is confounding our perceptions of what is true and untrue. Along with offering an incisive critique of the way medical doctors in general and psychiatrists in particular have used evidence to diagnose women's mental illnesses, Faber upsets the equation that links evidence to truth. The video insists that much of what we attribute to evidential material is in fact a function of the context and circumstances in which that material is produced and used. Like *Handsworth Songs*, *Delirium* sees representation as a political arena and sees evidence as a means of intervening in this particular arena.

Faber's candidness about the questionable nature of evidence is never as clear as it is in a sequence in which she exchanges roles with her mother, becoming herself the subject of the camera's curiosity. Toward the end of the video, we hear Mrs. Faber contradict her daughter's childhood memories of her mother's aggressive behavior: "Oh, Mindy, I don't remember that!" Then Mrs. Faber asks for the camera and points it toward her daughter, claiming for herself the authority that we normally attribute to documentary film and video makers. As the camera changes hands, Mindy looks a little uncomfortable, almost vulnerable, having become the subject of someone else's scrutinizing gaze. The sequence doesn't really undo the general argument presented in the video. Neither does it make Faber look less credible than before. But it reminds us that documentarians, too, have to struggle for their own truth.

Additional Filmography

Mondo Cane/It's a Dog's World (Paolo Cavara, Gualtiero Jacopetti, and Franco Prosperi, 1962)

Union Maids (James Klein, Miles Mogulescu, and Julia Reichert, 1976)

Selbe (Safi Faye, 1983)

The Good Fight: The Abraham Lincoln Brigade in the Spanish Civil War (Noel Buckner, Mary Dore, and Sam Sills, 1984)

Work in Progress (Luis Valdovino, 1990)

I is a Long Memoried Woman (Frances-Anne Solomon, 1990)

Lumumba: Death of a Prophet (Raoul Peck, 1992)

Fixer: The Taking of Ajmal Naqshbandi (Ian Olds, 2009)

Works Cited and Further Reading

Aristotle. *Rhetoric.* Trans. W. Rhys Roberts. Mineola, N.Y.: Dover, 2004.

Auguiste, Reece. "Handsworth Songs, Some Background Notes." *Framework* 35 (1988).

Bates, Peter. "Truth Not Guaranteed: An Interview with Errol Morris." *Cineaste* 17.1 (1989).

Corner, John. "Handsworth Songs." In *The Art of Record: A Critical Introduction to Documentary.* Manchester: Manchester University Press, 1996.

Flitterman-Lewis, Sandy. "Documenting the Ineffable: Terror and Memory in Alain Resnais's *Night and Fog.*" In *Documenting the Documentary: Close Readings of Documentary Film and Video*, ed. Barry Keith Grant and Jeannette Sloniowski. Detroit: Wayne State University Press, 1998.

Frisch, Michael. *A Shared Authority: Essays on the Craft and Meaning of Oral and Public History.* Albany: State University of New York Press, 1990.

Fusco, Coco. "A Black Avant-Garde?" In *Young British and Black.* Buffalo, N.Y.: Hallways/Contemporary Arts Center, 1988.

———. "An Interview with Black Audio Film Collective: John Akomfrah, Lina Gopaul, Avril Johnson and Reece Auguiste." In *Young British and Black.* Buffalo, N.Y.: Hallways/Contemporary Arts Center, 1988.

Gilroy, Paul. *There Ain't No Black in the Union Jack.* London: Hutchinson, 1987.

Hall, Stuart. "New Ethnicities." In *Black Film/British Cinema.* London: Institute of Contemporary Arts, 1988.

Mercer, Kobena. "Recoding Narratives of Race and Nation." In *Black Film/British Cinema.* London: Institute of Contemporary Arts, 1988.

Nichols, Bill. *Representing Reality: Issues and Concepts in Documentary.* Bloomington: Indiana University Press, 1991.

———. "The Question of Evidence, the Power of Rhetoric and Documentary Film." In *Rethinking Documentary: New Perspectives, New Practices*, ed. Thomas Austin and Wilma de Jong. Maidenhead: Open University Press, 2008.

Plantinga, Carl. *Rhetoric and Representation in Nonfiction Film.* Cambridge: Cambridge University Press, 1997.

Portelli, Alessandro. "The Peculiarities of Oral History." *History Workshop* 12 (Autumn 1981).

Ruby, Jay. "The Image Mirrored: Reflexivity and the Documentary Film." In *New Challenges for Documentary*, 2nd ed., ed. Alan Rosenthal and John Corner. Manchester: Manchester University Press, 2005.

Sekula, Allan. "The Body and the Archive." *October* 39 (1986).

Sheldon, James L., and Jock Reynolds. *Motion and Document Sequence and Time: Eadweard Muybridge and Contemporary American Photography.* Andover, Mass.: Addison Gallery of American Art, 1991.

Sontag, Susan. *Regarding the Pain of Others.* New York: Farrar, Straus and Giroux, 2004.

Stam, Robert. *Film Theory: An Introduction.* Malden, Mass.: Blackwell, 2000.

———. *Reflexivity in Film and Literature: From Don Quixote to Jean-Luc Godard.* New York: Columbia University Press, 1992.

Tagg, John. *The Burden of Representation: Essays on Photographies and Histories.* Amherst: University of Massachusetts Press, 1988.

Williams, Linda. "Mirrors Without Memories: Truth, History, and the New Documentary." In *New Challenges for Documentary*, 2nd ed., ed. Alan Rosenthal and John Corner. Manchester: Manchester University Press, 2005.

Winston, Brian. *Claiming the Real II: Documentary: Grierson and Beyond.* London: British Film Institute; New York: Palgrave Macmillan, 2008.

Zheutlin, Barbara. "The Politics of Documentary: A Symposium." In *New Challenges for Documentary*, 2nd ed., ed. Alan Rosenthal and John Corner. Manchester: Manchester University Press, 2005.

3

Authority

Documentaries are authored. They also generally speak with authority. And sometimes authorities give testimony on screen. Authority thus forms part of the complicated ways by which documentaries represent nonfictional reality. In fact, it is because documentaries speak to us with authority that we trust what they have to say. But where does that authority come from? And how can we recognize it?

It is easy to answer these questions when we look at documentaries that rely on voiceover narrations or when the documentarian appears in the film. Authority, in these cases, seems to emanate from a specific place; it can be associated either with the disembodied voice of an unseen narrator or with a visible entity. In *Bowling for Columbine* (2002), for example, Michael Moore does both things: he adds his own voiceover narration to the images and appears on the screen, playing the role of reporter and commentator. Moore's voiceover narration complements what we see and, every so often, provides information that is otherwise unavailable. Above all, it guides us through the film, helping us make sense of what we are watching. His screen appearances extend this presence to the visual track, creating a sense of rapport between the spectator and the filmmaker. They also situate the documentarian vis-à-vis the material recorded. We know where Moore stands in relation to his subjects. And we know what he does and how he does it.

But not all documentaries use voiceover narrations. And even fewer include the filmmaker's screen appearance. The sources of authority, in these other cases, seem more diffuse. What allows the films to "speak" authoritatively is usually a variety of things. As we saw in the previous chapter, evidence adds credibility to a film's truth claims, which in turn gives authority to the documentary. The same thing can be said about expert interviews, although these are clearly different in nature. Documentarians habitually call upon the knowledge of experts to back up their claims, or they combine interviews with evidential sources. Even seemingly unrelated material, such as fictional footage, can be used to illustrate or boost a particular point. Michael Moore knows this as well. In *Bowling for Columbine*, he draws not only on the power of his larger-than-life screen presence but also on various source materials that range from home movies to television news footage, from vintage commercials to fiction films, and from witness testimonies to interviews with authority figures.

In general, it is the combination of these different elements that gives authority to documentaries. Isolated sources can tell us a great deal about a particular subject, and they can reveal something about the way filmmakers approach the historical world. When we watch a documentary, though, we usually look at each source in relation to the others. It is the overall arrangement of the materials, the "dialogue" between them, that makes them meaningful.

More is involved in the concept of authority, however, than credibility. To say that a documentary "speaks" with authority is usually to assume that it provides a clear perspective on historical reality. Evidence is commonly deployed to substantiate a specific point of view. So are expert testimonies or any other source used by a documentary maker. There is no authority that is completely neutral. The question to keep in mind, then, may be not simply what documentaries can do to secure their authority but how that authority compels us to look at the referential world in a particular way. Who "speaks" to us, with what purpose, and to what effect?

Making an authoritative documentary may look like an easy task. The documentary maker finds source material that validates a certain point of view, then constructs commentary that conveys that viewpoint. The unity and coherence of the documentary's perspective should seem beyond all doubt. It should communicate information in a forceful and unambiguous manner, so as to leave little room for conflicting opinions.

While this kind of authoritative documentary is still made, contemporary filmmakers sometimes take a more nuanced approach to the historical world, acknowledging diverging points of view, refraining from making definitive statements, or letting it be known that what we are seeing and hearing are the personal views of the filmmaker. Some films explore the very nature of authority in nonfiction cinema, disclosing the means by which a documentary defines its perspective and inviting the spectator to assess the role of the filmmaker in this process. (Reflexive documentaries of the kind examined in the preceding chapter commonly do this.) Still others go beyond the effort to demystify the process of representation and, as we shall see shortly, extend the documentarian's authority to the people in front of the camera, allowing documentary subjects some measure of control over their representations. The idea of authority has not gone unchallenged in recent years.

These last two categories suggest a modern approach to nonfiction cinema, as documentary makers appear increasingly aware of their prerogatives and responsibilities. But these distinctions are not always clear-cut, and any given documentary might incorporate more than one approach. Michael Moore's films, for example, seem to expose the mechanisms by which the filmmaker frames the historical world for his audience. His authority, nonetheless, remains uncontested and his films hardly allow for diverging points of view.

This chapter looks at the way documentaries make authoritative statements about the historical world and how the effort to create credible representations contributes to relaying a film's outlook on reality. It also examines different attitudes toward authority in nonfiction cinema. And it explores the notion of authorship in documentary and the means by which documentary makers may share their authorial voice with the subjects documented.

Distinguishing Sources of Authority

One way of giving credibility to a particular representation is by using reliable sources. Documentarians draw from a vast array of materials. These materials can, however, function differently. Historians frequently distinguish between primary and secondary sources. By primary sources, they mean original documents and archival material contemporary with the subject being studied. The term secondary source, on the other hand, refers to later discussions of that same subject. A letter from an American Civil War soldier, for instance, would be considered primary material, while the ideas of a Civil War scholar reflecting on that letter or other aspects of the war would serve as a secondary source.

Documentaries, of course, are different from history books. Historians tend to privilege written sources, while documentary makers rely mostly on sound and image. For that reason, documentaries are more likely to give the impression that history is not constructed but merely recorded by the filmmaker. Documentaries are also more constrained by budget restrictions and exhibition patterns. And while they might have a more direct impact on the audience, they seldom enjoy the complexity of written accounts (Rosenstone).

Yet, for all these differences, the concepts of primary and secondary sources can be useful for us too. While documentaries do not generally quote extensively from written sources, they may use original footage, material shot by a witness contemporaneous with the events being explored. In this case, the footage plays a role analogous to that of the letter written by the soldier in the example above. Conversely, interviews with authority figures and expert opinions, which are standard in many types of documentary, remind us of what historians call secondary sources. A film scholar might be called upon to talk about the early days of cinema. And an astrophysicist might be invited to explain the birth of the universe.

These distinctions are meaningful because we tend to treat primary and secondary sources differently. Primary sources are closer to the subject under scrutiny and are, therefore, frequently perceived as more reliable. That is the case, as we saw in the preceding chapter, with most types of evidential material, which seem to bear an immediate relationship with the events represented. Documentaries that make extensive use of original footage draw their authority from this perceived closeness. By contrast, secondary sources have no direct connection to their subjects. Their authority has less to do with spatial or temporal proximity than with knowledge sanctioned by legitimate and publicly recognized institutions such as universities, research organizations, the publishing industry, and so forth.

In practice, documentaries tend to utilize both kinds of material. Expert testimony alone can be tiring and, depending on the circumstances, might also seem questionable. Documentary makers avoid these risks by supporting interviews with visual evidence, sometimes with the voice of the expert talking over the images. The primary source (the evidential material) is used, then, to illustrate, endorse, or uphold a secondary source. On the other hand, expert testimonies can help legitimize primary source information by explaining it and submitting it to the authority of a particular discipline or institution. They can also add eloquence to evidence that might otherwise appear inarticulate or incomprehensible.

The Panama Deception (Barbara Trent, 1992) relies on multiple sources to draw a picture of the 1989 U.S. invasion of Panama. One of the aims of the documentary is to discredit mainstream media reports that overlooked the military campaign's harm to the Panamanian civilian population and focused instead on strategic issues. To support her claims, Trent resorts to footage that had not been seen on U.S. network television. She also interviews American government officials, talks to Panamanian politicians, hears from scholars and activists, and records emotional testimonies from ordinary citizens. Much of the material comes from people who witnessed or participated in the events, although not all sources concur with one another. We watch a U.S. government spokesperson claiming that the operation was successful in minimizing damage to property and, more importantly, in minimizing casualties. Then the filmmaker shows us a Panamanian woman crying over the death of her daughter. Both sources were involved in the events—one as a representative of the government that planned and executed the campaign, the other as victim of the strikes that hit the civilian inhabitants. Yet they offer entirely different testimonies.

The effort to provide a counter-representation of the attacks benefits as well from the voices of experts who comment on the motives and consequences of the military campaign. We hear, for example, from authors and university professors who criticize the complicity between the media and the government and dispute the notion that the invasion was prompted by the need to protect American lives in Panama. We also watch human rights advocates denouncing the killing of thousands of civilians. In general, these authority figures were not directly involved in the events of 1989. They offer not evidential testimonies but carefully thought out arguments, legitimized by their status as writers, academics, or activists. To employ the same terminology, they function as secondary sources. But their voices are just as relevant.

The importance assigned to secondary sources in *The Panama Deception* reminds us that expert opinions enjoy a kind of cachet that evidential material or personal testimony by itself might lack. Distance from the events can produce a more reasoned or carefully pondered response to historical reality. Additionally, when we think about expert opinion, we assume that the material under consideration has been endorsed by established research criteria. Experts embody a type of social and cultural eminence that might elude the practical differences between primary and secondary sources.

Ultimately, the notion of cultural status demands that we look at credibility and authority from a different angle. As methodological and analytical concepts, primary and secondary sources suggest a sort of kinship between documentary filmmaking and history writing, but they hardly exhaust the discussion of what makes a source reliable. When the authority of expert opinion prevails over the voices of ordinary people, for instance, it is often because of socially established hierarchical distinctions that connect expert testimony to "legitimate" forms of knowledge. In fact, the documentary genre itself benefits from this association with authorized knowledge—otherwise we would not be drawing comparisons between documentary filmmaking and historical writing.

This is not to say, of course, that documentaries cannot reverse these hierarchies. Pelin Esmer's *The Play/Oyun* (2005), for example, deliberately locates the source of authority amongst "less prestigious voices," relying on the personal testimonies of peasant women in order to portray patriarchal society in rural Turkey. Shot in the village of Arslanköy, the documentary focuses on a group of women working with a local school principal to put together a play based on their life experiences. Most of them are agricultural workers, unfamiliar with the conventions of theatrical writing. And none have formal training as actors. Yet they all contribute to the making of the play, first by sharing their life stories with the principal and later by performing roles based on those stories. Esmer's documentary captures both the development of this process and the voices of those who participate in it.

In an early sequence, we watch a meeting between the school principal and the women whose stories are to provide the basic material for the play. One woman talks about the difficulties of giving birth alone; another complains of having to work in the fields while her husband sleeps at home. Despite their particularities, the stories revolve around the same themes: marriage, mothers-in-law, children, and work. Esmer documents these conversations and uses them not only as a record of the creative process but also as a way of getting to know the women in the village. She also interviews them outside the school: at home with their families, in the orchards, and in the fields. These interviews, together with the development of the play, end up being the main—if not the only—entry point to the sociohistorical world.

3.1. Village women discussing what should appear in their play, from the documentary *The Play/Oyun* (Pelin Esmer, 2005).

In another sequence, a young hairdresser recalls being forced out of secondary school by a father who expected her to get married. Unwilling to marry, she was given as a foster child to a family in Ankara but eventually decided to come back to the village. She now dreams of finishing high school and taking the university exam. The scene, shot while the hairdresser is applying makeup on a customer, underlines the significance of the personal, emotional stories shared by the documentary subjects. It also suggests a parallel between the making of the play—appropriately called *The Outcries of Women*—and the shooting of the documentary. Both the film and the play empower the village women by letting them speak for themselves.

The process of putting together *The Outcries of Women* helped the participants to understand their needs and analyze their desire for—and resistance to—change. Toward the end of the film, one of the women mentions that her thirteen-year-old son has been complaining that he has been neglected. The episode is part of an informal conversation that takes place in the home of one of the performers and involves several women from the play. As the mother expresses her guilt about not being able to fulfill her family responsibilities, one of her friends replies: "Make [your son] love the theater, and when he loves it as much as you do he'll hold on to it with enthusiasm. He won't ask you to cook for him anymore; he'll do it himself." "You favor him because he's a boy," she adds a little later, "that's what you saw your parents do. You're oppressed and can't get rid of it." Although we don't see them talking about the making of the documentary, the film does provide a public forum for understanding how the play has affected their daily lives. "You've been oppressed until now," the friend says, "but now you [have] started taking your freedom."

"The Voice of Documentary"

When all these testimonies are organized into a coherent whole, what we have is not just the record of individual experiences; it is a broader and more ambitious statement about those experiences. Like the women themselves, the documentary seems to "speak" in a distinctive way and from a particular point of view.

Bill Nichols has used the phrase "the voice of documentary" to designate the way nonfiction films "speak" to us, how they arrange different materials in order to address the historical world. The term "voice," of course, is not used literally (as, for example, in voiceover commentary). Rather, it refers to all "that which conveys to us a sense of the text's social point of view, of how it is speaking to us and how it is organizing the materials it is presenting to us." It involves the "interaction of all a film's codes" (18–19). In *The Play*, each testimony contributes decisively to the representation of the women's experiences. But it is the orchestration of these voices within the film that defines the way the documentary speaks to us.

Nichols's formulation is useful because it helps us think about the relationship between the source material and the documentary as a whole. It allows us to see how a film treats its different sources, whether or not it contains or controls their authority, and how it can play one source against the other. Sometimes different sources complement and support one another. In other occasions, they produce divergence and discrepancy. In *The Panama Deception*, the disagreement between sources creates a tension that defines the dominant perspective in the documentary. The juxtaposition of conflicting testimonies serves to expose the breaches in the U.S. government's official accounts of the military intervention, which in turn helps to shape the way the film speaks to us.

Rather than create contradictory statements, the use of conflicting sources can reveal the complexity of the subject under scrutiny. Nichols himself seems to favor documentaries that offer different entry points to the sociohistorical world. "History," he writes, "is not a monolith, its density and outline given from the outset" ("The Voice of Documentary" 26). Instead, it is a multifaceted process that involves diverse and, now and again, opposite points of view.

In some instances, though, the use of diverging source material can imperil the authority of the film as a whole. Andrew Jarecki's *Capturing the Friedmans* (2003) tells the story of a family from Long Island, New York, that was torn apart by charges of child molestation involving Arnold Friedman, his son Jesse, and youths from their hometown. The charges against the Friedmans seemed questionable from the beginning, and the documentary highlights the uncertainties of the case by using sources that contradict each other. Testimonies from law enforcement officials, attorneys, alleged victims, and family members both reinforce and discredit the charges. As a result, the spectator's desire to find out what really happened is never fully rewarded. Both Arnold and Jesse were sentenced to jail. But for those in the audience the case remains open.

What makes *Capturing the Friedmans* different from other documentaries that rely on conflicting sources is the absence of an overarching statement about the case. While we can talk about the existence of a "governing voice" in documentaries like *The Panama Deception* or *Rosie the Riveter* (in which not all sources agree with each other), in *Capturing the Friedmans* the dominant perspective seems to shift along with the materials used by the filmmaker. Jarecki never fully answers the questions raised in the film. On the contrary, he encourages us to think that truth claims can be ambiguous and are often contingent upon specific circumstances. Like the reflexive documentaries discussed in chapter 2, *Capturing the Friedmans* offers an opportunity to mull over the nature of nonfictional representation itself.

On the one hand, the film calls upon the spectators to fill in the blanks and come up with their own verdict. On the other, it runs the risk of suggesting that all testimonies are equally valid—or equally doubtful.

The Suspicion of Authority

When the film's point of view stands out, we may perceive the representational process as skewed and, sometimes, personal. By contrast, when documentaries refrain from making authoritative statements about the world, we are encouraged to believe that it is the world itself that speaks to us. The authority of the filmmaker seems overwhelmed by the events captured by the camera. While in practice nonfiction films always involve a particular point of view, the idea that documentaries might simply record the world as it is—rather than present a partial account of lived reality—has frequently served as a source of legitimacy for the representational process. To some documentary makers and critics, it is the purported absence of an authoritative perspective that gives credibility to nonfictional representations.

This suspicion of authority provided the basis for a powerful documentary film movement in the United States during the 1960s. The idea then was to document the historical world with minimal interference, so as to let things be what they would normally be like if the camera and microphone were not there to record them. To achieve these goals, direct cinema filmmakers—as they would eventually be known—used little, if any, voiceover narration (which could have appeared as an imposition on the subject matter), refrained from directing action, and avoided interviews and other types of interaction with their subjects. They merely "observed," like a "fly on the wall," as they said back then.

Whether or not we accept the idealism of this agenda, direct cinema films do teach us something about authority in documentary. For the sixties filmmakers, authority appeared as a way of distancing representation from reality, a means of distorting or, even worse, of corrupting lived experience. Gone from their films was, in theory, the gesture that submitted reality to a particular point of view. As theorist and critic Paul Arthur has noted, the noninterventionist ideal amounted to "a textual crisis of authority" (118). Direct cinema presumably removed the documentary record from conventional mechanisms of representation and turned the filmmaking process into an effort to simply make the world available to the audience.

Frederick Wiseman's *Titicut Follies* (1967) is typical of this aesthetic and ideological stance. It evokes direct cinema's philosophy to create a seemingly spontaneous portrait of everyday life in the Massachusetts Correctional Institution at Bridgewater, a hospital for the criminally insane. Like other direct cinema documentaries, it conveys a strong sense of immediacy, which in turn overshadows the existence of a perspective on the events represented. None of the scenes in the film seems to have been staged. Instead, what stands out in *Titicut Follies* is the impression of looking upon people who appear oblivious to the presence of the camera and, by extension, to the spectators as well. What happens at Bridgewater State, we are led to believe, has nothing to do with the making of the film. It is presumably what would have taken place even if Wiseman had not shown up with his crew.

Several sequences in *Titicut Follies* reinforce the notion that we are observing a world unaffected by the mediating process. Early in the film, for example, we watch a conversation between a psychiatrist and his patient, in which the latter is asked to talk about the sexual activities that led to his incarceration. The close shots of the conversation allow for a strong, almost intimate, connection between the viewer and the subjects. And yet at no moment do the people in front of the camera acknowledge the fact that they are being filmed.

It is surprising, then, to find one sequence in *Titicut Follies* in which the filmmaker's intervention seems both clear and purposeful. It happens when a patient who has been refusing to eat is force-fed by the staff in the hospital. As we watch the painful ritual unfold "in the present," Wiseman cuts to images shot later on, after the patient's death. The shot of the man being fed through a tube is intercut with the image of a corpse, which we recognize to be the body of the same patient. This flash-forward diverges from the dominant pattern in the documentary. Not only does it expose the possibilities afforded by the techniques of film editing, it also highlights the role of the filmmaker as a creative agent, an authority capable and willing to make a statement about the reality documented.

The sequence is also important because it foregrounds what had until then been an implicit assumption in the film: *Titicut Follies* provides a critique of the living conditions in the psychiatric hospital. It assesses the world from a particular point of view. As Bill Nichols has remarked, the sequence "[works] to make an editorial point . . . rather than allow events to unfold according to their own rhythm" (*Representing Reality* 41). Although we might occasionally forget, *Titicut Follies* does have an author, someone whose informed view of reality and whose voice of authority help give shape to what we see and hear.

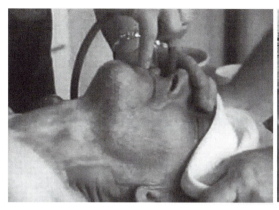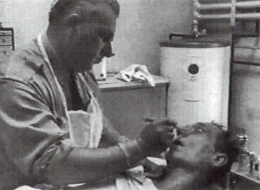

3.2. Force-feeding a patient in *Titicut Follies* (Frederick Wiseman, 1967). 3.3. Preparing the corpse for burial in *Titicut Follies* (Frederick Wiseman, 1967).

The Documentarian as Author

What is a documentary author? When critics talk about filmmakers as authors, it is usually to point out the distinctive attributes of the work of a certain artist or, more commonly, to highlight the significance of personal vision in a specific film. Authorship appears as synonymous with artistic originality, creativity, or inventiveness. It is easy to see why this can pose difficult questions for documentary makers. To documentarians, the emphasis on authorship might suggest a departure from the genre's commitment to representing reality, a shift toward individual expression. Instead of conferring prestige to a particular documentary, as happens when we talk about fictional cinema, authorial intervention could in theory endanger the credibility of the representational process.

Yet artistic vision is not alien to documentary; nor is the notion of authorship antithetical to nonfictional representation. *Triumph of the Will/Triumph des Willens* (Leni Riefenstahl, 1935), for instance, uses noticeably stylized camerawork to represent Hitler's visit to Nuremberg during the 1934 Congress of the National Socialist Party. Think of the sequence, toward the beginning of the film, in which we see Hitler standing on a moving vehicle as it rides past an enthusiastic crowd. The shots are taken from near the subject, who has his back turned to the camera. Standing in the foreground, isolated in the frame, Hitler ends up taking most of the screen space and appears as a sort of demiurgic figure. By contrast, the crowd that greets the passing motorcade is usually seen from afar, often in high angle shots that highlight the people's submissiveness to their leader. This contrast helps define the way we see the events in the documentary. Aesthetics and politics come together to create a film that is both impressive and well suited to Nazi ideology.

Other documentaries might not stand out as models of artistic expression, but they, too, can reveal the existence of a distinctive authorial voice. Frederick Wiseman's work, to return to a familiar filmmaker, is both personal and consistent, even though in this instance the author appears to "hide" behind a seemingly impersonal, noninterventionist mode of filmmaking. His interest in documenting the workings of institutions like hospitals and schools, and more recently the American Ballet Theater and Central Park, together with specific stylistic features (self-effacing camerawork, lengthy shots with synchronous sound, loosely structured narratives), add an easily recognizable authorial quality to his films.

So does the recognition of an authorial style threaten or boost the authority of documentary representations? Authorship need not distract us from the referential world. The contrary, in fact, is often the case. Distinctively authorial voices can, for example, expand our understanding of historical reality by suggesting new ways of looking at events with which we might already be familiar. Compare the authorial treatment of racial tension and urban violence that we have in *Handsworth Songs* with what we normally find in news reportage. The film stands out, in part, because it offers an uncommon view of the world and a highly stylized account of incidents known to the British public through ordinary media coverage. *Handsworth Songs* allows us to perceive the conflicts between the police and the people in Handsworth in a way that would hardly have been possible through official media channels. In this case, an authorial perspective is also likely to be seen as uncompromised by journalistic interests and demands, and therefore as *more* reliable. Instead of giving us less—because they fail to conform to standard notions of balance and objectivity—documentaries with a clear authorial perspective can give us more, by supplying unique insights into the subject explored.

Marlon Riggs's *Tongues Untied* (1989) is another good example of how a strong authorial voice can expand our appraisal of social reality. The film offers a poignant response to the impact of the AIDS epidemic on African American gay men, and its power as a documentary has as much to do with the seriousness of the subject matter as with Riggs's, at times, intensely personal and poetic approach to it. Departing both from the conventions of observational filmmaking and investigative reportage, it uses verse, music, and dance as representational tools, and explores sentiments such as sadness, anger, and outrage. Like many other documentaries, *Tongues Untied* relies on various individual testimonies to deliver its message. But here the testimonies become moments of self-dramatization that add intensity to the film. Similarly, the voiceover narrations in *Tongues Untied* provide more than commentary or explanation for what we see on the screen. They serve as expressive devices that draw on inflection and rhyme to articulate the film's message. Finally, Riggs's use of rhythmic editing and slow-motion photography also differs from documentary cinema's traditional ways of recording and organizing information.

As a result, *Tongues Untied*'s look at the lives of African American gay men seems both fresh and provocative. Rather than portray its subjects simply as victims of HIV and social discrimination, it shows them as progressive, creative, and active agents (starting with Riggs himself, the author, who also appears in the film). *Tongues Untied* eschews impersonal and seemingly objective approaches to the AIDS crisis and substitutes them with a text that is simultaneously solemn and sensuous, serious and exhilarating. In doing this, the film ends up speaking not of helplessness but of strength. And it solicits not pity but solidarity.

A documentary's authorial voice can be closely related to its subject matter, as happens when a film focuses on the personal experiences of the filmmaker. In these occasions, the author stands out not only as an agent capable of shaping the documentary material but also as someone who has privileged access to the reality documented, a sort of insider whose knowledge is based on concrete, lived experience. These are films with a strong autobiographical component, in which subjectivity poses no danger to authenticity but serves instead, as theorist Michael Renov nicely put it, as "the filter through which the real enters discourse" (176).

To be sure, documentarians never completely control the subject matter in their films. Nor is any one person the sole creator of a documentary. In fact, both film and literary theorists have taught us that authorship in general involves not one but many voices, all of which contribute to the construction of meaning. However unique or innovative it might be, the creative gesture usually presumes some form of "dialogue" between the creator and the social world, and the creator and the spectator. This is particularly true of documentaries, in which the filmmaker records and represents the thoughts and opinions of others. We can think of a film like *The Play*, with its self-effacing authorial presence and strong emphasis on the voices of ordinary women. We can also think of *Tongues Untied*, in which Marlon Riggs aligns his assertive voice with those of other African American gay men.

One interesting manifestation of authorial expression in documentary is the presence of the film or video maker on the screen, acting as participant, performer, or provocateur. In general, we do not need to see or hear the documentarian to associate authorial expression with lived experience. Nor does the visible or aural presence of the documentary maker necessarily suggest any direct involvement

in the events documented. (We sometimes hear the voice of an offscreen interviewer without identifying who is talking.) But being able to recognize the documentarian as "actor" in a particular situation does make it easier for us to connect
authority and authorship in nonfictional representation.

Think again of Michael Moore's documentaries. Or, more specifically, think
about the role played by the filmmaker in those documentaries. Michael Moore,
the everyman, the ordinary guy in the gravy-stained T-shirt whose job it is to look
after our interests, seems to be the authority that is no better than we are but who
has more guts. Smart but appearing to be unschooled, he performs an act that
says as much about his role as filmmaker, polemicist, and populist advocate of liberal causes as it does about the historical world. And the act itself adds credibility
to his films. Moore's documentaries depend on his screen persona to convince us
of the veracity of his claims.

Moore's screen act can be self-mocking at times, but it is ultimately reassuring. In *Roger and Me* (1989), his first feature-length documentary, he uses his
working-class background and his apparent lack of sophistication to forge an alliance with the average citizen, who is both a subject in his film and, in theory at
least, a member of the audience. The documentary examines the consequences of
the layoffs of thousands of workers from General Motors in the 1980s. It is also a
sort of autobiographical film, set in Flint, Michigan, Moore's hometown. Insofar
as he sides with the unemployed workers of Flint, Moore reveals a deep suspicion of established authorities like General Motors CEO Roger Smith, whom he
chases in the film. This suspicion, in turn, helps establish Moore's own authority
as documentary filmmaker. Good humored but always defiant, he works hard to
be "one of us." Moore wants us to believe that he knows what it is like to be out
of work.

The on-camera presence of the filmmaker suggests that the film is actually
about the gathering of information. Even though much of what we see is mani-
festly staged, it may also seem to emphasize a local and situated knowledge, available through the filmmaker's contact with other people in the documentary. Underlying this encounter with the world, however, is a more complex source of
authority: the self that is performed for the camera. To a large extent, it is this constructed, "enacted" self that secures the bond with the referential world and lends
a particular voice to the documentary. Michael Moore has few probing on-camera
interviews. Rather than introduce new information or produce suitable evidence,
the interviews serve to illustrate Moore's audacity and superiority and make us
aware of the contingencies of the moment. In Christopher Sharrett and William
Luhr's words, he's "a simple guy looking for answers to a few simple questions"

(254). His interviews are frequently impertinent (he hurls ridicule at politicians and gets under the skin of celebrities) and hold very little authority in the film's argument. They do, however, buttress the author's persona. Moore's persona, in a way, functions as the voice-of-God commentary did in days of old. Despite the persona's limited understanding, it gives the appearance of authoritative certainty and frequently seems to be extremely informational and, therefore, believable.

An ongoing contrivance in the film is Moore running up against a retinue of security guards and public relations personnel in an attempt to meet with Roger Smith. As Richard Schickel has noted, Moore the journalist certainly knows that getting in to see movers and shakers without an appointment is nearly impossible (77). But Moore's persona needs the encounters to fortify its own identity and illustrate his own authority. Interviewing Tom Kay, a spokesman and lobbyist for General Motors, who seems to be trying to dispel difficult questions with vacuous optimism whenever we meet him, Moore, suffering through Kay's glib assertion that there are still opportunities in Flint, hurls a useless question at him, "Do you mean that?" All Kay can answer is, "Yes, I do." In lieu of offering an appropriate response, Moore chooses to share with the viewer the energy of his delinquency. His interviews are sources not of authority but, like fiction films, of character. Yet his persona feeds off the glow of the authority it condemns.

Roger and Me lets us see what other nonfiction films tend to conceal: the role of the filmmaker as author and authority in the documentary process. Moore, the author, plays himself as documentary filmmaker. And it is the documentarian, the author of the film, whom we choose to believe, more so than the film itself. As Stella Bruzzi points out in another context, there would be no film without the filmmaker's interventions (207).

Shared Authority

In most other documentaries, the roles of documentary maker and documentary subject remain clearly distinct. Moreover, the relationship between one and the other has traditionally assumed an unequal distribution of authority, with the documentary maker enjoying the greater share. For this reason, documentary subjects have been demanding a more direct role in the filmmaking process. Those who have regularly been the subject of representation—non-Western people, ethnic and sexual minorities, women, the poor, and so on—have become more and more involved in production. In some cases, they have successfully taken up the roles of film and video makers. But even when they haven't turned themselves into documentarians, some have challenged conventional models of representation in which the maker and the subject occupy separate positions.

A common way of sharing authority is the documentary interview. In addition to being a useful source of information, interviews can help foster a genuine dialogue between documentary makers and their subjects. They create opportunities for spontaneous exchanges that can, in turn, help shape the documentary. That is the case with *The Play*, as we saw earlier. Instead of offering quick sound bites, *The Play* revolves around lengthy conversations that capture the interviewees' mood, opinions, and attitude toward the world, as well as their relationship with the filming process. The documentary subjects become participants in the making of the film, even if they do not have direct access to the filmmaking apparatus.

Apart from the interview format, nonfictional subjects can also participate in the filming process by acting out their lives. An interview is a sort of performance, an act staged for the camera. But it is not the only type of performance available to nonfictional subjects. Documentary reenactments, for example, serve a similar purpose. They involve staged events, which call for some form of acting on the part of the documentary subject. Here the subjects are asked to play themselves—or even other people—as if they were reliving a particular event or situation. And the acting determines, in part, how that event or situation will be represented.

We will have an opportunity to discuss the idea of nonfictional performance at length in a subsequent chapter about the profilmic. Here we look at a film in which the subject's screen act serves to expose the power relations that normally connect the documentary maker and the person in front of the camera.

In Kazuo Hara's *Extreme Private Eros: Love Song 1974/Gokushiteki erosu: Renka 1974* (1974), the documentary subject and her performance literally usurp the authority that we normally expect from the filmmaker. The film starts out as an autobiographical piece, the young Hara's effort to reconnect with his estranged girlfriend after their break-up. The woman in this case is Miyuki Takeda, a strong-willed independent feminist with whom he lived for three years. Some time after their break-up, Takeda left for Okinawa and took their baby son with her. As the film begins, we hear Hara's voice over a series of still photographs showing Takeda, the couple, and their child: "One day she told me she was going to Okinawa. I got really upset and agitated because if she went to Okinawa I would not be able to deal with feelings I still had for her. I felt I had to do something. . . . The only way to stay connected with her was to make this film." What follows, however, has less to do with Hara's emotions than with Takeda's daily life, her personal feelings toward him, and her relationships with people she has met in Okinawa. We watch her as she looks after the baby, interacts with new romantic partners, expresses her opinions about men, and intermingles with the women who work in bars frequented by American GIs stationed in Okinawa. We also see and hear her resentment toward Hara. Present in virtually every scene, Takeda is the main subject in his autobiographical film. She is also a sort of "collaborator" in the documentary, deciding—through her speeches as well as her actions—what we should know about her and how we should know it. Takeda's response to the presence of the camera is a lot more explicit than in many such observational films.

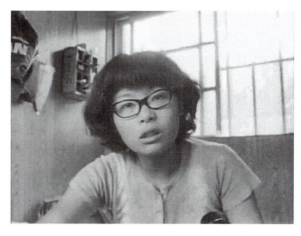

3.4. "I don't want to do this if you're getting upset." From *Extreme Private Eros: Love Song 1974/Gokushiteki erosu: Renka 1974* (Kazuo Hara, 1974).

In his first visit to Okinawa, Hara finds out that Takeda and her son had been living with a woman named Sugako and her infant. The nature of the women's relationship, we hear in his voiceover commentary, remains unclear to the filmmaker. But the footage recorded establishes a general pattern for the film. What we watch concerns not Hara's desire to continue his relationship with Takeda but Takeda herself and her new circumstances. The sequence opens with an argument between the two women. His name is never mentioned, his presence never acknowledged. Hara does not intervene or participate in the argument, and his role is limited to a few explanatory voiceover comments toward the end of the sequence, suggesting that his visit was the cause of their fight.

Eventually, the two women separate, and Hara's second visit finds Takeda living with Paul, an African American GI, who will also leave her after a few weeks. The brief sequence in which we see Paul and Takeda together suggests a more studied posture on her part, Takeda now self-consciously playing herself for the camera. At this point, we also know that she is two months pregnant, but the identity of the father seems to be of little importance to her. The sequence ends with what turns out to be the only open confrontation between her and the filmmaker. Yelling from offscreen, obviously furious with jealousy, Hara questions the motives of her relationship with Paul. But here, too, her presence eclipses the forcefulness of his voice. Before the sequence is over, we see Hara crying, microphone still in hand, shot in profile in one of the few times in which he appears on camera.

The most explicit manifestation of hostility toward him comes a few minutes later, when we are shown footage from his third visit to Okinawa. This time he shows up with Sachiko Kobayashi, a new lover, who becomes his sound recorder and producer for the documentary. Uncomfortable with her presence, Takeda uses the opportunity to humiliate Hara: "I don't trust him," she says nonchalantly. "He's good with words. That's why I don't trust him. . . . He just wants to have sex. You [Kobayashi] were an easy target for this guy." Takeda also questions his integrity as a documentarian: "If he is not trustworthy, how can the film be any good?"

Less apparent than her speeches but equally important are the actions she performs in the film. Much of Hara's job consists of recording what Takeda does. We watch her, for example, as she runs a nursery for the children of bar girls in Okinawa. Later, when she decides to adopt a bar girl's son, we follow Takeda in her unsuccessful search for the boy and his mother. Finally, just before returning to Tokyo, she takes us on a mission to educate the bar girls about their relationships with the GIs. Disappointed by her own experience with Paul, she writes a pamphlet—"from a woman of the mainland to women of Okinawa"—and distributes them in the bars and streets. In these scenes, the film becomes a sort of mouthpiece for her conscience, a way of recording and promoting her actions, a means for her to express her interests and concerns.

Takeda's authority finds an especially striking illustration in the scene in which she gives birth to her second child. Early in the film, she had told Hara that she wanted to get pregnant, travel to Central Asia, and have a child all by herself. Moreover, she wanted Hara to record it on film. Eventually Takeda does give birth to a baby girl by herself, with Hara shooting and Kobayashi holding the mike. The scene, however, takes place not in Central Asia but in Hara's Tokyo apartment. We first see her going into labor and preparing to deliver the child. Takeda lays out newspapers, plastic, and towels. Then comes a frontal image, a lengthy, uncompromising shot aimed between her legs, somewhat blurred, that shows the baby being born. Takeda does it without anyone's intervention, as Hara watches from behind the camera. ("I was so nervous. I was sweating so much, and I didn't know the picture was out of focus.") Later on, she recalls her feat with pride, turning the birth scene into yet another instance through which she asserts herself both as a woman and a documentary subject.

Extreme Private Eros: Love Song 1974 is particularly noteworthy in its approach to authority because it combines two distinct, albeit interconnected, forms of power relations: the exchanges between the documentarian and his subject, on the one hand, and the relationships between men and women, on the other. Neither the traditional codes of documentary filmmaking nor the conventions of patriarchal society seem to be on Takeda's side. But she manages to confront these rules by playing a part that contradicts standard expectations. Takeda uses the documentary in order to tell her own story, addressing issues that are relevant to women's role in society and settling unresolved problems with Hara. It is the nature of her act, the way she rises as an authority figure in the film, that makes *Extreme Private Eros* such a compelling documentary.

The Subject as Author

At its most ambitious, sharing authority with the documentary subject can turn the person in front of the camera into a sort of coauthor whose role might include other aspects of filmmaking as well. What if, for example, the subjects could make decisions regarding the structure of the documentary? Or if they could take the camera in their own hands? Several documentaries have tried to answer these questions by extending the tools of film and, more often, video making to the documentary subject.

These issues have concerned thoughtful documentary makers, especially since the introduction of portable video equipment in the 1960s, with its potential for more democratic participation in the communication process. In 1966, the National Film Board of Canada inaugurated Challenge for Change/Société nouvelle, a production incentive that was meant to address social problems, spur dynamic social change, and, increasingly, put cameras and production decisions in the hands of community members. One of their works, Mort Ransen's 1969 *You Are on Indian Land*, addressed current events from the Mohawk viewpoint. Tribal members served on the crew, and Mike Mitchell, a member of the community, spoke the narration in the first person plural. In recent years, this kind of project has been facilitated by the availability of technology that is not only more affordable but also easier to operate. It is now relatively common to see documentarians sharing the camera with their subjects and teaching them how to use it. Documentary subjects also participate in the editing of their works, thus extending their input to the videos' organizational structures. The making of the documentary ends up involving much more than an effort to represent the sociohistorical world. It becomes a pedagogical and communal project, the result of which can be a multi-authored account of a particular experience.

Any list of documentaries in which the subjects become the authors or coauthors of their representations would be incomplete, but it's worth mentioning a few examples from the past couple of decades. Spencer Nakasako worked in a San Francisco youth center with Southeast Asian teens, giving them the means to represent themselves. The Mirror Project in Somerville, Massachusetts, later relocated to Atlanta, Georgia, under Roberto Arévalo's supervision, also gave video cameras to inner-city teens to record their community. From 2004 to 2007, the Scribe Video Center coupled community groups in the greater Philadelphia area with humanities scholars and filmmakers for four months of video training and research, culminating in forty-two short, community-made videos that give voice to local residents to tell the world about their neighborhoods. In China, Wu Wenguang has been handing small digital video recorders over to farmers to make their own documentaries. In the Philippines, Kidlat Tahimak has been instructing Ifugao hill tribes on the use of video. The traditional people ethnographers usually study—such as the Aboriginals in Australia and the indigenous people of the Amazon forest—are now producers of studies themselves. And even when they do not have total control over the means of representation, many indigenous groups can dictate how they are represented and what aspects of their culture can be represented, restricting access to certain ceremonies and information. Groups attempting to establish and maintain a sense of community and to assert their social and political claims to the larger world are challenging the right of established institutions to control the representation of their lives.

Taking Aim (Monica Frota, 1993) documents one of these efforts to share video technology with indigenous groups. In 1985 Frota, an independent film and video maker, and anthropologists Renato Pereira and Luis Rios started teaching the Kayapo in the Brazilian Amazon how to use video cameras. Having been the subject of documentary films and television reportage, the Kayapo understood the nature of the recording technology and were familiar with its results. But the new project, known as Mekaron Opoi D'joi (He Who Creates Images), aimed at giving them access to the means of production and therefore power over how they would be represented. The first Kayapo group with which the documentarians worked, the Metuktire, responded enthusiastically to the idea and soon began learning how to use the video equipment. They also recognized the political significance of video recording. Frota recalls in an article about Mekaron Opoi D'joi that during a malaria crisis in 1985, while the Metuktire were waiting for government assistance, one of the leaders asked for visual documentation of what was happening in his village, in order to, in the words of Frota, "demonstrate and denounce the negligence of the authorities" (266). In *Taking Aim*, we hear the Metuktire explain that making videos is a way of appropriating the white man's tools. We also see them recording everyday events and watch images shot by the Kayapo themselves. Frota incorporates their footage into *Taking Aim* and credits them at the end of the documentary.

This association between "primitive" cultures and video technology has surprised those accustomed to traditional ethnographic images of indigenous people. But the indigenous groups themselves have been quick to find uses for the new tool. In *The Spirit of TV/O Espírito da TV* (Vincent Carelli, 1990) we see the Waiãpi, another indigenous group in the Brazilian rainforest, discussing the usefulness of video recording both to preserve the essential practices of their culture and to convince others, especially the gold miners in the region, of their ability to defend the communal possession of their land. Their agenda is both cultural and political. "After I have died," one man contemplates in a close shot, "my grandchildren will still see me on TV. . . . Now the young can see their elders and learn from them." They also comment on other indigenous groups they have seen on TV, including the Kayapo. And they debate if it is useful to be recorded drunk: "I don't want people to see us drunk, especially the gold miners. . . . When you show these pictures, tell them: 'These people are dangerous. They are killers when they're drunk.'" And they definitely do not want the camera to show that there are few of them left in the village.

The Waiãpi have noticed that documentaries (in the case of *The Spirit of TV*, made through Vincent Carelli's Video in the Villages/Vídeo nas Aldeias project of the Centro de Trabalho Indigenista) can be a useful tool for negotiating identity and cultural self-preservation. This is especially important in locales where the dominant, mass-produced media have penetrated. Videos can also be a useful tool to speak to whites about the indigenous people's struggle for survival in the fight against land dispossession and genocide. This is vital in areas where gold miners, loggers, road builders, ranchers, and other nonindigenous groups have brought in industry, animals, arms, and disease.

But technology is more than simply hardware. And some from within the communities, as well as some from outside, are worried that the use of video technology by indigenous people might supplant traditional modes of communication by making them seem insufficient and obsolete (Ginsburg "Indigenous Media"). Others, however, see indigenous knowledge systems in the videos themselves. Although *The Spirit of TV* does not use footage shot by the Waiãpi, the Video in the Villages project provides technical assistance to Indians in making their own videos. Carelli sees a different aesthetic in the videos made by the Indians. For example, he notes that they tend to eschew the kind of editing he uses and have more respect for the duration and repetitive aspects of ceremonies and rituals (cited in Aufderheide 91).

The use of video cameras by indigenous peoples recalls a common pattern in the history of recording technologies. While technological innovations alone do not change the politics of documentary, they can make it possible for documentarians to redefine the way authority is distributed in nonfictional works. Frota admits, for instance, that the economic advantages afforded by portable video technology and the capacity to instantly play the recorded material were key to the success of Mekaron Opoi D'joi (259–260). In the past two decades, this redistribution of authority found renewed impetus with the availability of digital recording equipment and the advent of novel forms of exhibition. Digital cameras and cell phones with video capabilities allow individuals with virtually no professional training to create their own representations of sociohistorical reality. And the Internet has enabled nonprofessionals to make their works widely accessible for public consumption. It has also encouraged more interactive forms of exchange between documentary makers and users.

As the promises of these technologies begin to be fulfilled, more and more people will have authority over nonfictional material. And more and more people will take responsibility for the images and sounds that represent their world.

Additional Filmography

Housing Problems (Edgar Anstey and Arthur Elton, 1935)

Operation Snow Ball/Opération boule de neige (Bonnie Sherr Klein, 1969)

Two Laws (Carolyn Strachan, Alessandro Cavadini, and the Borroloola Tribal Council, 1982)

Children of Shatila (Mai Masri, 1998)

Maquilapolis: City of Factories (Vicky Funari and Sergio De La Torre, 2006)

We Struggle But We Eat Fruit/A gente luta mas come fruta (Bebito Piãko and Isaac Piãko, 2006)

Stranger Comes to Town (Jacqueline Goss, 2007)

I've Already Become an Image/Já me transformei em imagem (Zezinho Yube, 2008)

Works Cited and Further Reading

Arthur, Paul. "Jargons of Authenticity (Three American Moments)." In *Theorizing Documentary*, ed. Michael Renov. New York: Routledge, 1993.

Aufderheide, Patricia. "The Video in the Villages Project: Videomaking with and by Brazilian Indians." *Visual Anthropology Review* 11.2 (Fall 1995).

Berry, Chris. "Wu Wenguang: An Introduction." *Cinema Journal* 46.1 (Fall 2006).

Bruzzi, Stella. *New Documentary.* 2nd ed. New York: Routledge, 2006.

Burnett, Ron. "Video: The Politics of Culture and Community." In *Resolutions:*

Contemporary Video Practices, ed. Michael Renov and Erika Suderburg. Minneapolis: University of Minnesota Press, 1996.

Frota, Monica. "Taking Aim: The Video Technology of Cultural Resistance." In *Resolutions: Contemporary Video Practices*, ed. Michael Renov and Erika Suderburg. Minneapolis: University of Minnesota Press, 1996.

Ginsburg, Faye. "Aboriginal Media and the Australian Imaginary." *Public Culture* 5.2 (1993).

———. "Indigenous Media: Faustian Contract or Global Village?" *Cultural Anthropology* 6.1 (1991). Reprinted in *Rereading Cultural Anthropology*, ed. George E. Marcus. Durham, N.C.: Duke University Press, 1992.

———. "The Parallax Effect: The Impact of Indigenous Media on Ethnographic Film." In *Collecting Visible Evidence*, ed. Jane Gaines and Michael Renov. Minneapolis: University of Minnesota Press, 1999.

———. "Shooting Back: From Ethnographic Film to Indigenous Production/ Ethnography of Media." In *Companion to Film Theory*, ed. Toby Miller and Robert Stam. Malden, Mass.: Blackwell, 2004.

Grant, Barry Keith. "Ethnography in the First Person: Frederick Wiseman's *Titicut Follies*." In *Documenting the Documentary: Close Readings of Documentary Film and Video*, ed. Barry Keith Grant and Jeannette Sloniowski. Detroit: Wayne State University Press, 1998.

Jordanova, Ludmilla. *History in Practice.* London: Arnold, 2000.

MacDougall, David. *Transcultural Cinema.* Ed. Lucien Taylor. Princeton, N.J.: Princeton University Press, 1998.

Mamber, Stephen. *Cinema Verite in America: Studies in Uncontrolled Documentary.* Cambridge, Mass.: MIT Press, 1973.

Nichols, Bill. "Frederick Wiseman's Documentaries: Theory and Structure." In *Ideology and the Image: Social Representation in the Cinema and Other Media.* Bloomington: Indiana University Press, 1981.

———. *Representing Reality: Issues and Concepts in Documentary.* Bloomington: Indiana University Press, 1991.

———. "The Voice of Documentary." In *New Challenges for Documentary*, 2nd ed., ed. Alan Rosenthal and John Corner. Manchester: Manchester University Press, 2005.

Renov, Michael. "New Subjectivities: Documentary and Self-Representation in the Post-verité Age." In *The Subject of Documentary*. Minneapolis: University of Minnesota Press, 2004.

Rosenstone, Robert A. "History, Memory, Documentary: A Critique of *The Good Fight*." *Cineaste* 17.1 (1989).

Ruby, Jay. "Speaking for, Speaking about, Speaking with, or Speaking Alongside."
In *Picturing Culture: Explorations of Film and Anthropology.* Chicago: University of Chicago Press, 2000.

Schickel, Richard. "Imposing on Reality." *Time*, January 8, 1990.

Sharrett, Christopher, and William Luhr. "*Bowling for Columbine:* A Review."
In *New Challenges for Documentary*, 2nd ed., ed. Alan Rosenthal and John
Corner. Manchester: Manchester University Press, 2005.

4

Responsibility

Documentary makers bear responsibility for what they represent. Their films and videos can help us understand the world we live in, shape our perception of historical events, and influence our opinions about current issues. They can also affect the lives of the people represented. Documentaries turn private matters into public affairs, exposing their subjects to the scrutiny and judgment of an audience. More than simply asking if what we see and hear is credible or authentic, we should think about what interests a documentary serves, what impact it might have on the spectators, and whether or not it takes into account the welfare of the people represented.

In an often-mentioned scene from Claude Lanzmann's *Shoah* (1985), the filmmaker asks a survivor from a Nazi extermination camp to recount his experience as a barber in Treblinka. The interview takes place halfway into the nine-and-a-half-hour film, demonstrating with remarkable clarity why responsibility is such an important issue in documentary filmmaking. Abraham Bomba, trimming a man's hair in a Tel Aviv barbershop, recalls that he was forced to cut the hair of women right before they were put to death in Treblinka's gas chamber. With unyielding determination, he explains in detail how the women came into the room, what they were like, and how long it took to cut their hair. He also demonstrates with gestures how much hair was taken off. Most of the time, Bomba speaks without looking at the camera, framed in a medium shot that allows us to see a little bit of the barbershop, as well as his image reflected in a mirror. He responds to Lanzmann's questions in a monotone voice that reveals no hint of emotion. Then, all of sudden, as he starts telling the story of a friend, a barber like himself, whose wife and sister came into the gas chamber, Bomba's voice begins to falter. He stops talking, the camera zooms into his face, and he wipes his tears with a piece of cloth. There is a long moment of silence, eventually broken by Lanzmann's off-screen command: "Go on, Abe." Bomba resists: "It's too horrible." The filmmaker, however, continues shooting and insists that the barber finish his story. In the four minutes that follow, we see Bomba struggling with his emotions while the filmmaker waits for an answer. Lanzmann seems determined to get the story on record, no matter how painful that might be for the subject in the film.

The scene is unsettling not only because it deals with heinous crimes but also because it forces the interviewee to relive the events that took place nearly four decades earlier. It is as if, in order for the audience to learn about those atrocities, a man should suffer them again. Had Lanzmann chosen to spare the barber from reliving his experience, the interview would not produce the same effect on the audience. Neither would it convey the horror of a Nazi extermination camp with the same intensity. It is the undying pain in Bomba's voice and tears that makes it so gripping. Yet Lanzmann's choices raise complicated questions about the ethics of documentary filmmaking and viewing. It is important to inform the public about the death camps. But at what cost? Is it ethical to evoke this painful recollection knowing that it will cause more sorrow? Does the public's right to know justify causing harm? When the filmmaker arouses Bomba's tears, he is not only bringing the barber's suffering to light; he is bringing distress to the audience as well by inviting us to have empathy, compassion, or benevolent concern for his pain. Whether it is anxiety, anger, sadness, or resentment, the scene calls for a response.

Bomba's tears are also disconcerting because they bring to mind the potency of the desires that viewers bring to a film. We want chilling evidence, heart-warming evidence, even sensational evidence. We want the "I was there." We want the witness to remember and to be here now to tell the tale (Hartman 69–70). Looking at Abraham Bomba in a Tel Aviv barbershop, we see a compelling individual and infer humanizing abstractions. And because this is a documentary, we also want to believe that he was performing his usual actions, in his natural environment, and recalling the incident for us. In actual fact, Bomba had emigrated to the United States after the war and settled in New York City, working as a barber in a shop beneath Pennsylvania Station. Lanzmann had spoken to him in his cottage in the Catskill Mountains. Now retired, Bomba had recently immigrated to Israel. The filmmaker rented that Tel Aviv barbershop and posed him in it for the interview ("Seminar with Claude Lanzmann" 95–96).

Lanzmann has criticized some films of the Holocaust for their unflinching gaze on the unimaginable, for offering a means of access to the radically inaccessible. His own film offers no archival images and no re-creations, no visual representations of the past. Instead, *Shoah* is built out of shots of the Polish landscape (a "deceptively peaceful" landscape, to quote the literary scholar Geoffrey H. Hartman) and many encounters with survivors, bystanders, perpetrators, and even a historian, leaving the viewer to imagine the impossible. Lanzmann draws on the testimony of a number of people like Abraham Bomba. At one point, he interviews friendly Polish peasants, somewhat complicit witnesses, some voicing antisemitic fantasies, while a Jewish man who survived the camp in their hometown stands among them. "Lanzmann seduces, lures, and cajoles the protagonists," writes Gertrud Koch,

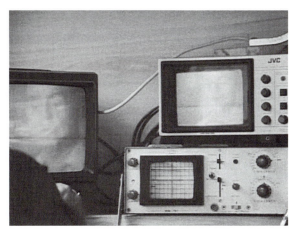

4.1. Inside the van parked outside Walter Stier's house recording his interview. From *Shoah* (Claude Lanzmann, 1985).

"into doing and saying things that would otherwise have remained silenced and hidden" (130). And he also interviews with a hidden camera and microphone people who did not wish to be on record. The film employs methods that some might consider troubling. But others, the documentary maker Marcel Ophüls, for example, feel that one cannot be a "gentleman" and be a documentary filmmaker (83).

Making a documentary calls for consideration of not only truthfulness but also obligation. There are always judgments involved. Filmmakers need to weigh their actions to see if they cause damage to the subject or the audience. The public does as well.

This chapter looks at the circumstances of documentary film and video production, representation, and reception as social acts—and as acts that have ethical consequences. Here we borrow from Raymond Williams, who suggests that we look "not for the components of a product but for the conditions of a practice" (48). He recommends that when we look at a work, we pay attention to the nature of the social practices that produce and receive the work. Whether we are talking about conditions of production, conditions of representation, or conditions of reception, documentaries are traversed by social relationships. Think of the relationship between filmmakers and their funders, between filmmakers and their subjects, and between filmmakers and spectators. These relationships are frequently unequal. It is because of this inequality that responsibility is an important issue.

In matters of production, we might want to ask ourselves, as in the previous chapter, if there is a way to make the relationship between the filmmaker and the participating subject more equitable, or to make the creative process more balanced. What kinds of production interventions take place? And are they ethical? In matters of representation, we should think about who controls the choice of subject matter, the selection of what aspects to show and how to show them. In matters of reception, the filmmaker's choices affect how and by what means the audience members make sense of the documentary.

In any social relationship, issues of power are inevitable. Therefore it is useful to think of documentaries as exercises of power and examine the political and social consequences of this power. Michel Foucault has argued that it is a mistake to describe social power as simply a negative force that operates through refusals, repression, and prohibitions. The relations of power are productive. "In fact, power produces; it produces reality; it produces . . . rituals of truth" (*Discipline and Punish* 194). What counts as truth depends on the conceptual systems—or discourses— in operation, our ways of knowing, ordering, and describing the world. For Foucault, power is associated not with particular institutions (the State, the police), but with practices, techniques, and procedures. And the exercise of power creates new knowledge, new forms of discourse, and new bodies of information.

The Case of "Harvest of Shame": Making Choices, Acting Responsibly

Production, representation, and reception are artificial separations, of course. When watching a documentary we do not experience three separate stages. But these separations are helpful to the analytical process. "Harvest of Shame," an episode of *CBS Reports*, a prestigious, hour-long U.S. television documentary series, is a good place to start our inquiry. Broadcast on November 25, 1960, "Harvest of Shame" explores a concrete situation in a specific time and place: the immiseration of migrant farm labor in the United States in a time of unprecedented prosperity. And it asks its audience to imagine themselves as able to remedy the situation.

If we use the terminology familiar from the preceding chapter, this is a documentary that does not disavow its authority. Nor do host Edward R. Murrow and producer David Lowe hide their presence. They appear on screen questioning migrant farm workers, farmers, and officials. Murrow speaks directly to the camera, addressing the audience. He also expresses his point of view on the plight of migrant workers fervently in the commentary. Confident and authoritative narration such as this seems to be the result of empirically accurate observation. Documentarians do research, learn facts and details, find supporting evidence, and share their information and insights with the audience.

But what happens when this godlike authority is used to describe people with little authority of their own? What responsibilities do filmmakers have when they speak on behalf of those who are seldom given a voice or presence in the public arena? In "Harvest of Shame" the journalists speak for those whom they perceive as having no voice, and they delineate the manner in which those people are to be understood. David Lowe squats down next to Aylene King in the field, microphone in hand, and asks, "How much did you earn [today]?" Looking at Lowe, not the audience, she replies, "One dollar." "How much will your food cost you today?" "About two dollars." He continues, "Aylene, how old are you?" "Twenty-nine." "How many children do you have?" "Fourteen." Aylene King's self-awareness and self-understanding are not part of the way we get to know her. Lowe has both defined her and confined her. And he has defined and confined her by her hardships and deprivations. The setting is limited to adversity and neediness.

This way of framing the subject has a long tradition in American documentary expression. William Stott, commenting on documentary work in the 1930s, points out how little we see of these people: "They come to us only in images meant to break our heart. They come helpless, guiltless as children and, though helpless, yet still unvanquished by the implacable wrath of nature—flood, drought—and the indifference of their society. . . . Never are they vicious, never depraved, never responsible for their misery. And this [approach], of course, was intentional" (58). The camera in Aylene King's cabin shows us the rat holes in the mattress. Lowe interviews her nine-year-old son, Jerome, at home tending his three younger sisters, and asks him if there is any food for lunch. Jerome answers "yes" and the film cuts to an image of a pot with a small amount of beans in it.

Lowe and Murrow may have been acting in good faith by trying to raise consciousness about the migrant workers' living conditions. But by doing so, they decided how Aylene King and her family would be presented and they sketched a portrait of frail, suffering, injured parties. This is an image of victimhood that is far removed from the lucid agency we are presented with in a documentary such as *The Nation Erupts* (Not Channel Zero, 1992), in which people in Los Angeles are interviewed about the racial disturbances after the verdict in the Rodney King beating. A man in South Central, for example, commenting on the television images of parents and children looting together, points out a biting paradox: "I can explain . . . to my kids why poor people steal. But I can't explain racism to my kids." Here "the person on the street" analyzes his own situation, rather than simply responding to the host's agenda.

"Harvest of Shame" is a clear editorial statement. The program is as much the story of Edward R. Murrow's moral indignation about the problems of seasonal farm workers as it is the story of migrant labor. Murrow was, at the time, a celebrity, a celebrity made by the media. He had reported from London on the radio during World War II and since 1951 had appeared regularly in American living rooms on television hosting *The CBS Evening News, See It Now, Person to Person*, and *Small World*. One thing that makes "Harvest of Shame" different from documentaries shown as shorts in movie theaters is the appearance of people with whom viewers were acquainted, people who had entered their homes before, voicing their opinions and interacting with the subjects. It is important to recognize the power in Murrow's persona and how forcefully that might have been received in American living rooms that Friday after Thanksgiving. "The people you have seen have the strength to harvest your fruit and vegetables. They do not have the strength to influence legislation. Maybe we do." When Murrow slips easily into the first-person plural, when he looks directly into the camera and asks the viewers to write to their legislators, he calls on the viewers' good intentions and compassion, their empathy, by touching their feelings of harmony and commonality, not with Aylene King and her family, but with the liberal views of the reporter and narrator. And rather than implicating them in the problem, the onscreen anchor beseeches viewers to take action and see themselves as part of the solution.

Questions of responsibility were also part of the way the documentary was received. Some viewers objected to the fact that the show took such a strong stance. Television journalists, however, defended it vigorously. Richard Salant (the head of CBS News at the time), in a 1961 speech to the affiliate stations, remarked: "The price of avoiding angry letters is blandness; the price of blandness . . . is public indifference." Reuven Frank, then an NBC News producer, also defended "Harvest of Shame" in an interview in *Television Quarterly* in the fall of 1962: "Selection always creates a point of view. The question is not one of objectivity—but responsibility. Objectivity is a screen we hide behind. It's just a word. These programs cannot be done by computer. They have to be done by people. . . . [We] are looking . . .

for people who are sufficiently disciplined to approach a subject responsibly. 'Fairness' is not an objective criterion" (both quoted in Bluem 105–106).

"Harvest of Shame" shows us that documentarians have to make decisions about how they approach the subjects in their works, and these decisions help define both the representations and the effects that the documentary may have on audiences. Because the camera and microphone do not simply deliver an unmediated trace of some preexisting truth, and because truth is neither unproblematic nor easily accessible, the issue for scholars is how we can analyze the decisions film and video makers make and their consequences on both the subjects of the documentary and the spectators. More relevant than "Is it the truth?" is "Whose truth are we getting? What ideological forces are in operation?"

The filmmaker brings myriad expectations, feelings, interests, and desires into this process, filtering everything through his or her own values and interpretive schema, as do the subjects of the documentary and its viewers. Many of these are shared concerns about not only representation, but politics, ethics, and historical relevance. But there can also be potential contradictions in the interests of media makers, their subjects, funders, and viewers. ("Harvest of Shame" was sponsored by R. J. Reynolds Tobacco, and, indeed, tobacco-growing areas are sparsely documented in the program.) We explore these questions in the rest of the chapter.

Questions of Production

We begin by asking where the documentarian is situated. Who is he or she? How is she or he defined in relation to those she or he is studying, recording, and representing? How is he or she defined in relation to the intended audience? What effects does she or he anticipate the documentary may have? In *Chronicle of a Summer/Chronique d'un été* (1961), an early synchronized-sound documentary, Jean Rouch and Edgar Morin, an anthropologist and sociologist, respectively, set out to register the attitudes of some Parisians in the summer of 1960—Frenchmen studying the French. The film begins with generic shots of Paris in the summertime and a voice commenting that we will be seeing men and women who are not actors, who are devoting their time to a new experience in cinema truth, "*cinéma vérité.*" Then we are presented with Rouch and Morin talking to Marceline, one of their helpers, about the possibility of getting sincere replies from interviewees, people speaking in a relaxed and natural manner. When Marceline says that she thinks she would be intimidated by the filmmaking process, they assure her that anything she objects to can be edited out. The film shows clearly the role of the filmmakers in the production and post-production process: their concern for their subjects and how they arbitrate the recording and editing. The relations of production are evident.

Marceline and another helper go out to question passersby on the street: "Are you happy?" Then, more successfully, delving deeper, the filmmakers interview people who had agreed to participate in the film: a couple of artists, a worker in a factory, an Italian immigrant, a West African student, Marceline's ex-boyfriend, and so on. They introduce the factory worker to the African student; they take a bunch of them on vacation to Saint Tropez; and they film Marceline, who had been interned in a German concentration camp during World War II, talking to her departed father about her experiences while walking through a Paris street. Then they project an edited workprint for the participants and film their responses. This scene is worth looking at more closely because, once again, Rouch and Morin are seen setting the agenda for discussion, and cinema truth is part of that agenda. The group debates the honesty of the revelations. "When I was speaking, I forgot the camera was there. . . ." Was Marceline acting when she talked about her deportation? It becomes clear that the participants realize that the film, while representing reality, has become a reality of its own, and that reality is what is being debated. At the end of the film, we see Rouch and Morin walking the halls of the Musée de l'Homme, musing about the reactions of the participants to the screening ("We were criticized for not being real enough and we were reproached for being too real") and debating what effect their film might have.

This is a very different approach toward their subjects from what we saw in "Harvest of Shame." *Chronicle of a Summer* was, according to Morin, an "experiment in cinematographic interrogation" (6). But we might also see it as an experiment in "shared anthropology" ("*anthropologie partagée,*" in Rouch's words) where a learned and sensitive authorial presence, and insistent probing, provokes some interesting ruminations on the possibility of happiness and fulfillment. The filmmakers' attitude toward their subjects is neither patronizing nor condescending. Without being deferential, they have faith in their subjects' intelligence and judgment, inviting their contributions to the making of the documentary.

This is not to say, however, that the filmmakers no longer control the production process. Rouch and Morin gave up some of the social scientist's monological authority. Yet, in Brian Winston's words, they continue to "manipulate and condition the film at every turn . . . by insisting that the topics they think significant are dealt with by the other participants" (185). They set the program and influence the answers merely by posing the questions. No matter how magnanimous (or acutely politically aware) a filmmaker is, power in the filmmaking encounter is shared only partly, with much caution, and, as filmmaker Trinh T. Minh-hà observes, generally on the condition that the share, or the voice, is *given*, not taken ("Outside In Inside Out" 134).

Chronicle of a Summer demonstrates that production is not a neutral practice. The intervention of the filmmakers and the filmmaking process always inflects the production itself. Rouch acknowledges the intervention and celebrates the presence of the filmmaking apparatus as a psychological stimulant, a catalyst encouraging people to do things they might not ordinarily do, or reveal things that they might ordinarily keep hidden. Describing the scene in *Chronicle of a Summer* where Marceline is walking through the streets of Paris and talking about being deported, Rouch said in an interview: "It's false—no one walks along talking out loud. But I suddenly discovered that this released a series of confessions that Marceline had never made during a direct, face-to-face interview, simply because she was suddenly in a totally different element. . . . [The filmmaking process] stimulated something she would never have said without it" (Levin 137).

But sometimes the camera's intrusion does seem more problematic, counterproductive, and occasionally even irresponsible. In *Titicut Follies* it is possible that the camera's presence incited some of the behavior we see. While they never acknowledge the presence of the crew, the men handling the patients at times seem to be showing off for the camera. What is disturbing is that it appears that some of the cruelty we witness may have been provoked by the filmmaking situation.

The film also makes us wonder about whether the subjects were properly informed when they gave their consent to be documented. If the administration and caretakers really understood what the documentary was going to be about, would they have consented to being filmed? What are the ramifications of aiming a camera at someone? Or at someone's personal life and then showing it to the populace at large? "People don't immediately realize what it means to speak to the camera," director João Moreira Salles reminds us. "They believe they are talking to a friend, but when they speak to the camera they are speaking to an audience, to perfect strangers" (Dieleke and Nouzeilles 144). In Jean Rouch's words, "Every time a film is shot, privacy is violated" (quoted in Winston 187). Do documentary subjects realize that later generations will be looking at them? How do the sons and daughters, grandsons and granddaughters, of those criminally insane inmates in *Titicut Follies* feel about seeing their family members abused—or naked—on film?

It is important to recognize that the ethical implications of documentary production also include the aftermath of the public exhibition of a work. When people consent to being recorded, do they understand the implications and consequences of becoming public figures? To put it bluntly, something happens when you turn someone into a movie star. There are side effects to celebrity. A person's world cannot be business as usual after that person is transformed into a character in a documentary. No matter how willing an individual was to be a subject of the documentary, no matter whether the person is famous or obscure, the reality of that person's life changed simply by having been photographed and included in a public event. Producer Craig Gilbert disclosed the Loud family's anger after the broadcast of his observational twelve-episode series *An American Family* (National Educational Television, 1973). The daily lives of the family members had been recorded by Susan and Alan Raymond and Joan Churchill over a period of seven months. After the series was televised, people responded to what they saw by commenting not so much on how they perceived the documentary, but how they perceived the Louds themselves. The act of documenting has the ability to turn what might have been ignored into something more significant, worthy of attention, appreciation, or investigation. As Gilbert retrospectively acknowledged, the filmmakers were "*using human beings* to make a point. To invoke the harsh but accurate word, we [were] 'exploiting' them to make our films, and no matter how sensitive, caring, or understanding we may be, the fact [was] that our incomes and our careers often depend[ed] on our ability to conceal the truth of this exploitation from our subjects" (44; emphasis in original).

A great deal of power—and accountability—lies in the hands of the filmmaker. Reconciling the trust the subjects give the filmmaker with his or her power to use and interpret their image, words, and actions is a complex task that often calls for sensitivity, humility, and forethought.

Questions of Representation: Representing Ourselves

Traditionally, it is the filmmaker who takes responsibility for the representational process. But what happens when the person making the film is also a subject of the documentary? In other words, what kind of ethical issues are involved in the act of representing oneself? One reason why documentary subjects have demanded authority over their representations is the need to take responsibility for the way they appear before others. Sometimes this includes a conscious attempt to "correct" existing images of a particular social group, especially when that group has been denied access to contemporary means of representation. At other times, though, self-representation can turn into a more ambitious project, an effort to question the very hierarchies that had created the exclusion in the first place. Each approach has specific implications for the discussion of responsibility in nonfiction film and video.

Consider the early feminist film *Joyce at 34*, by Joyce Chopra and Claudia Weill (1972). The representation of women had been a concern for the American feminist movement since the mid-1960s. There were many stereotypes of women as beautiful, sexy, highly emotional, weak, dependent, deficient in intellectual ability, and capable of little more than domestic service. The women's movement had been represented in the popular media as a bunch of angry, middle-class bra burners. At the time, many feminists were working toward getting more jobs for women in filmmaking and television, hoping that putting them in positions of power or creativity would affect the (mis)representations of women. It is useful to see *Joyce at 34* in this particular historical moment, as a reaction to the mass media's representation of the so-called liberated woman, and as an effort to deal with some issues that the filmmakers felt were important.

The film's methods and commitments appear superficially straightforward: a small, intimate film, a portrait that begins at the later stages of the filmmaker Joyce Chopra's first pregnancy and includes the birth of her daughter and some of the events of the following year. It looks confidently and directly into her world as if gazing through a window at reality. Chopra and Weill counter the stereotypical view of the liberated woman with an excruciatingly honest depiction of family life. They are frank and candid in the way they represent Chopra's personal experience, even when it is unflattering. Joyce confesses to the camera that raising a child has been difficult and she doesn't think she will be having a second. Her husband looks at the camera and tells how he resents having to shop for food when he needs to work on a screenplay.

Chopra and Weill counter stereotypical images of femininity. By representing both Joyce's mothering and her commitment to her work, they also undercut the idea of an *essential* femininity. The complexity of Chopra's daily struggles between job and family suggests a different view of "reality" and "experience" than that of the mainstream media. Yet, in trying to "correct" a misrepresentation, Chopra and Weill also took reality for granted. Much like *The Life and Times of Rosie the Riveter*, another early feminist documentary, the film assumes truth can speak for itself. *Joyce at 34* seems to be a transparent portrait of the "real world" of a modern feminist filmmaker. After seeing the film, viewers might feel that they know Joyce. But, of course, they only know what Chopra and Weill present. The character "Joyce" is constructed by mechanisms of representation (Kaplan 87).

In the desire to seize authority, to define oneself and to express oneself, documentary makers sometimes substitute a new vision of the real for the inadequate one. Representing oneself may be a valuable practice, but it is not necessarily a "solution" to the problem of authorial hierarchy because sometimes it serves to reverse the hierarchies without destroying them. In these cases, indeed in most cases, documentarians make use of all the persuasive devices at their disposal to convince the viewers of the veracity of their image of the world. But as Jay Ruby put it, "So long as our images of the world continue to be sold to others as *the* image of the world, we are being unethical" ("The Ethics of Image Making" 211; emphasis in original). Even when dealing with our own lives or the lives of those with whom we feel closely aligned, we have ethical and political responsibilities toward showing that our representations result from a particular point of view. A view of the world looks quite different depending on where and when one locates oneself.

Rather than simply celebrate what had theretofore been deemed marginal, some documentaries attempt to deconstruct and undermine the authority that distinguishes between centrality and marginality. In video maker Pratibha Parmar's words, they "expose the tyranny of the so-called center" ("That Moment of Emergence" 4). Parmar's *Sari Red* is an interesting contrast to *Joyce at 34*. The 1988 video is a short memorial piece for a young woman who was the victim of a racial murder in England three years earlier. It explores certain concerns of later feminists, particularly concerns about what means of representation are used and how they may contribute to a more radical viewing experience. *Sari Red* also questions the possibility of ever being able to re-present "reality" and "experience" unambiguously.

The video doesn't see reality as unproblematic. And it suggests that experience is not so easily re-presented. In fact the video implies that Asian women living in England experience a multiplicity of identities and the reality of these identities may involve contradictions, ambiguities, and even confusions. For those women, identity formation is a multifaceted experience partially because of the way that Asian women have generally been depicted in Western film and television: disadvantaged people represented as objects—objects of pity—and as "a problem." The video, then, can be seen as a site where aesthetics retain their complexity in order to engage the audience in the process of signification. Images of children playing in the street and images of women walking on the sidewalk appear to be captured at random. Yet there are also images that are clearly carefully arranged for the camera. The video works most sharply, however, by repetition and accumulation. The phrase "blood against the wall" reoccurs on the sound track, and red liquid splashed on a brick wall reiterates as an image. These are not nature's consoling repetitions. They are cold, piercing warnings. At times images overlie each other, reducing simplicity and complicating reality. And at times voices tumble, echoing, vibrating, suggesting various perspectives on the awful event.

The complexity of the aesthetics, including the visual superimpositions and overlapping of sounds, in addition to the poetic, repetitive quality of both the images and the voiceover commentary, makes us aware of representation *as representation*. The vision of the world we see in *Sari Red* is clearly contingent on the where and when of the video's maker. As if she were following Ruby's directive, Pratibha Parmar gives *her* images of the world in such a way that we understand them to be dependent on her political and social situation, as well as her intellectual and aesthetic mission. Born in the resistance and opposition to singular views of lived experience, the video is part of a larger social movement to query the construction and proliferation of one-dimensional views of cultural identity.

Both *Joyce at 34* and *Sari Red* are works that have a double agenda: they are at once a critique of the mainstream media's representation of women and an attempt to take charge of one's own image, to represent the complexity of women's experience. Yet the two works are notably different. Each of them is representative of concerns of feminist filmmaking in their time. *Joyce at 34* is from the early 1970s and is indicative of certain trends of the period, such as attempting to correct misrepresentations of women. *Sari Red*, a video from the late 1980s, explores concerns of poststructuralist feminists, particularly concerns about the signifying process and the politics of representation. In *Joyce at 34*, the ready-made subject, "Joyce," appears to be easily knowable. And Joyce Chopra and Claudia Weill have brought her to us. Not so in *Sari Red*. The subject is not given but is produced historically through discourses. And identity is a social construct, always in the process of becoming.

On the one hand, *Sari Red* is a reply to the dominant media; and, on the other, it constitutes an alternative understanding. But what means of representation does this alternative understanding use? How *do* you portray the many-sided aesthetic and political meanings of the culture of people removed from their homeland? In *Sari Red*, we see and hear a contrapuntal interweaving of tellings. Unlike traditional storytelling, this is not a monophonic performance. The visual and aural means used—the fragmentation of the image track, the poetic voiceover commentary, and the repetition of certain sounds and images—evoke a multiplicity of tellings and a variety of interpretations. For political reasons, Parmar avoids closure. Considering that the video is about a death—probably the ultimate of all closures—it is amazingly open-ended. Rather than sweeping us up in a story and moving us toward the murder of the woman, the openness of the ending creates space for critical reflection—and anger.

The video stresses agency—in particular, resistance—along with victimization: "For her dignity and pride, she shouted back. For her self-respect, she shouted back. For such violation in public, she shouted back." The inclusion of images of demonstrations by a group of women called the "Sari Squad" shows the collective history and vibrancy of that agency and resistance. And the video reclaims the nature of the sari, from clothing that marks difference and that can incite harassment to an article of both sensuous beauty and affirmation. This is a self-conscious effort to use a language different from TV news reports. The news claims to bring us *the* truth, a coherent unified "story." *Sari Red*, in contrast, is not a single coherent whole. Indeed, the video questions whether we live in a coherent world. Or perhaps the video works against *the illusion* that we live in a coherent world. A mere reworking or reversal of television's

4.2. Sensuous superimposition from *Sari Red* (Pratibha Parmar, 1988). Photo courtesy of Women Make Movies.

discursive characteristics in order to tell the "real story" would remain locked within the same terms it aims to shatter. In Audre Lorde's words, "The master's tools will never dismantle the master's house." *Sari Red* seeks to introduce us to a totally different experience.

The choice of aesthetic means is a calculated act—and an ethical act. Calvin Pryluck puts it well: "More than morality is involved; ethical assumptions have aesthetic consequences, and aesthetic assumptions have ethical consequences" (195). What Pratibha Parmar gives us is clearly only one view of reality and a clearly partial view. The video questions whether there is a single explanation for racism. Eschewing an essentialist realism, Parmar's representation of this racist murder uses aesthetic means that point to how we construct categories and how we produce understandings. And because she does not present us with a unified corpus of symbols awaiting interpretation, we, like her, cannot pretend to know the whole truth.

Questions of Representation: Representing Others

Anthropologist James Clifford reminds us that culture is not an "object" to be described. "Culture, and our views of 'it,' are produced historically, and are actively contested" (18). Likewise, no one can describe others as if they were discrete or seamless objects, or as if one could see the whole picture from any one point.

In the cases of *Joyce at 34* and *Sari Red*, the documentary makers were consciously or self-consciously representing a culture with which they were intimate. Their representations of difference and their representation of self are firmly grounded in the politics and history of lived experience. But sometimes difference (racial, ethnic, class, sexual, gender . . . difference) is transformed into "Otherness" and exploited, or treated with disdain. When one culture represents another, especially when an explorer or an anthropologist represents a so-called exotic culture, the result often tells us as much about the representer as the represented. We frequently learn as much about the values, prejudices, ideology, culture, and self-image of the explorer or anthropologist as about the culture they are filming. And sometimes, of course, Europeans or Euro-Americans reinforce their identity through the construction of a serviceable primitive Other—or the serviceable primitive as their Other. The term "serviceable" is from novelist Toni Morrison's collection of essays *Playing in the Dark*. She discusses how whites construct blacks as the kind of people that whites require them to be in order for whites to have the identity they themselves desire. Likewise, literary theorist Edward Said has found that Westerners have imagined Orientals in a fashion that serves them well. The Orient has been "textualized" in ways that allow the Western observer to see without being seen. The Western observer is coded as the invisible "norm," the universal against which "deviance" or "Otherness" is measured.

In documentary, this production of identity through difference is a discursive dynamic for securing sovereign subject status for the observer. Objectifying the other, displacing desirable or undesirable traits on to another, or, borrowing from Albert Memmi, assigning values to "real or imaginary differences," benefits those doing the representing by justifying their own power and privileges (186). But it also damages those who are demeaned or exoticized by influencing how they see themselves. In Pratibha Parmar's words, "Images play a crucial role in defining and controlling the political and social power to which both individuals and marginalized groups have access. The deeply ideological nature of imagery determines not only how other people think about us but how we think about ourselves" (quoted in hooks 5).

In anthropology, white scientists no longer portray nonwhite peoples with unchallenged authority. And new positions of knowledge have been constructed through careful negotiations between the self and the Other. Elizabeth Bird compares ethnographic research seen as "an objective scientific exercise" with a more modern approach. Research here is seen as "an interpretative, humanistic enterprise, in which the subjectivity of the researcher is crucial in both fieldwork and writing, and in which the ethnographer's claim to speak in the name of the other is increasingly brought into question" (252). The same modern approach can be employed with ethnographic filmmaking and documentaries made about other cultures. But much documentary filmmaking, consciously or not, rests on a distinction between subject and object, generally a hierarchical distinction, recording and analyzing from a critical distance.

As we have seen, most documentaries are concerned with trying to capture or preserve the authentic. And to do this they often attempt to (or pretend to) eliminate subjectivity, "a stance in which one stands at a distance from one's own experience and from one's own emotions" (Gabriel 78). But Edward R. Murrow did not do so when he expressed his dismay at the plight of migrant farm workers. Nor were Rouch and Morin disengaged or detached from the process of making *Chronicle of a Summer*. And Pratibha Parmar certainly does not attempt to describe objectively. Can we ever eliminate subjectivity? Can we ever step outside our skins, the mental habits with which we do our thinking? For Trinh T. Minh-hà, the separation of the knowing subject from the object known is never possible. We always know things through our particular point of view because "the subject filmed and the subject filming are so interrelated that one cannot separate them" (Penley and Ross 96). The notions of subjectivity and objectivity are more useful when they are viewed not in terms of dualities or conflicts but in terms of degrees and movements within the same concept, as always coexisting and interrelating ("Of Other Peoples" 140). There is necessarily a subjectivity in every objectivity, and the acknowledgment of that subjectivity is part of Trinh's effort to create ethical representations of other cultures.

Trinh T. Minh-hà wrestles openly with the ethical questions raised by filming another culture in her 1982 documentary on rural women in Senegal, *Reassemblage: From the Firelight to the Screen*. The film offers a critique of the so-called objectivity of documentaries and, as Constance Penley and Andrew Ross point out, suggests that ethnography might be more a matter of "unacknowledged voyeurism than it is scientific fact-finding" (87). Rather than a transcendent observer, Trinh is self-consciously partial and committed.

In *Sari Red* and many other postmodern documentaries, the ground from which filmmakers have securely represented others has been dislodged. There is no longer a place from which to affect an overview. By revealing the moving ground on which they stand, these filmmakers do not suggest giving up facts or accurate reporting. They acknowledge, however, that representation is historical, contingent, and contestable. In *Reassemblage*, Trinh takes it even further. She uses strategies of deliberate frustration, digression, and incompleteness. She uses ellipsis, concealment, and limited disclosure in order to undermine the normally hermetic surface of an ethnographic account. She gives us gaps, a series of fragments. Trinh admits that some shots are too short in duration, or too close, or too far for the viewer to take full possession of the content (Penley and Ross 90). Some are out of focus. One is taken through a water-spotted lens. Some of the camera's pans are "unfinished," movements that travel without clear departure points or end points. (Cinematography manuals suggest the camera rest for a brief moment on a preselected point of interest before beginning the panning movement and, at the end, after the movement is completed, come to rest again on a point of interest.)

Trinh employs a similar strategy in the way she edits sounds. The film begins with nearly a minute of Joola percussion music and natural location sounds over black leader. Then there is silence, as we see close shots and medium-close shots, some barely recognizable, of people performing daily chores. Then all of a sudden, as the images continue, a first-person voiceover narration begins, followed by a slight jump in the image track as the narration ends and the music returns. In other places there is untranslated talking over black leader. The music sometimes provides continuity; but it also sometimes disrupts continuity.

Absolute silence comes as a shock when we are used to synchronized sound. In an interview, the filmmaker talks about her use of silence not as the negation of speech but as a sound itself ("Questions of Images and Politics" 22). In another, she says that her sound editing is often "an acknowledgement of the filmmaker's manipulations, a play on factualism and authenticity" (Penley and Ross 91). At one point in *Reassemblage* there is a playful illusion of synchronized sound as we see a woman pounding maize and hear a drum beating. But in most of the film, recorded natural sounds, people talking, percussive music, voiceover commentary, and silence are cut together with no attention to corresponding with the images.

By frustrating expectations and reveling in digression, Trinh makes it difficult for the audience, like the filmmaker herself, to possess sure knowledge of the subject on the screen. The Other is not easily available to us; Trinh lets us know less than we might have wanted. This might seem like a high price to pay; however, it is what enables the filmmaker to establish a less authoritative relationship with her subject and her audience. She is very careful not to impose meaning on a people, not to define them. Trinh T. Minh-hà is not the sympathetic, authoritative observer telling us all about the Sereer or the Peul or the Bassari. Rather than an all-knowing voice of authority, an objective voice of knowledge, her first-person commentary acknowledges the filmmaker's presence on the spot, her active role in bringing the village women of Senegal to us, and some of the dilemmas she encountered in the filming.

Trinh's storytelling is fluid, storytelling that constructs not truth but, admittedly, situated, conditional experiences. Because of this, spectators often have to draw connections themselves. But there is no point where they can see the whole picture since it is constantly emerging, being challenged and renewed. "My approach," she notes, "is one that avoids any sureness of signification" (Penley and Ross 93). Although she relates anecdotes from the adventures of a Peace Corps volunteer and an ethnographer, she does not attempt to draw conclusions from them. This is an inherently imperfect model of storytelling. As she points out in the outset of the film, she does not intend to speak "about," just "nearby."

Yes, *Reassemblage* looks at some of the local women of rural Senegal. However, as Penley and Ross suggest, the film might just as well be about *the act* of looking at the Senegalese village women as it is about their lives (Penley and Ross 87). And importantly, Trinh divulges that these women of rural Senegal were also looking at her. Unlike the gaze of the spectator, her look is returned. Toward the end of the film, the filmmaker tells us that her appearance in a large hat made the Senegalese laugh. This use of the first person in the commentary is not uncommon in anthropological or expedition films. What makes Trinh T. Minh-hà's commentary unusual is that it questions itself.

More traditional ethnographic and expedition films take a completely different route, relying on a hierarchical distinction between *us* and *them* to produce knowledge that seems deceptively simple and complete. The 1961 Academy Award–winning documentary *The Sky Above, the Mud Below/Le Ciel et la boue* provides a poignant instance. The film follows French filmmaker Pierre-Dominique Gaisseau's seven-month adventure among the indigenous people on the island of New Guinea. The expedition is narrated in the first person. "I am determined not only to succeed but to film the whole story as we go." It begins on an airplane, introducing the participants, and finishes as they reach their destination: "We made it! The impossible!" The film recognizes the observers' presence, both affecting and affected by the incidents and lives they are exploring. But it is also a spectacle of the so-called primitive. This is a story that strongly positions the spectator as the "we" in a we/they, self/other opposition. "We are off. To insecurity, uncertainty, and adventure." "We are just here as observers and, if they will let us be, as friends." And the "they" are introduced to the audience as "bizarre," "terrifying," "terrible," and "cruel." There is, for example, an image of a crowd of native people turning the bend in several long, dugout canoes calling out in untranslated language, as the commentator exclaims, "I could hardly believe it was possible. Real savages . . . proud, free, and dangerous." Later, we see the preparation for a peace-making ritual, and the voiceover narrator whispers, as if hiding this information from the native participants, "We must be the first strangers to witness such a ceremony." The voiceover commentary anchors the meaning of the images, fixing them with the words of the author. It also aligns the spectator with the authority of that author.

As in *The Sky Above, the Mud Below*, in many ethnographic films it is often the voiceover commentary that expresses the scientists' fundamental urge to fix meaning. The voiceover in Robert Gardner's ethnographic film *Dead Birds*, for example, explains what we are seeing and the meaning of what we are seeing. It even goes so far as to describe what people we see are thinking.

Some ethnographic filmmakers have dispensed with voiceover narration and substituted subtitled dialogue of native-language speakers filmed synchronously with the actions being observed. The decision to subtitle or to dub, even not to translate, is a tricky one, loaded with ethical connotations. For some it is respect for sounds. For some it is respect for local inflections. Others prefer to provide a voiceover translation (sometimes aurally superimposing the translation over the sounds of the native speaker), paraphrase, or summary, justifying that it makes information more accessible to the spectators. But the decision is ultimately based on the documentary's agenda. It is frequently determined by political and ideological criteria. In *Reassemblage* the words of the local women are not translated. Everyday language is treated more like music. The untranslated conversations, according to Trinh, are "one way of bringing out the music in the language and challenging the tendency to consume language exclusively as meaning" (Penley and Ross 90).

But is this necessarily a more responsible position? Some may feel that by neglecting the meaning of their words, Trinh objectifies the Sereer, the Peul, and the Bassari. This is not collective filmmaking; she did not ask her subjects what they wanted translated, or even what they wanted to have filmed. Nor did she ask them how they would like to be filmed, how they wanted to be represented. She did not give the cameras to her subjects. How and when should a documentary maker yield control? What are the potentials and quandaries of collective filmmaking? Does sharing authority, as we saw in some of the films in the previous chapter, indicate a more responsible involvement on the part of the filmmaker?

Some filmmakers show rushes to the people in their films. *Who Says It's Fate!/ Von wegen Schicksal!*, Helga Reidemeister's 1979 film, shows the mother of the family at a flatbed editing table viewing footage of her daughters talking about her marriage. And we see and hear her reactions. But just showing rushes does not necessarily give subjects precise ideas of how they will be seen when the film is completed. It is usually the way the film is edited, the final sequencing and juxtaposition of shots, that defines how a particular subject will be seen. Thus George Stoney shows some stage of edited workprints to the people in his films and tries to incorporate their thoughts and insights on them (Pryluck 203). Lin Tay-jou as well showed edited work to his subjects in *The Secret in the Satchel.* Wanting to protect the identity of the students whose personal lives formed the basis of his video, he told their turbulent stories through re-creations and animations. And when he was finished, he interviewed the students on camera about the accuracy of his portrayals, obscuring or framing out their facial features to assure their anonymity. We saw, too, how Jean Rouch and Edgar Morin showed footage from *Chronicle of a Summer* to their participants and recorded their responses. But as we have also seen, there are real limits to how much Rouch and Morin shared their authority.

A more ambitious way of incorporating the subjects' input, as we mentioned in the preceding chapter, is to get them involved in the production process itself. *A.K.A. Don Bonus* (Spencer Nakasako and Sokly Ny, 1995) is an autobiographical video made by a Cambodian high school student in Spencer Nakasako's San Francisco youth program. The video is a powerful example of a work in which the subject has the means to represent himself. Sokly "Don Bonus" Ny sets up the camera and looks into it to tell us his personal thoughts. He gives a strong account of his family's life, their aspirations and their anguish. We see his home filled with family members and their dreams. We see individuals weighed down by the social service and legal systems, but also struggling to take charge of their own lives by making difficult choices. We see the divisiveness of racial antagonisms in their housing project. We hear of his father giving himself up to the Khmer Rouge in hopes of saving

4.3. "Sometimes I wish that . . . why can't I have another family . . ." From *A.K.A. Don Bonus* (Spencer Nakasako and Sokly Ny, 1995).

his family. And the family, fifteen years later, not haunted by his mute presence but having forgotten him. We also hear the teen sobbing and telling us about how much he misses his recently married older brother, as he aims the camera, not at himself, but out the car's windshield.

When we turn the camera on ourselves, the subject is an active voice deciding how he or she will be presented to the world. But we must be careful not to assume that when a subject portrays him or herself the questions of responsibility are automatically resolved. Or that the "reality" represented is necessarily generic to others of that race, class, profession, age, gender, or ethnicity. Differences exist not only between cultures but also between individuals. What makes *A.K.A. Don Bonus* so compelling is not simply the fact that the "native" is presenting his point of view, an insider speaking with authority about his own culture, but also the fact that the video does not represent Cambodians as a homogenous group.

Neither does the video oversimplify the individual. Just as a culture is seldom consistent or uniform, there are multiple facets to any individual and one's identity is always in the process of being reshaped, remade. The contradictions, the uncertainty, the confusions the video maker expresses, along with his hopes and desires, offer a complexity that is rarely seen when a filmmaker is observing another culture. Some aspects of the video may be culturally specific and therefore not accessible to everyone in the audience. And some audience members may view his uncertainty as weak storytelling. But this complexity is exactly what makes *A.K.A. Don Bonus* so rich.

Questions of Reception

So far we have talked about documentaries made *by* and *about* certain people. But we have spoken less about whom they are made *for*, and what people might make of them. When we watch a documentary, if we watch critically, there is always a tug of war—in Roland Barthes's words, an "infinite dialogue"—between the receiver and the work (xii). Spectators strive to make some sort of coherent interpretation of what they see and hear. We saw what people made out of the Louds' lives. And we can imagine the reaction to Abraham Bomba's tears. More often than not, documentary filmmakers strive to sway the audience in certain ways.

John Grierson, back in the late 1920s, aspired to public education, to influence people through film by transmitting an assemblage of facts and opinions. What Grierson—and many other filmmakers at the time—had in mind was the idea that documentaries might serve as a medium of persuasion and an agent of public transformation.

Another way documentaries can affect the public is by serving as an instrument of community, helping foster affiliation among people who have little physical contact. An important goal of the Video in the Villages project discussed in chapter 3 was the documentation of rituals and customs so that the younger generation will have a record after their elders are gone. A second ambition was to communicate with nonindigenous groups. A third objective of the works was intertribal relations, to introduce one isolated Tupi-speaking group to another, so that they can see and hear about common experiences. And as we saw in *The Life and Times of Rosie the Riveter*, the wartime experiences of the "Rosies" served an integrating function, joining the five individuals interviewed in the film (five individuals from diverse racial, regional, social, and work backgrounds who most likely did not know each other at all) and potentially some of the audience as well. Seeing and hearing the experiences of women in the past, women in the present may recognize something of themselves in their foremothers. Elizabeth Corbett, a retired librarian, who heard that this book would be dealing with *The Life and Times of Rosie the Riveter*, talked about the occasion when she had first seen the film and declared enthusiastically, "I was a Rosie! Did you know?" Representations can be strong unifying forces in social life, a basis for social bonds.

Joyce at 34 seems to have been motivated as much by the idea of bringing women together in fellowship and commonality as by the desire to send a message. There are two group scenes in the film that might be seen in this light: a scene of a consciousness-raising session, in which several women discuss both mothering and their relations to their own mothers, and a reunion of some teachers, Joyce's mother included, talking about their working lives and reconciling work with their household and family responsibilities.

In this last scene, the teachers share their feelings of guilt over not being at home with their children *and* their feelings of guilt over being bored when they are at home with their children. For some in the audience who have these same feelings, the scene might be making clear what they had been taking for granted. Some experiences can become so commonplace that we no longer recognize them. Seeing commonalities can be moving, but, perhaps even more importantly, it can cause us to think about what these experiences portend. A documentary such as *Joyce at 34* can force these experiences into the foreground for consideration. After her first viewing of the film, Julie Par Cadenhead, at the time a New York City college student with a preteen daughter, almost involuntarily blurted out, "It's like that!"

This type of identification with the subject matter can be stronger than our awareness of the fact that what we are looking at is a representation. As Bill Nichols points out, bonds of identity transcend the "constructedness" of the text (*Representing Reality* 172). Although we may understand a text as a fabrication, an artificial construct, feelings of empathy can triumph. These bonds tend to be seen as indications of common problems, emotions, and situations, even when time and social differences may seem to separate us.

At best, identification can be a way to resist the simplistic logic of a we/they opposition. But it can also be patronizing, as sometimes happens when filmmakers tempt their audiences to feel sorry for a person or situation portrayed. Shared experience turns into pity. Or even worse, condescension. The communal bond is reduced to stooping to the level of the suffering subject.

Not having faith in an audience's ability to engage with intricate narratives, psychological complexity, or aesthetically challenging work can be equally paternalistic. Yet many film and video makers not only have respect for their viewers, they see them as able to process information and use it to effect transformations. While not reducing expression to political or social work, some media activists do think of their documentaries as social and political agitation. Connie Field, for example, said that, when considering a subject, she thinks about whether the film could be used as an organizing tool and if there are groups that would actually use it (Zheutlin 164). *Doctors, Liars, and Women: AIDS Activists Say No to Cosmo* (Jean Carlomusto and Maria Maggenti, 1988), a documentary with useful medical information about the transmission of HIV, also imagines its audience members not merely as receivers of that information but as agents of change.

In practice things can work somewhat differently since there is no guarantee that the public will turn their newly acquired knowledge into action. Awareness does not necessarily lead to social change, just as proposing a solution to an existing problem is not the same as solving the problem. In recent years several documentarians have tried to inform the public about the dangers of climate change and have offered convincing arguments about the need for environmentally responsible consumer habits. But if we really expect to see effective action, we might need to do more than simply alert the public about the impending risks of environmentally related disasters. Jay Ruby notes that there is little "empirical verification" of the impact that documentaries have on their audiences ("Speaking" 199). The assumption that watching documentaries about problems, or even subsequent indignation, will motivate spectators to action (and the concurrent fantasy that social problems can be changed by making documentaries about them) is comfortable for the makers as they move the responsibility for change to the audience. It is also a way of making the populous feel not unsettled, but satisfied. They are made to feel powerful.

But what if you combined the screening of the documentary with face-to-face social activism? New digital imaging systems, camcorders, and cell phones make documentary production more accessible, and experimental, grassroots, politically engaged, or oppositional works more vitally possible. Even before these innovations, however, some film and video makers saw themselves using documentary as an insurgent form of communication in order to make information available either as a public service or as a part of their political activism. Before cable, or Internet distribution, these works were carried by their makers and shown at rallies, demonstrations, and union meetings. *The Hour of the Furnaces/ La hora de los hornos* (Fernando Solanas and Octavio Getino, 1968) was made in sections so it could be conveniently stopped for discussions at clandestine meetings and assemblies during Argentina's military dictatorship. In Cuba, trucks with generators projected newsreels and documentaries in the countryside soon after the overthrow of Fulgencio Batista in 1959 in order to engage rural people in the ongoing revolution. Even a later work such as *Doctors, Liars, and Women*, in addition to being aired on the Gay Men's Health Crisis's public access cable program *Living with AIDS*, was screened by its makers at universities, conferences, bars, social clubs, schools, and libraries. These events were meant to urge debate, a sort of forced entry into "the master's house," to use Audre Lorde's metaphor one more time.

Doctors, Liars, and Women aims not only at AIDS advocacy but also at group empowerment. Women are seen discussing the issues, deciding what is important, making posters, marching and reacting at the demonstration, and confronting not only the police but a television talk show host as well. Then they are seen talking about it afterward, reviewing, rehashing, and reaffirming the validity of their actions. This is a video of solidarity for more than the women in the video. It is a video of solidarity for those in the audience as well.

In its responsibility to the audience, *Doctors, Liars, and Women: AIDS Activists Say No to Cosmo* is a return to the Griersonian ideal: socially useful documentaries. But it is also an attempt to build alliances, reminding us of the common root of the words "communication" and "community."

Additional Filmography
The Hunters (John Marshall, 1958)
"Hunger in America," *CBS Reports* (Martin Carr, 1968)

The Wedding Camels (Judith and David MacDougall, 1980)

Forest of Bliss (Robert Gardner, 1985)

A Kiss on the Mouth/Beijo na boca (Jacira Melo, 1987)

Joe Leahy's Neighbours (Bob Connolly and Robin Anderson, 1988)

DiAna's Hair Ego: AIDS Info Upfront (Ellen Spiro, 1989)

The Five Obstructions (Jørgen Leth and Lars von Trier, 2003)

Works Cited and Further Reading

Anderson, Carolyn, and Thomas W. Benson. "Direct Cinema and the Myth of Informed Consent: The Case of *Titicut Follies*." In *Image Ethics: The Moral Right of Subjects in Photography, Film, and Television*, ed. Larry Gross, John Stuart Katz, and Jay Ruby. New York: Oxford University Press, 1988.

Barthes, Roland. *Critical Essays.* Evanston, Ill.: Northwestern University Press, 1972.

Bird, Elizabeth. "Travels in Nowhere Land: Ethnography and the 'Impossible' Audience." *Critical Studies in Mass Communication* 9 (1992).

Bluem, A. William. "News Documentary: The Ongoing Crisis." In *Documentary in American Television: Form-Function-Method.* New York: Hastings House, 1965.

Boltanski, Luc. *Distant Suffering: Morality, Media and Politics.* Cambridge: Cambridge University Press, 1999.

Clifford, James. "Introduction: Partial Truths." In *Writing Culture: The Poetics and Politics of Ethnography*, ed. James Clifford and George E. Marcus. Berkeley: University of California Press, 1986.

Corbett, Elizabeth, conversation with Louise Spence, December 27, 2004.

Dieleke, Edgardo, and Gabriela Nouzeilles. "The Spiral of the Snail: Searching for the Documentary, an Interview with João Moreira Salles." *Journal of Latin American Cultural Studies* 17.2 (August 2008).

Foucault, Michel. *Discipline and Punish: The Birth of the Prison.* New York: Vintage, 1995.

———. *Power/Knowledge: Selected Interviews and Other Writings 1972–1977.* New York: Pantheon, 1980.

Gabriel, Teshome H. "The Intolerable Gift: Residues and Traces of a Journey." In *Home, Exile, Homeland: Film, Media, and the Politics of Place*, ed. Hamid Naficy. New York: Routledge, 1999.

Gilbert, Craig. "Reflection on *An American Family*." *Studies in Visual Communication* 8.1 (Winter 1982).

Hartman, Geoffrey H. "The Cinema Animal." In *Spielberg's Holocaust: Critical Perspectives on "Schindler's List,"* ed. Yosefa Loshitzky. Bloomington: Indiana University Press, 1997.

hooks, bell. *Black Looks: Race and Representation.* Boston: South End Press, 1992.

Kaplan, E. Ann. "Theories and Strategies of the Feminist Documentary." In *New Challenges for Documentary*, ed. Alan Rosenthal. Berkeley: University of California Press, 1988.

Koch, Gertrud. "The Aestheic Transformation of the Image of the Unimaginable." In *Claude Lanzmann's "Shoah": Key Essays*, ed. Stuart Liebman. New York: Oxford University Press, 2007.

Lanzmann, Claude. "Seminar with Claude Lanzmann, 11 April 1990." *Yale French Studies* 79 (1991).

———. "Why Spielberg Has Distorted the Truth." *Guardian Weekly*, April 3, 1994.

Lesage, Julia. "Political Aesthetics of the Feminist Documentary Film." In *Films for Women*, ed. Charlotte Brunsdon. London: BFI Publishing, 1986.

Levin, G. Roy. *Documentary Explorations: Fifteen Interviews with Filmmakers.* Garden City, N.Y.: Doubleday, 1971.

Lorde, Audre. "The master's tools will never dismantle the master's house." *Sister Outsider: Essays and Speeches.* New York: Crossing Press, 1984.

Memmi, Albert. *Dominated Man.* Boston: Beacon Press, 1968.

Morin, Edgar. "Chronicle of a Film." *Studies in Visual Communication* 11.1 (1985).

Morrison, Toni. *Playing in the Dark: Whiteness and the Literary Imagination.* New York: Vintage Press, 1993.

Nichols, Bill. *Representing Reality: Issues and Concepts in Documentary.* Bloomington: Indiana University Press, 1991.

———. "The Voice of Documentary." In *New Challenges for Documentary*, 2nd ed., ed. Alan Rosenthal and John Corner. Manchester: Manchester University Press, 2005.

Ophüls, Marcel. "Closely Watched Trains." In *Claude Lanzmann's "Shoah": Key Essays*, ed. Stuart Liebman. New York: Oxford University Press, 2007.

Parmar, Pratibha. "That Moment of Emergence." In *Queer Looks: Perspectives on Lesbian and Gay Film and Video*, ed. Martha Gever, John Greyson, and Pratibha Parmar. New York: Routledge, 1993.

———. "Woman, Native, Other: Interview with Trinh T. Minh-hà." *Feminist Review* 36 (Autumn 1990).

Penley, Constance, and Andrew Ross. "Interview with Trinh T. Minh-hà." *Camera Obscura* 13–14 (Spring-Summer 1985).

Pryluck, Calvin. "Ultimately We Are All Outsiders: The Ethics of Documentary Filming." In *New Challenges for Documentary*, 2nd ed., ed. Alan Rosenthal and John Corner. Manchester: Manchester University Press, 2005.

Rowbotham, Sheila. *Hidden from History.* London: Pluto Press, 1974.

Ruby, Jay. "The Ethics of Image Making." In *New Challenges for Documentary*, 2nd ed., ed. Alan Rosenthal and John Corner. Manchester: Manchester University Press, 2005.

———. "Speaking for, Speaking about, Speaking with, or Speaking Alongside." In *Picturing Culture: Explorations of Film and Anthropology.* Chicago: University of Chicago Press, 2000.

Ruoff, Jeffrey K. "'A Bastard Union of Several Forms': Style and Narrative in *An American Family*." In *Documenting the Documentary: Close Readings of Documentary Film and Video*, ed. Barry Keith Grant and Jeannette Sloniowski. Detroit: Wayne State University Press, 1998.

Said, Edward. *Orientalism.* New York: Pantheon, 1978.

Snyder, Robert L. *Pare Lorentz and the Documentary Film.* Norman: University of Oklahoma Press, 1968.

Stott, William. *Documentary Expression and Thirties America.* Chicago: University of Chicago Press, 1986.

Trinh T. Minh-hà. "Documentary Is/Not a Name." *October* 52 (Summer 1990).

———. "Of Other Peoples: Beyond the 'Salvage Paradigm.'" Transcription of a discussion in the Dia Art Foundation's *Discussions of Contemporary Culture*, ed. Hal Foster. Seattle: Bay Press, 1987.

———. "Outside In Inside Out." In *Questions of Third Cinema*, ed. Jim Pines and Paul Willemen. London, BFI, 1989.

———. "Reassemblage: Sketch of a Sound Track." *Camera Obscura* 13–14 (Spring-Summer 1985).

———. "Questions of Images and Politics." *The Independent (Film & Video Monthly)*, May 1987.

Trinh T. Minh-hà, and Harriet A. Hirshorn. "Interview." *Heresies* 22 6.2 (1987).

Williams, Raymond. "Base and Superstructure in Marxist Cultural Theory." In *Problems in Materialism and Culture.* London: Verso, 1980.

Winston, Brian. *Claiming the Real II: Documentary: Grierson and Beyond.* London: British Film Institute; New York: Palgrave Macmillan, 2008.

Zheutlin, Barbara. "The Politics of Documentary: A Symposium." In *New Challenges for Documentary*, 2nd ed., ed. Alan Rosenthal and John Corner. Manchester: Manchester University Press, 2005.

PART TWO

Structural Organization

5

Argument

Documentaries are cohesive units, not unstructured bits of information. Most follow a characteristic and somewhat predictable organizational pattern. They order different events, assign importance to specific subjects, and propose answers to posed problems. (In *Poetics*, Aristotle called this organization of events "plot.") Documentaries, in other words, have an overall structure that helps determine the way the sociohistorical world is transposed to the screen. And it is because of this structure that we understand the "messages" in the film.

This is not, however, the way we experience real-life situations. The real world is messy and undisciplined, and oft times maddeningly contradictory. We struggle to recognize relationships between specific events. Different subjects compete for our attention. And linear progression is undermined by the apparent randomness of our lived experiences. Compared to this, most documentaries appear artificially neat. Information about the world is amassed, arranged, and presented to an audience in an articulate and efficient manner, with each new sequence affecting the way we understand previous and future sequences. Whereas real-life situations might lack a definite course, documentaries create specific structures of meaning. They organize knowledge and give shape to what might have otherwise lacked a specific plan or design.

It is easy to overlook the importance of a documentary's overall structure because what usually stands out in nonfiction films are their referential aspects, their special relation to the real. Many people would choose to watch a documentary based on their affinity with its subject matter—not its narrative virtuosity. Yet a documentary's ability to say something about the historical world depends largely on the effectiveness of its structure. When we fail to understand the events in a particular film, it is usually because the structure itself is complex or confusing. The opposite is true when a documentary communicates its message easily and effectively.

Another way of looking at this, of course, would be to acknowledge that there are different ways of telling a story. While the subject matter might be the same, the manner in which the events that make up the film are presented can vary greatly. And, consequently, how we look at those events will also change. As with other types of nonfictional representation—television news or historical narratives, for example—there is nothing natural about the structure of a documentary. On the contrary, even when filmmakers claim to follow an organizational pattern that already exists in real life, theirs is a new design, a form of intervention in the world of lived experience. Documentarians are not free to reinvent the world as they please; however, any given set of events that actually occurred can be arranged in any number of ways. And like their counterparts in the entertainment industry, documentary makers rely on different strategies to arrange the various materials in their films.

This chapter examines how these strategies help filmmakers put forward their arguments about the sociohistorical world. It treats the overall structure of a film not only as a tool for reporting but also as a means of persuasion. The problem that these filmmakers face is how to fashion the social world into a form that might incline the public to reach a desired opinion. The form they choose, the way they assemble their argument, far from being neutral or innocent, entails choices with distinct ideological and even specifically political implications. We saw in chapter 2 that facts seem to have a natural organization once the filmmaker arranges them into a story or an argument. The documentarian's task consists precisely in discovering that organization. Indeed, as in all art and much science, a documentary is a blend of detailed observation and imaginative reach.

Think about a documentary such as *Prelude to War* (Frank Capra, 1942). It is a World War II propaganda film—the first part of the *Why We Fight* series—produced by the U.S. government to teach their soldiers, defense workers, and the general public why they were at war (prints were distributed free of charge to movie theaters). Propaganda films are partial and unbalanced representations of the sociohistorical world. They are committed to promoting a specific agenda and are likely to offer an exceedingly limited perspective on the events they represent.

Yet in many ways they also fulfill documentary cinema's noblest purposes. Propaganda films serve not only to inform but also to educate. And like most activist documentaries, they are expected to have immediate and significant impact on their audiences. Rather than dismiss them as biased—and therefore unworthy—accounts of lived experience, we should try to understand how they represent the world and, more important, what they can teach us about nonfiction cinema in general.

Propaganda films usually arrange their materials carefully so as to avoid ambiguous or confusing messages. The argument tries to influence the audience to accept the film's propositions on the basis of the reasons offered. It is a carefully crafted case for a conclusion. In these films, the work of persuasion is seldom subtle or self-effacing. *Prelude to War* is not built on hints and whispers. On the contrary, the film renders obvious what other documentaries might try to disguise: the role of rhetoric in the process of nonfictional representation. As important as the subject matter is the way it is treated. And the treatment, in this case, involves an argument that puts the overall structure of the film at the service of a particular point of view. Propaganda films have an attitude, and that is one reason why they might upset some people. They are generally less restrained than most documentaries. Overall, though, they are not as exceptional as they might appear. While the emphasis on persuasion might set them apart from other films, their argumentative strategies end up showing us some of the mechanisms that are available to all documentary filmmakers.

Comparisons and Contrasts

Let's look at the way *Prelude to War* builds its argument. The film is organized around the contrasts between the "free world" and the "slave world," and much of the effect of the documentary depends on this structural pattern. The people of the "free world" are almost always shown as individuals, a single person in the frame, and usually working people, the little man, John Q. Public. There is, for instance, a nearly one-minute montage sequence from public opinion interviews in 1939 Pathé newsreels that shows fourteen individual Americans, alone in the shot, giving their opinion on the American entry into the war. Most are recognizable as working men and women, some shown with the equipment of their trade (a carpenter and a gas station attendant, a butcher, a cab driver). As in his fiction films, the director, Frank Capra, seems to be saying, "God loves you little man. Hang in there!"

5.1. "If war breaks out in Europe, I think that this country should heed the advice of the first president and avoid all foreign entanglements." From *Prelude to War* (Frank Capra, 1942). 5.2. *Prelude to War*'s "human herds."

Those in the "slave world," on the other hand, are generally represented by masses of people, the "human herds." The Germans, Italians, and Japanese are described as having "given up their rights as human beings" and are almost always shown on the screen as a group, in huge numbers. We see, for example, extreme long shots of crowds of Japanese bowing and cheering, and we hear the commentator, Walter Huston, in a tranquil, cool voice saying, "Yes, in these lands, the people surrendered their liberties and threw away their human dignity." In the background, the assembly shouts, "Bansai, Bansai!" We see similar shots of a crowd of Germans ("Sieg Heil! Sieg Heil!") and a throng of Italians ("Duce! Duce!"), while the commentary continues. Later the enemy is referred to as "deadly serious, . . . out for world conquest, . . . 70 million Japanese, 45 million Italians, and 80 million Germans, all hopped up with the same idea." The leaders are practically the only enemy shown as individuals, and are constantly referred to in a disparaging manner. Benito Mussolini is described as "an ambitious rabble rouser," Adolf Hitler as a "gangster," sinister and cunning, and the Japanese warlords as "honorary Aryans" and "buck-toothed pals." The film's treatment of the Axis leaders is best illustrated by a collage of Hitler, Mussolini, and Hirohito. It begins with newsreel footage of Hitler making a speech, then the camera pulling back to reveal the threesome as the commentator warns, "Take a good close look at this trio. Remember these faces. Remember them well. If you ever meet them, don't hesitate. . . ."

The message is, of course, powerful and easily understood: the enemy represents an evil force and therefore needs to be stopped. But what makes it particularly effective is not simply its contemptuous view of the Axis powers, nor its unambiguous treatment of the conflict. Rather, it is the way it turns supposedly conflicting values into structural opposites that makes *Prelude to War* such a good example of propaganda cinema. The simplicities of the polarities we see in *Prelude to War* are based on suppressing uncertainty and weaving seemingly unrelated data into a coherent whole. The message itself depends on this particular organizational principle, a pattern that turns out to be as compelling as it is predictable.

In addition to contrasting individual American working people with hordes of fascists, *Prelude to War* uses this structural pattern to address other subjects. The children of the "free world," for example, are also contrasted with the children of the "slave world." A sequence of a boys' choir shows a quick long shot of the group, then changes significantly to a tracking shot, passing each individual child's shining face as he sings "Onward Christian Soldiers." The children of the "slave world," however, are shown in masses, training and playing war games with dirge-like hymns or drum beats in the background. The most spectacular treatment of the subject is a long montage sequence—four minutes (almost 8 percent of the film)—showing groups of enemy children marching, first tiny children in uniform, then older, and still older, all marching to the same rhythm. The sequence is introduced with Huston's almost paternal delivery in the voiceover commentary: "Yes, take children from the faith of their fathers and teach them the state is the only church, and the head of the state is the voice of God." The rest of the sequence has no voiceover, just martial music with a heavy drumbeat.

This is a film that needed to make an impact on its audience, to convince both the military and civilian populations of its argument. On August 12, 1941, just a few months before the attack on Pearl Harbor, the U.S. House of Representatives voted on whether the draft army instituted the year before should be extended. The tally was 203 for and 202 against, demonstrating a clear reluctance for international commitment. The "draftees" themselves were hardly at fighting pitch. *Time* magazine in August 1941 described uniformed troops in a Mississippi camp "booing newsreels of President Roosevelt and General Marshall and cheering a speech by isolationist Senator Hiram Johnson" (Bohn 93). It was also reported that the word "OHIO" (Over the Hill in October, the month the draft was supposed to have ended) was scrawled on barracks walls. It was because of this opposition that the film needed to explain what the war meant to the American people and why the country was fighting.

At every new set of events, with every new opposition, *Prelude to War* seems to insist: We are not like them, we are better than they are, and therefore we must win this war. Contrast is used as both a rhetorical figure of speech and a structuring device to organize the narrative. It is what allows us to understand the particular scenario presented in the film, the way *Prelude to War* makes its argument about the sociohistorical world, the way the film answers the question, "Why are we fighting?" A documentary that portrayed the enemy in a strongly negative light without resorting to the oppositions used by Capra could, of course, have directed our sympathy toward the Allies. But it would lack the power to explain, or justify, the war as a conflict between the virtues of the "free world" and the dehumanizing values of the "slave world." Even worse, it could fail to promote the idea that the Allies were destined to win the war because "good" was on their side. The war would have been the same, and the principles embraced by the film, too. Yet the message would have been different.

The way a documentary is structured regulates what will be shown, what will not, and in what order things appear on screen. In *Prelude to War*, the placement of information is an important influence on how we understand the events leading up to World War II and an important aspect of the film's persuasive work. For instance, the fact that the United States had never joined the League of Nations (the precursor to the United Nations) is included as one of "our mistakes"—along with Prohibition—following "Beautiful Dreamer" on the sound track. Imagine how different the message would have been if that had been mentioned in the sequence where the Japanese walk out of the League of Nations, followed by the sound of gunfire on the sound track! *Prelude to War* is a compilation film. About eighty percent of it consists of archival footage. But what was made of the archival footage has little relation to its original usage or meaning.

The beginning of *Prelude to War* quotes the first sentence of a famous 1942 speech by Vice President Henry A. Wallace: "This is a fight between a slave world and a free world." But there are significant differences in the message: Wallace's speech (given just six months after Pearl Harbor) used the contrast of the free world and the slave world to point out the necessity to liberate the slave world. "We shall not rest until all the victims under the Nazi yoke are free" and "the peace must mean a better standard of living for the common man not merely in the United States and England, but also in India, Russia, China and Latin America— not merely in the United Nations, but also in Germany and Italy and Japan." Wallace believed that the United States failed in its job after World War I: "We did not build a peace treaty on the fundamental doctrine of the people's revolution. . . . We can not perpetuate economic warfare without planting the seeds of military warfare." And: "Our duty is to build peace—just, charitable, and enduring." For Wallace, trying to inspire the people to the war effort meant stressing the prospect of a peace that would unify common people everywhere (quoted in Blum

635–640; the speech became known as "The Century of the Common Man," a reference to and rejection of Henry Luce's "American Century").

Prelude to War had the same objectives; however, the film used an argument that stressed contrast in order to establish a presumed threat to the American way of life. If we lose the war, "we lose everything, our homes, the jobs we want to come back to, the books we read, the very food we eat." The organizational system that Frank Capra used contrasted "their" way of life with "ours," and explained why the United States needed to fight by emphasizing what it was fighting *against*—not what it was fighting for.

Prelude to War is never subtle about its particular worldview. Like Michael Moore's documentaries—to use more recent examples—it has a point to make, and it makes it forcefully. Most documentaries, however, tend to avoid such biased accounts of the world for fear of losing their credibility. When people refer to a documentary as "pure propaganda," it is usually to question its legitimacy, not to praise its achievements. But even if they manage to escape the charge of propaganda, documentaries, whether dogmatic or enigmatic, can only offer partial representations of the world, as we argued in the beginning of this book. More interestingly, many rely on structural patterns that are similar to those used in *Prelude to War*.

Comparisons and contrasts are popular rhetorical strategies. But the "we/they" contrast we saw in *Prelude to War* is just one kind of opposition. Contrasts can also be employed to shape a story by altering tone. Consider, for instance, *Paradox*, Leandro Katz's 2001 video. Unlike *Prelude to War*, whose powerful voice-over commentary tells you how you are supposed to think about these contrasts, *Paradox* has no verbal commentary at all. But the wash of industrial sounds and the feverish activity of the workers in the sequences of banana harvesting and processing, juxtaposed to the quiet, contemplative tone of the natural sounds of the jungle and lengthy static shots of Mayan altars and local people, tell quite a bit about contemporary Latin American life. The components of film language (camerawork, editing, sound design, and so on) become building blocks for the larger pattern of contrast.

In *Paradox*, conflicting blocks alternate and it is implied that the distinctions between these blocks are significant. Contrast creates a conscious and deliberate incongruity and, in doing so, begs us to compare the two terms. The intentional dissonance affected by such juxtapositions evokes mental pictures or perspectives that reach beyond the immediate sounds and images. And most importantly, whether the connections are inherent or more artificial, such contrasts function to create a distance between the associated terms, sharpening distinctions. It is sounds and images of serene tropical forest life that make commercial banana production seem so intense and inhumane. The factors being contrasted must be similar enough for viewers to appreciate the association, but it is the dissimilarities that are in the spotlight. In *Prelude to War*, it is because Americans are shown as individuals that the enemy "hordes" seem so repulsive.

The two works we have looked at use contrast as a rhetorical device to persuade spectators of their particular point of view. That rhetoric should be of interest to documentarians becomes clear when we recall that documentaries do not simply provide information; they also have to convince us that their information is truthful and legitimate. As Bill Nichols puts it, documentaries seem "destined to bear propositions" (*Representing Reality* 114). This is where the use of rhetorical strategies comes into the picture. Rhetoric, as we will see, helps us find the most efficient way of presenting our arguments.

Rhetoric

Rhetoric is the art of persuasion. It does not belong to one particular branch of knowledge or "class of subjects" but serves, instead, as a tool that can be applied to almost any subject (Aristotle, *Rhetoric* 6–7). Political rhetoric might be different, say, from forensic rhetoric, but both rely on similar principles to achieve their goals. Rhetoric serves as an aid to present an issue effectively and to make a case convincingly. It is less concerned with the message itself than with the effects that the message might have on the audience. For a long time, rhetoricians were interested primarily in the use of *speech* as a means of persuasion, since this was how most arguments were presented. For us, though, the realm of rhetorical argumentation seems much vaster. It includes not only speech but also images, as well as music and sound effects. And it involves different media, genres, and formats. There is rhetoric in television commercials, news reports, editorials, and, of course, in many documentaries.

Because they usually serve to prove or disprove something, rhetorical strategies are familiar tools both to lawyers and politicians. But rhetoric is also part of ordinary communication, and we end up using it whenever we need to support a particular position. Take an adage such as "Wisdom is a privilege of age." It seems reasonable, but it is not a self-evident claim. One way to establish its legitimacy is to find evidence that substantiates it: instances in which elderly people have acted wisely or, conversely, those in which young ones have behaved foolishly. Another way to convince our audience would be to present a series of statements that logically lead to a desirable conclusion, as classical rhetoric has taught us. In lieu of resorting to particular examples, we could present our case as follows: Wisdom is a natural result of one's capacity to accumulate experience. Young people have not had the time or opportunity to accumulate such experience, and therefore wisdom remains a privilege of age. No examples were used here, and yet by using a set of logically coordinated propositions we were able to present our case in a clear and convincing manner.

Presenting an argument in a documentary can be a little more complicated, but documentarians have used both strategies extensively. *Prelude to War*, to reference Capra's film one more time, combines carefully orchestrated ideas with examples that illustrate the documentary's central proposition. If the Axis powers win the war, the documentary postulates, American freedom and democracy will be in danger. Therefore, the United States has to stop them. The film reinforces this point with examples that demonstrate how the leaders of the "slave world" had banished freedom from their countries. And if they did it at home, we conclude, they would certainly do the same in the rest of the world. The examples here serve to set up the contrasts that justify the explanation for the American involvement in World War II.

Documentaries strive to prove that things are as they say they are. And they use different means to achieve this objective. Sometimes, however, they build up arguments not by demonstrating a particular point but by disputing an existing claim. They prove their proposition by disproving a widely held one. In Aristotelian parlance, they use a *refutative* argument. In this case, it is a good idea to start our presentation by revisiting the proposition we want to dispute. First we restate our opponents' claims. Then we expose the flaws in their claims and go on to introduce an argument of our own. More than simply an effort to assert one's rightfulness, what we have here is an attempt to show what is wrong with someone else's approach to a given subject. To put it differently, we prove the legitimacy of our case by opposing something that we believe to be wrong, inaccurate, or illegitimate. This strategy is particularly useful when our argument goes against a well-established proposition. The more flawed one proposition appears, the stronger the other will become.

The Life and Times of Rosie the Riveter, discussed in chapter 2, is a good example of this form of argument. The film shows us how women's experiences working in war plants during World War II differed from official government propaganda about their motivations and working conditions. The use of the government footage introduces a number of themes (such as child care) that serve to put forth

5.3. "Why did I take a defense job? That's a funny question. . . . We're in a jam, aren't we?" From *The Life and Times of Rosie the Riveter* (Connie Field, 1980). 5.4. "You'd think you make more in a day than you used to make all week. . . . I was buying fox furs!" From *The Life and Times of Rosie the Riveter* (Connie Field, 1980).

a view on the lives of these working women. But these "facts" are undermined by the testimonies of the former workers interviewed by the filmmaker. When one of the "Rosies" looks back and remembers something dissimilar from the government footage that punctuates the film, she provides a subversive undercurrent to the official story of glorious patriotic duty, inviting the viewers to take an ironic distance from the historical material. Its main rhetorical strategy depends on the juxtaposition of contrasting elements in order to refute the one that is disputed. Here each particular element is only fully realized when it is juxtaposed to a second—and ideologically opposed—"building block" of information. We are presented with disparate views of the same historical moment.

As we will see in our discussion of editing, Peter Davis's *Hearts and Minds* (1974) is another potent example of how this method can be used by nonfiction filmmakers. The film makes a strong case against the American intervention in Vietnam and disputes official accounts of the conflict. Davis begins his documentary by presenting a standard view of the reasons that led the United States to get involved in Vietnam: the fear that communism would spread all over Southeast Asia and the Pacific, the alleged obligation to support the fight for "freedom" in the region, and so on. Little by little, these arguments begin to crumble, making room for a different view of the conflict. Contradicting the notion that the United States could secure freedom in the region, Davis offers testimonies from Vietnamese men and women in which they argue that the American presence in Vietnam represented a threat to their own independence. Davis also disputes the idea that the intervention was justified, showing us the tragic effects of the bombing on Vietnamese villages. And he confronts typical notions of patriotic duty with images of service men whose lives were literally crippled by the combat experience.

Both demonstrative and refutative arguments tend to rely on generalizations. They draw broad scenarios out of particular situations and turn individual stories into expressions of collective experience. *The Life and Times of Rosie the Riveter*'s argument about women's experience during World War II is particularly compelling because the case is based on concrete examples. Yet the examples themselves—the testimonies of five women—only have a significant impact because we see them as exemplary of a collective past. Similarly, a film such as *Joyce at 34*, examined in the preceding chapter, would be little more than a chronicle of the filmmaker's approach to motherhood if we failed to make some form of generalization. Because we see the protagonist's experience as representative of a larger experience, however, the documentary ends up also speaking about other women's struggle to balance career opportunities and family life in the early 1970s. Generalizations thus appear as a common tactic for different documentaries, regardless of their style or subject matter.

While documentaries might occupy a niche of their own, they share a number of features with cultural practices that, at first sight, may have little in common, such as political speeches, scientific papers, and economic reports. Bill Nichols refers to these practices as "discourses of sobriety," since they are "seldom receptive to 'make-believe'" (*Representing Reality* 3). Like many TV commercials, though, documentaries also appeal to our senses in a way that seems reminiscent of fantasy and entertainment. Even if they rely on data, facts, and statistics to present their cases, they use sounds and images as well in order to convey their messages, resources that may be only marginally available, say, to a scientific report. Moreover, these sounds and images are organized in a manner that can alternately move, infuriate, excite, and even entertain us. Often what we find most compelling in a documentary—the very core of our experience—is precisely what produces the strongest emotion.

Emotions are key to different types of persuasive communication and can be particularly relevant to documentaries. Because audiovisual media in general combine rational and emotional stimuli, and because our thoughts and feelings are tightly interwoven, documentarians can never neglect the role of the latter in the work of persuasion. Michael Moore's films, for example, are less notable for the artistry of their

5.5. "Mr. Heston, please don't leave. Mr. Heston, please! Take a look at her. This is the girl." From *Bowling for Columbine* (Michael Moore, 2002).

arguments than for the passions they arouse. *Bowling for Columbine* might not provide a definitive answer to the question that prompts the filmmaker's investigations (Why is there so much gun violence in the United States?), but it never fails to produce a strong emotional impact on the audience. The nearly nine-minute sequence toward the end of the film, in which Moore visits actor Charlton Heston, then head of the National Rifle Association, in his Beverly Hills home is a noteworthy instance. While the interview itself adds little to the ideas already articulated in the film, it contains one of the documentary's most powerful moments. Holding the photograph of a six-year-old girl who had been shot by a classmate a year earlier, Moore asks the chief of the NRA to take a look at the picture. Heston refuses, leaving it up to the audience to respond to the filmmaker's appeal.

Even when they seem subdued or impartial, documentaries tend to capitalize on this affective connection with the spectator. They turn what might have otherwise looked like straightforward data into opportunities to explore the audience's emotional involvement with the material documented. Frederick Wiseman's *Titicut Follies* has none of the excesses that we seem to find in Moore's documentaries. Like other films by Wiseman, it offers a meticulous and seemingly detached study of the subject represented. Yet no one who sees the film will fail to recognize its emotional appeal. When *Titicut Follies* captures the everyday routines of the patients and personnel in a Massachusetts psychiatric hospital and exposes the dismal conditions to which society subjects the criminally insane, we feel sorry for the inmates, horrified by the kind of treatment they receive, and angry at the institutional apparatus that subjects them to this kind of life. Significantly, it is because the documentary can stir up these emotions that it commands such an intense response. Rather than see reason and feeling as opposite and mutually exclusive states of mind, we should then see them as working in tandem as instruments of understanding.

There is one more form of persuasion that contributes to the work of rhetoric, although it has less to do with the way information is presented than with the source of that information. Besides reasoning and emotional appeal, rhetorical discourse, as Aristotle saw it, relies on moral character, the trustworthiness of the speaker (*Rhetoric* 7–8, 59–60). This may be less apparent in nonfiction films than it is in ordinary speech, but it is not without relevance in documentaries. We saw in chapter 4, for instance, how Edward R. Murrow's character and reputation as a war correspondent boosted the credibility of "Harvest of Shame." His role as reporter and commentator, as well as his on-camera appearances, helped establish the legitimacy of the documentary by adding moral weight to it.

While it is possible to single out one specific feature in documentary rhetoric—Edward R. Murrow's goodwill, for example, or the emotional appeal that we find in *Titicut Follies*—nonfiction films are likely to rely on more than one form of persuasion. And as we will see shortly in our discussion of *The River*, they can employ different aesthetic means to achieve the desired results.

The Movement toward a Solution

Although *Titicut Follies* appeals to our emotions when it points to terrible conditions that need to be changed, it does not offer a resolution to the problem. But some documentaries investigate a predicament or difficult situation in order to try to sell us a solution. *The River*, a 1937 film by Pare Lorentz, for instance, carefully poses a problem, examines its historical origins, and then proposes a solution to the dilemma. Like *Prelude to War* and *Paradox*, it uses comparisons and contrasts. But the paramount organizing principle, a common one, is this problem/solution argument. All the reasons put forth as the cause of the predicament provide evidence that make credible the solution the film proposes. The film is meant to be a vehicle of persuasion; therefore the data support the conclusion offered.

Made by the U.S. government's Farm Security Administration during the Great Depression, *The River* tells the story of the flooding of the Mississippi River. The film is arranged, plotted, in four main sections. The first three are trips down the river, from the source in Minnesota to the delta. We begin with a glorious celebration of the native resources. The tributaries of the Mississippi and the towns and the trees on its banks are enumerated, almost catalogued, with an obvious relish for not only the richness of the resources but also the "Americanness" of the names. One is reminded of Walt Whitman's delight in the word Monongahela, as if it were the real America hidden behind the diction of superficial culture: "Monongahela—it rolls with venison richness upon the palate." (See F. O. Matthiessen's discussion of Whitman's language experiments, *American Renaissance* 519.)

Then in a parallel structure, we go down the river again. But this time the abundance of natural resources is joined by an enthusiasm for the lumber industry, mining, and steel production. The third time, we see the results of this enthusiasm, the ecological devastation caused by the harvesting of lumber and other industrialization: the flooding that was destroying the Mississippi delta. In the final section, the fourth, the film offers a solution to the problem: progressive government action, the Tennessee Valley Authority (one of the Farm Security

Administration's main initiatives at the time) with its locks and dams, new homes on the reclaimed lands, and rural electrification.

It would be helpful to consider the documentary's rhetorical strategies more carefully. When *The River* takes us down the Mississippi three times, it underlines the changes, not only the changing buildings and activities on the river's banks but also the physical change of the rising river. The second and third time we see those banks, the contrasts modify the meaning of previous sequence(s). We retroactively understand that the fervor for industrial production has ravished and destroyed those very resources the film had passionately greeted earlier. Order has been disrupted. The causality does not need to be stated directly; it is clearly implied that the changes on the banks have brought forth the changes of the river. These changes, in turn, call for some kind of action, which should lead to the resolution of the problem.

The changes in the river are also articulated aurally through the film's use of repetition, and then a variation, in both the music and the voiceover commentary. These point us to the problem (sometimes in a decidedly emotional manner) and build momentum that leads us to the solution. On the first trip down the river, for example, the music begins with a trumpet fanfare, and the narrator describes

5.6. "We left the mountains and hills slashed and burned—and moved on." From *The River* (Pare Lorentz, 1937).

the Mississippi River from its sources, its tributaries, down 2,500 miles to the Gulf, "carrying every drop of water that flows down two-thirds the continent." The second trip down the river begins again with the trumpet fanfare, and the narrator lists, "Black spruce and Norway pine, / Douglas fir and Red cedar, / Scarlet oak and shag bark hickory," intoned with pride, evoking majesty. We see close shots of bark and axes and more distant shots of trees falling. At the end of the second trip, the narrator says, "We built a hundred cities and a thousand towns." St. Paul, Minneapolis, Davenport, Moline, Cincinnati, St. Louis. . . . Then later, on our third trip, narrator Thomas Chalmers repeats the line and adds to it, "We built a hundred cities and a thousand towns—but at what a cost." His delivery this time is slower, more deliberate, almost somber. Going down the river this time, we hear many of the same words as before, but at a different pace and with an intonation that

is measured, unhurried, almost mournful. And then, "We cut the top off the Al-
leghenies / and sent it down the river. / We cut the top off Minnesota / and sent
it down the river. / We cut the top off Wisconsin / and sent it down the river. /
We left the mountains and hills slashed and burned—and moved on." The images
here are unbalanced compositions, acute angles full of stumps silhouetted against
a light grey sky. The music is the trumpet again, but the fanfare turns into piercing, dissonant chords, unstable and jarring. This final time going down the river
the list of tributaries is also reiterated; however, this time the narration is ponder-
ous, the image is full of rushing waters, and the score is heavy with tympani and
foghorns.

These repetitions function almost like a river, as an indication of the possibility of continuity and the potential for union even while ever changing. And the
variations, the changes of wording, the changing music and instrumentation, the
changing graphics, and the changing buildings and activities on the banks, are not
only catalogues of diversity; they, too, are unified by rhythm and cadence, and by
the echo of words and phrases.

Much of the lyric quality of the film's voiceover commentary derives from these
uses of repetition, especially at the beginning of lines. "We made cotton king /
We rolled a million bales down the river for Liverpool and Leeds. . . . / Rolled them
off Alabama / Rolled them off Mississippi / Rolled them off Louisiana / Rolled
them down the River." (In poetry this is called "epanaphora"; it is used extensively
by Walt Whitman in *Leaves of Grass*.) The sonorous baritone delivery of Thomas
Chalmers has the recitative quality of oratory: "Down the Yellowstone, the Milk,
the White and Cheyenne, / The Cannonball, the Mussekshell, the James and the
Sioux, / Down the Judith, the Grand, the Osage, and the Platte. . . ." Then, "Down
from the Cumberland Gap, / Over from Georgia and South Carolina, / Over
from the tidewaters, / Over from the old cotton lands west of the big river, / West
of the steamboat highway, / Down the highway to the sea, / Corn and oats, /
Down the Missouri, / Tobacco and whisky, / Down the Ohio, / Down from Pitts-
burgh, / Down from St. Louis, / Hemp and potatoes, pork and flour / We sent
our commerce to the sea."

The images frequently move from small to large, from a single tree being felled
at the beginning of a sequence to a frame full of logs at the end, from a melting ici-
cle's drop of water to rushing floods. Words, place names, and images rhythmically
accumulate, "mounting," in William Alexander's words, "to an awe-inspiring sense
of the movement down a continent of America's great and powerful river" (138).

The music, composed by Virgil Thomson, often employs the raw energy of
American popular idioms, especially the melodies of familiar hymns and folk

songs. Only a small proportion of the music is original, some of which uses the banjo and pentatonic folk-like melodies. All the music is meant to establish an American sound that comments on the subject pictured, frequently drawing out distinctions. For example, in logging sequences, as log after log course down the river, the music is a sprightly, energetic rendition of "Hot Time in the Old Town Tonight." Then the music in the next segment, accompanying the steel mill scenes, is full of cacophonous, dissonant tone clusters. The music, like the voiceover commentary, helps to express the predicament and lead the viewers toward the idea that the Mississippi is a national resource, a broken national resource, that must be fixed.

The film works to forge a community of caring viewers, challenging that community to solve the community's problems. Notice the film's use of the first-person plural, the comradely "we." "We built a hundred cities and a thousand towns." "We mined the soil for cotton until it would yield no more." "We built new machinery and cleared new land in the West." The first person plural of the narration summons us to that union, perhaps even to a shared identity as Americans, uniting us under the wing of the New Deal. It is inclusive. The emphasis on the Mississippi's tributaries carrying "every brook and rill, rivulet and creek," and "all the rivers that run down two-thirds the continent," lets us know that this is an American problem, "our" problem. The river flowing from north to south, from a drop of melting ice to the swells of the delta, unifies the North and South, as well. Flooding is the responsibility of all Americans (not a regional problem as it might have seemed).

Like Walt Whitman, Willard Van Dyke, one of *The River*'s camera operators, also experienced sensuous pleasure in place names, Anglo names, Native American names. While on location in Arkansas he wrote home to his wife, Mary, "Today I have been studying maps, and the names I have seen—names my father knew and loved—have assumed a new meaning for me. American names, rich with the color of hard men and patient women who built a country. Names they took from their daily lives and the Indians who lived around them—Broken Pine, Rolling Fork, Little Red River, Coal Creek . . . , Ouachita, Wabbeseka, Winona, Okolona. . . . Long rolling names for the great plains and wild sweet rivers" (54). We hear this, too, in the commentary written by Lorentz after the film was edited, "The Cannonball, the Mussekshell, the James and the Sioux." The familiarity and Americanness of the musical score, cadences rich with both joy and melancholy, also function in a similar way: to rejoice in the vitality and the range of tones and nuances of American folkways—as envisioned by the filmmakers.

This affective dimension, of course, contributes to the film's persuasive force. It permeates the overriding thrust toward resolution, which serves as a structuring principle in *The River*. Ordinarily a film like this might offer a statement of the problem, the explication of what brought it about, and the proposal of a solution. Although *The River* does follow this strategy, it also, significantly, changes the pattern. It begins not with the problem, but with the celebration of what the nation had. And the solution proposed does not imply the restoration of the virgin state, the celebrated state, but something new, a remedy. Rather than shrill patriotic bombast or a bleak view of the ecological malaise of modern society, Pare Lorentz paints an elegiac *and* optimistic view, a full savoring of both the bounty of American life and the possibility of progress, progress that leads to a reasonable resolution, the projects of the Tennessee Valley Authority. Order is restored. Our expectations are satisfied.

Through its narrative structure, its plotting, *The River* invokes an inevitability. This is how it was; this is what we did to it; this is what happened; this is what we can do to fix it. We *can* solve the problem. "We had the power to take the valley apart—we have the power to put it together again."

The solution to the problems in *The River*, the renewal that is the promise of the future, may be a utopian ending, a utopianism haunted by a sense of social entropy and social need. But it is also a utopian ending that follows logically from the argument. It is a utopian ending that resolves the mounting disequilibrium of the first three parts. And, as Brian Winston points out, the ending is the culmination of the previously seen history of the river (78). The historical analysis in the rest of the film leads us to the specific social solution.

In many ways, the footage is fairly abstract. Pare Lorentz's camera teams brought him shots of water, trees, clouds, cotton, floodwaters, power lines. . . . Early in the shooting, Van Dyke wrote, "I haven't gotten the feeling of a picture yet, and of course I didn't expect to have one, but somehow I feel that in the back of Lorentz's mind, there is far more structure than appears on the surface" (42). The story was built—structured—in the editing room. The film is a Whitmanesque celebration of the value of multitude. With his innovative use of free verse, the brash independence of his poetic voice, but, most importantly, his use of repetition and variation, Pare Lorentz carefully regulated aural and image patterns and rhythms with the aim of producing an organic vision of decay and resurrection.

The River is not simply a representation of reality; it is a rhetorical operation on reality.

Irony

We saw an occasional hint of irony in *The River*. Every once in a while the film invites us to infer meaning different from the literal meaning. Think, for instance, of the way the alarm blasts for the flood mimic the factory whistles. Or the time we hear the roll call of trees and see the denuded hills. Or, in the sequence just before the utopian solution, when the narrator describes a generation, "Growing up without proper food, medical care, or schooling, / Ill-clad, ill-housed, and ill-fed—/ And in the greatest river valley in the world."

But irony is sometimes used less as tone or an indication of attitude than as a structuring device. In the remainder of this chapter, we will examine *Strange Victory* (Leo Hurwitz, 1948) and *Avenge But One of My Two Eyes/Nekam achat mishtey eynay* (Avi Mograbi, 2005), two works that use the rhetorical device of irony—the intentional use of an idea, words, or an image in such a way to convey meaning opposite to the literal meaning—in a strategic manner to create cognitive dissonance that calls into question the "reality" portrayed. Both documentaries employ irony as a tool for enhancing critical consciousness.

In *Strange Victory*, irony creates a double-voiced discourse on "victory," so that two senses of victory coexist simultaneously. Instead of posing a problem and suggesting a solution, the film presents us with the United States' successful defeat of the fascist enemy in World War II and then asks if this is really a victory. Like *Prelude to War* and *The River*, *Strange Victory* contains statistics and an authoritative voiceover. It, too, summarizes a period of American history. But this film was not made by the federal government; in fact, it was made by a group of people who were questioning government policy and social attitudes and yearned for better times.

The documentary begins with the defeat of the Nazis and a view of what life looked like after the war. Then, halfway through the seventy-two-minute film, it performs a magical feat. The technology of reverse motion brings us back to the war, reconstructing what was just demolished. We watch the rise of the Nazis and are confronted with the question "Remember how it was?" By running the sequence in reverse, the film literally deconstructs the allied "victory." *Strange Victory* also shows us images of gaunt corpses, amassed dentures, hair, and eyeglasses from the concentration camps, which are interwoven with images of postwar American infants—Italian babies, Jewish babies, black babies—in their cribs and basinets. And we see posters, placards, and graffiti about "Pope-lovers" and "niggers," or declaring "No Jews," as well as signs for restricted housing developments and whites-only entrances. "A strange victory, with the ideas of the losers still active in the land of the winner." This ironic parallel between World War II atrocities and postwar prejudice strongly condemns the incongruous triumph of racial discrimination in U.S. social life, the same attitudes toward others that gave rise to Nazism.

Strange Victory uses irony to explore a second layer of meanings. The heard and seen (with their explicit meanings) and the unheard and unseen (the meanings that are being implied) exist side by side, or, as in the case where Hitler's face is superimposed on the image of ordinary Americans going to work, one atop the other, inviting the audience to infer the relationship between the two (Hutcheon 12–13; 39; 64). Made just three years after the end of World War II, *Strange Victory* and its voiceover's recurring refrain, "Remember?" must have spoken strongly to audiences at the time.

There is a short enacted scene of an African American—or "Negro," as they were called in polite circles at the time—flyer returning from the war, trying to secure a job as a commercial pilot and being turned away. "On the airlines of postwar America, there are no Negro pilots, no co-pilots, no navigators. Only a thousand Negroes flew in the war against Nazi Germany. We only *let* a thousand fly. But the old job mopping the floor in the men's room is still open." Then, over the faces of individual African Americans, eyes uplifted: "A Negro flyer, a million soldiers, a people of fourteen million who are still waiting for their share of the victory, still living out the old statistics. Of twenty thousand architects in the United States, less than one hundred are Negro; of eighty thousand civil engineers, less than one hundred are Negro; . . . the Germans put a yellow star on the Jew. But we keep the yellow star hidden in quotas for Negroes, for Jews, for Italians."

The enacted scene functions as an allegory for all those Americans who are "still waiting for their share of the victory." As a rhetorical operation, allegory employs people, things, and events to make larger "moral, ideological, or even cosmological statements," in James Clifford's words (98). Allegory has a "continuous double structure" (101) that allows the particular, as Jonathan Kahana (arguing from Clifford) puts it, "to retain its specificity . . . while serving as the medium for a lesson of general significance for others" (7). *Strange Victory* has a clear moral message: the promise of an abundant future is not available to all.

Aristotle itemizes three forms of persuasion, "appeals" to the audience: ethos, pathos, and logos (*Rhetoric* 7–8). Ethos uses the authority invested in the speaker's character to appeal to the audience; pathos engages the emotions of audience members; and logos persuades by employing logic and reasoning to make arguments. *Strange Victory*, like many other persuasive documentaries, employs all three. They are used to build a special relationship with spectators, turning them into confederates who understand the intricacies of the irony being explored. Of course, there is no guarantee that a viewer will interpret the irony the way the filmmakers intended. But the film uses those "appeals" to try to mold that special intimacy. It crafts an argument that petitions our emotions, as well as our reason and respect for convincing research and information. Using the indirection and critical edge of irony (in both the film's language and its form) as a tactical weapon, the documentary calls on our sympathies, feelings, judgment, and common sense, as it points out the ironic discrepancy between what Americans fought for abroad and their social practices at home.

The word "rhetoric" may seem like an old-fashioned term. And the kind of tightly argued narrative that we see in *Strange Victory, The River,* and *Prelude to War* may also seem a thing of the past. Indeed, much of the persuasive power of these films lies in their use of omniscient voiceover commentary, which is not very popular anymore. Yet, as we noted earlier, and as *Paradox* demonstrates so vividly,

rhetorical strategies can soundly structure a work even without voiceover commentary. Take another recent documentary, Avi Mograbi's *Avenge But One of My Two Eyes.* The video uses the ethical force of the irony to drive home its message. It looks at the Israeli celebration of sacrifice in the Masada myth (960 Jewish zealots killed themselves rather than submit to Roman capture) and Samson's biblical suicide (martyred to deliver the Israelites from the Philistines, saving the tribe of Judea

5.7. A Palestinian citizen appeals to an Israeli soldier at one of the checkpoint watchtowers in *Avenge But One of My Two Eyes/Nekam achat mishtey eynay* (Avi Mograbi, 2005).

from extinction), then juxtaposes these bloody stories' use as legends of nation building and national freedom with how modern-day Israelis treat Palestinians in the occupied territories. *Avenge But One of My Two Eyes* shows the watchtowers where the Roman soldiers stood guard, alongside the checkpoint towers and tanks from which Israeli soldiers bully Palestinian citizens. Although aggressive acts of Palestinian rebellion are only alluded to, the spirit of resistance is revealed to be part of daily life.

The opening titles appear over a circling helicopter shot of the remains of the walled fortress on Mount Masada, and an hour and a half later the documentary closes with images of uniformed school children behind a fence and gate, needing to cross the "closed military zone" to return home. Their parents and Mograbi entreat the soldiers to let the youngsters through. In between, we had frequently heard Palestinians declaring that it is better to be dead than to live under these conditions. And there were regular telephone calls to the documentary maker from a Palestinian friend describing the curfew, daily life during the occupation, and his preoccupation with death. "Believe me," he says just before we see the schoolchildren, "I don't mind if I die. My problem is how to live." The episode of the barricaded schoolchildren quotes quotidian reality. But the documentary never shows the children reunited with their families. Instead, the final shot is a guide at Masada pointing out that now an Israeli flag "proudly waves" at the site of one of the greatest defeats of the Jewish people, and the Romans, people who came to murder and rob, are relegated to history books. This is followed by a title dedicating the work to Mograbi's son and his friends, "who refuse to learn to kill."

The dark absurdity of contemporary political realities is brought into stark relief not so much by contrast, as in *Paradox*, as by correspondence. Although the narrative structures of *Avenge But One of My Two Eyes* or *Paradox* may not seem as goal-obsessed as *Strange Victory*, *The River*, or *Prelude to War*, their arguments are equally moving and effective. They, too, are carefully constructed cases for the conclusion they want their audiences to accept.

Additional Filmography

Land without Bread/Las Hurdes (Luis Buñuel, 1933)
The Battle of Midway (John Ford, 1942)
Listen to Britain (Humphrey Jennings, 1942)
Indonesia Calling (Joris Ivens, 1946)
You and Many a Comrade/Du und Mancher Kamerad (Andrew and Annelie Thorndike, 1955)
The Battle of Chile/La batalla de Chile: La lucha de un pueblo sin armas (Patricio Guzmán, 1975)
Isle of Flowers/Ilha das Flores (Jorge Furtado, 1989)
Africa Rising (Paula Heredia, 2009)

Works Cited and Further Reading

Alexander, William. *Film on the Left: American Documentary Film from 1931 to 1942*. Princeton, N.J.: Princeton University Press, 1981.
Aristotle. *Poetics*. Trans. Malcolm Heath. London: Penguin Classics, 1996.
———. *Rhetoric*. Trans. W. Rhys Roberts. Mineola, N.Y.: Dover, 2004.

Arthur, Paul. "Jargons of Authenticity (Three American Moments)." In *Theorizing Documentary*, ed. Michael Renov. New York: Routledge, 1993.

Blum, John Morton, ed. *The Price of Vision: The Diary of Henry A. Wallace.* New York: Houghton Mifflin, 1973.

Bohn, Thomas William. *An Historical and Descriptive Analysis of the "Why We Fight" Series.* New York: Arno Press, 1977.

Clifford, James. "On Ethnographic Allegory." In *Writing Culture: The Poetics and Politics of Ethnography*, ed. James Clifford and George E. Marcus. Berkeley: University of California Press, 1986.

Hutcheon, Linda. *Irony's Edge: The Theory and Politics of Irony.* New York: Routledge, 1994.

Kahana, Jonathan. *Intelligence Work: The Politics of American Documentary.* New York: Columbia University Press, 2008.

Lerner, Neil. "Damming Virgil Thompson's Music for *The River*." In *Collecting Visible Evidence*, ed. Jane Gaines and Michael Renov. Minneapolis: University of Minnesota Press, 1999.

Matthiessen, F. O. "Only a Language Experiment." In *American Renaissance: Art and Expression in the Age of Emerson and Whitman.* New York: Oxford University Press, 1968.

Nichols, Bill. *Representing Reality: Issues and Concepts in Documentary.* Bloomington: Indiana University Press, 1991.

———. "The Voice of Documentary." In *New Challenges for Documentary*, 2nd ed., ed. Alan Rosenthal and John Corner. Manchester: Manchester University Press, 2005.

Plantinga, Carl. "Roger and History and Irony and Me." *Michigan Academician* 24 (1992).

Snyder, Robert L. "The River." In *Pare Lorentz and the Documentary Film.* Norman: University of Oklahoma Press, 1968.

Van Dyke, Willard. "Letters from 'The River.'" *Film Comment* 3.2 (Spring 1965).

Winston, Brian. *Claiming the Real II: Documentary: Grierson and Beyond.* London: British Film Institute; New York: Palgrave Macmillan, 2008.

6

Dramatic Stories, Poetic and
Essay Documentaries

An argument is only one way to organize a documentary. Some nonfiction films rely on dramatic conventions familiar from fiction storytelling, focusing on the events that surround a particular individual and the actions taken by that individual to accomplish a specific goal. Others use less conventional structures and arrange information in a personal or poetic manner. Both types differ from the films we discussed earlier but are no less compelling.

In this chapter we look at these two types of films. As we exemplify shortly, they span the entire history of documentary cinema, from the silent era to the present. First we discuss documentaries that use dramatic conventions to tell their stories, building narratives that are rich in character and action. Then we examine nonfiction films that aim at developing experimental or poetic ways of arranging story information. At the end of the chapter, we also see how new digital media have expanded the possibilities of documentary experimentation through database formats. The form each work takes involves a particular manner of treating nonfictional reality and offers a distinctive way of exploring the historical world.

Telling Stories

As we saw in the previous chapter, many documentaries start off from a specific issue that the filmmaker feels the need to investigate or explain. The investigation is likely to go on all the way to the end of the film, when a statement or verdict must be offered, lest the case proposed by the filmmaker lose some of its persuasiveness. These documentaries tend to play with our expectations, raising questions and putting off answers, forestalling closure, so that the last minutes in the film will coincide with the resolution of a particular issue or problem. Another way to create a forward thrust is to treat the documentary as a kind of dramatic narrative in which an event or series of events progresses toward a conclusion. Think of the Lumière brothers' 1895 film, *The Demolition of a Wall/Démolition d'un mur.* We begin with the wall standing perpendicular, slightly to the left of the frame. The workers push from the far side of the wall; the wall begins to crumble; it falls in the center of the frame; and we see a screen full of dust as it is demolished. The one-shot film has a beginning (that establishes the state of affairs as it existed), a middle (in which that state is disrupted, the wall is struck and falls), and an end (the conclusion, the wall is no longer; we see the space where it had been). *Demolition of a Wall* predates the use of the term "documentary." But even such a simple record of a specific event reveals the attractiveness of storytelling for nonfiction filmmakers. The film is "ordered" by a coherent system of causality. And as audience members, we, too, relate to the dramatic developments and respond accordingly to the prospects raised by the film.

6.1–6.3. The narrative form of *The Demolition of a Wall/ Démolition d'un mur* (Lumière brothers, 1895).

From this perspective, documentaries do seem to share a great deal with fictional stories. Both introduce a series of causally related events and seek a conclusion for their developments, offering a teleological trajectory (from the Greek *telos*, meaning finality) that motivates and justifies many of the filmmaker's choices. The storytelling itself, the plotting, proceeds toward this finality. Those films that are about competitions, for example, thrust us in the direction of the inevitable moment when someone wins. Think of *Spellbound* (Jeffrey Blitz, 2002), a film about a national spelling bee, or *Mad Hot Ballroom* (Marilyn Agrelo, 2005), which follows New York City public school kids as they prepare for and participate in a ballroom dancing contest.

But even films that center on an individual who is not in competition can indulge in a narrative resolution. In *The Wild Parrots of Telegraph Hill* (Judy Irving, 2004), the protagonist, Mark Bittner, is obliged to leave his cottage on Telegraph Hill and thus abandon the wild parrots. The documentary, however, concludes with Mark finding a new interest in birds indigenous to San Francisco, and also happily informs the audience of Mark's romance with the filmmaker: "And Mark and I became a pair."

Another common structuring device involves the use of a quest to organize story information, with a payoff at the end of the pursuit. In *Another Road Home* (2004), Danae Elon takes us on a search to find an elderly man she called Moussa, a gentle, nurturing Palestinian who took care of this Israeli woman throughout her childhood and young adulthood in East Jerusalem. Early in the film, she locates Moussa's sons in Paterson, New Jersey, and interviews them about their father. We learn about Moussa's dedication to his children as well as his devotion to the Elon family. We also hear the grown-up sons speak of homeland and exile, personal relationships and political conflicts. As we watch *Another Road Home*, we grow increasingly curious about the man at the center of these conversations. And our curiosity is rewarded in the second half of the film, after Moussa takes a long and difficult trip from his Israeli-occupied village to meet with his children and the filmmaker in the United States.

Touching on such wide-ranging subjects as the conflict between Israelis and Palestinians, *Another Road Home* does involve more than a personal quest for one's history. It offers a unique entry point to the social fabric that connects Jews and Muslims in the Middle East. But it is that quest, Elon's effort to reconnect with Moussa, that provides a structuring principle for the documentary and, ultimately, helps us understand the social and political issues that permeate the filmmaker's family history.

Relying on effective dramatic conventions can prove particularly useful when the events represented are already familiar to the audience. *Bus 174/Ônibus 174* (José Padilha, 2002) tells the story of a young man who hijacked a bus in Rio de Janeiro and held eleven passengers captive for several hours. The ill-fated episode, which ended with the death of the hijacker and one of his hostages, was well known to Brazilian spectators, who had seen it live on television. But the filmmaker managed to retain the attractiveness of the account by creating a dramatic narrative that turns increasingly suspenseful as we approach its tragic conclusion. Toward the end of the film, Padilha intercuts television footage of the bus with testimonies from police officers, the hijacker's family members, and the surviving victims. More than simply broadening our understanding of the event, the testimonies delay its closure, increasing our interest in the story's developments. Even though we may foresee what will happen in the end, we continue to watch the film with growing anticipation.

Documentaries that utilize dramatic conventions do not necessarily eschew the rhetorical strategies that we find in films such as *The River* and *Prelude to War*. But those strategies are less noticeable here, or are overshadowed by the line of action that constitutes the backbone of the film. For this reason, documentaries that are rich in dramatic elements often seem less manipulative than those that openly force an argument on the spectator. They can, however, be more insidious, since the particular worldview they embrace—the message in the film—is eclipsed by the seemingly natural quality of the plotting.

Many of these documentaries wrap the complexities of the sociohistorical world in a series of conflicts involving one or more subjects. As happens in most fiction films, individual characters have a major role in these narratives and are portrayed as agents capable of altering a certain state of affairs. Early on, we find a general characterization of the individual, the obstacles he or she is likely to face, and the situation that serves as the basis for the narrative. What follows is, normally, a development of the initial conflicts, with the action pushing us further and further toward a conclusion. Along the way, there are frequently insights and sometimes revelations. And in the climactic moments, increasing dramatic tension and a great sense of urgency dominate, culminating with the resolution of the conflicts outlined earlier.

Man on Wire (James Marsh, 2008) turns Philippe Petit's 1974 tightrope walk between the World Trade Center's Twin Towers in New York City into what the director has described as a "heist movie." The story, which involves the clandestine use of the towers as a stage for Petit's stunt, was widely reported at the time. In Marsh's hands, it reemerges as a thrilling documentary that owes as much to the venerable narrative conventions used in the film, including the picturing of Petit as an ambitious individual, as it does to the uniqueness of the event. We hear about his determination to perform what looks like an impossible feat; we watch footage of his preparations; we hear testimonies about the difficulties involved in the project. All along, we get a close look at Petit's personality and motivations. As with *Bus 174*, the outcome of the episode might have been familiar to some viewers.

But the way the story is presented—a suspenseful succession of events centered on the goals of a main character—makes it hard for us to lose interest in the film.

There are, of course, important differences between a documentary and a fiction film narrative. Documentaries are not scripted the same way fiction films are and the people onscreen usually appear as themselves. Even when nonfiction films rely on prefabricated scenarios, a certain measure of spontaneity and unpredictability tends to distinguish them from their fictional counterparts. Moreover, the narrative expectations that characterize a fiction film might be only partly fulfilled in a documentary. A particular line of action might remain incomplete, for example, or a certain conflict might yield a resolution that is less than satisfying. (Take, for instance, the issue of Mark's eviction from his home in *The Wild Parrots of Telegraph Hill*.) None of these differences, though, can undo the fact that dramatic documentaries owe part of their "attractiveness" to the audience's familiarity with a formula common to many fictional narratives, in particular to Hollywood films.

Life as Drama

Nonfiction filmmakers have sometimes argued that the dramatic quality of their films is not solely the product of artistic design but can also be found in real life. It is up to the filmmaker to discover it. Rather than call upon existing formulae, one should look for those moments in which drama is likely to arise naturally, situations that already involve a potential for discord and emotional intensity, as happens in the competition documentaries we mentioned above. In this case, the notion of "discovered drama" replaces the concept of dramatic artifice, and the aesthetic treatment of the narrative events follows a pattern already defined in real life.

But filmmakers do not merely come across the subject of their films. They pursue them actively and choose to present them in a certain way. Even if one is right to assume that drama is already part of ordinary life, the dramatic structures that we see in some documentaries are a product of the creative choices made by the filmmakers. Just as the events captured by the camera are built into a series of developments with a certain order, rhythm, and finality, this act of discovery is also an act of re-creation. Situations that exist in the sociohistorical world are given a definite shape.

Robert Flaherty, a sort of father figure in the history of nonfiction film, introduced many of the existing ideas about real-life drama. Back in the silent period, when documentary cinema was not yet a clearly defined concept, he set out to record the lives of people living in "remote" parts of the world. And for that, Flaherty chose not the detached attitude that one might have found in the travelogues and nature films made at the time but rather the emotional approach that one tends to detect in a fiction film. Drama appeared, then, as a key to lived experience. Flaherty believed that life already contained dramatic moments, and that the filmmaker should "carve" them out of the raw material of the historical world (Calder-Marshall, quoted in Mamber 11).

His first film already exemplified this interest in drama. *Nanook of the North* (1922) was shot in the semi-arctic region of northern Ungava (on the northeastern border of the Hudson Bay), Canada, and captured the life of an Inuit hunter whose "adventures" constitute the heart of the film. The idea was to document traditional aspects of Inuit life that were disappearing or had already vanished. Yet rather than simply focus on the general features of the landscape and the people—an indistinct account of his subject—Flaherty filmed the experiences of one particular individual, a hero so to speak, to whom our attention is directed throughout the film. Thanks to the man Flaherty named "Nanook," we do learn something about Inuit life. But we also rejoice at the dramatic opportunities offered by his screen appearances. We empathize with Nanook as he struggles to survive, share moments of tenderness with him and his family, and laugh at the antics of his children. Unlike a cold exposé of Inuit life and culture, *Nanook of the North* has many of the ingredients that contribute to the making of a good dramatic film: pathos, humor, and even suspense.

That these qualities were largely a product of the filmmaking process is revealed by Flaherty's own shooting methods. Several of the scenes in *Nanook* were staged for the camera, produced specifically to fit the purposes of the film. The subjects and the setting are genuine, but the events were re-created at the moment of shooting. Flaherty also makes a deliberate effort to present his subjects in a way that matches the overall narrative concept of the film, attributing to them features that are common to dramatic characters. Early in the film, for example, an intertitle describes Nanook as "Chief of the 'Itivimuits'" and "a great hunter famous through all Ungava." The idea is later reiterated by the various actions recorded by the camera, with Nanook playing the role announced earlier. The promise of real-life drama—when it exists—is thus fulfilled by the filmmaker's "artistic" intervention, his effort to match what he saw as authentic experience with conventional forms that are generally recognizable to film audiences. Needless to say, it is the specific design that results from this intervention that gives shape to the film's compelling message and, to a great extent, accounts for its lasting power.

The motor of the narrative in *Nanook of the North* is the clash between the individual and the environment. We find no real villains in the film, but in the absence of a human antagonist, Nanook's inhospitable surroundings provide the necessary obstacles for the development of narrative momentum. As William Rothman has noted, *Nanook of the North* is the story of "a man's heroic efforts to keep his family alive in a harsh natural environment" (25). Much of what we see in the film grows out of this initial conflict. As with many dramatic narratives, here we have a protagonist, a goal, and the difficulties that are likely to stand between him and his objectives. Will Nanook overcome the challenges imposed by the unforgiving landscape of the North? Will he be able to feed his family? These are the questions that drive the narrative forward. And it is our desire to know the answers that keeps us involved in the story events.

The film's overall pattern is established early on. *Nanook of the North* does not have one central plot line, which the spectator is expected to follow all the way to the end. Instead, Flaherty's film is divided into various episodes, all of which have a somewhat autonomous line of action, with a specific subject matter and the developments and complications that pertain to it. One of the early scenes in the film is introduced by an intertitle that reads: "A wandering ice field drifts in from [the] sea and locks up a hundred miles of coast. Though Nanook's band, already on the thin edge of starvation, is unable to move, Nanook, great hunter that he is, saves the day." The title is followed by images of Nanook in his kayak, trying to find his way through various ice blocks. Later, he walks on the large white field and looks for a place to fish. Using two pieces of ivory in lieu of bait, he manages to bring home a large catch and, as Flaherty had announced, saves the day. The scene is simple, almost predictable. But it fulfills the film's dramatic promise. Brave and ingenious, Nanook takes up the challenge facing him and proves, already toward the beginning of the documentary, that he can prevail over the obstacles that come his way.

This pattern repeats itself over and over again, as Flaherty presents different situations in the life of Nanook and his family. Whether Nanook is facing the adversities of the weather or involved in hunting exploits, the dramatic treatment of the story events remains basically the same. An initial challenge sets the action in motion, leading to a struggle against a specific "enemy." Once the struggle is over, Nanook emerges victorious, the prize being his own survival. With each episode, we have a provisional resolution, which in turn gives way to a new challenge and a new set of complications.

The most spectacular rendition of this pattern is a walrus hunt in which Nanook is joined by a few of his fellow Inuit men. Shortly after the fishing scene, an intertitle announces: "For days there is no food. Then one of Nanook's look-outs comes in with news of walrus on a far off island." What follows is a suspenseful sequence comparable to many found in fiction films. Flaherty shows us the Inuit

near the shore, then a herd of walruses lying on the beach, followed by a shot of Nanook and his companions walking toward their prey. As the men approach surreptitiously, the action is held still for several seconds. Then, all of a sudden, it changes into a fast-paced battle. Aware of imminent danger, the walruses rush to the water, but one of them ends up being hit by a harpoon. From then on, we see what is probably the film's most literal representation of the struggle be-tween man and nature. On one end of the line, the walrus swims for its life; on the other, the men struggle to drag it out

6.4. "Rolling the dead quarry from the undertow." From *Nanook of the North* (Robert Flaherty, 1922).

of the water, their own lives at risk if they lose the battle. In the end, the hunters win the fight, the confrontation now rewarded as they cut open the walrus and share the prize.

This sequence also demonstrates with unusual clarity how narrative conven-tions help shape our perception of the world depicted by Flaherty. All the central ideas in *Nanook* are condensed in this dramatic confrontation: the fascination with a generally inhospitable environment, the bravery of the Inuit men, and the struggle for survival are all underlined by these images. Perhaps most importantly, the battle scene draws attention to the distance that sets the "primitive" world of the Inuit apart from the white man's "civilization." Every trace of the industrial world has been deliberately avoided in this scene, as the hunters revive an ancient ritual that was no longer in place when Flaherty made the film. Hunting with harpoons instead of rifles was a traditional practice that put the lives of the Inuit "performers" at greater risk. To do otherwise, though, would be to compromise the pristine world evoked by Flaherty's camera. Instead, the walrus hunt scene preserves that ideal, as it puts dramatic intensity at the service of what Flaherty sees as the authentic Inuit way of life.

Flaherty's vision of the Inuit world is, of course, a romantic looking back, and for that he has been much criticized. Rather than show us how Nanook's people lived at the time he made the film, he chose to represent a world that might have existed *before* white explorers arrived in the land of the Itivimuits. In this sense, *Nanook of the North* cultivates a certain fascination with the primitive, one that is itself reminiscent of the white man's colonial imagination. As Fatimah Tobing Rony puts it, the film's "appeal was the myth of authentic first man" (103). What is striking for us here is the way this particular vision fits the dramatic concept of the film and how that concept seems to mold the reality we see on the screen. Had Flaherty chosen a different approach, or structured his film in a different way, his idealized vision of Inuit life might have been lost. As it is, the film projects and celebrates that vision. It honors the nobility of the "primitive," exalts their bravery, and adds a sensational quality to the real-life drama of survival.

Flaherty's influence in general and *Nanook*'s legacy in particular are immeasurable, but one of their obvious contributions is precisely this emphasis on drama as a way of approaching nonfictional reality. Many years after the making of *Nanook*, the idea of "discovered drama" continued to reverberate among documentary makers who claimed to find in real life the structures that we often attribute to a fiction film. In the early 1960s, for example, a group of American filmmakers, soon to be associated with the label of *direct cinema*, embraced an attitude toward nonfiction that recalled Flaherty's interest in capturing dramatic situations. Robert Drew, who produced some of these films, explains: "Dramatic logic works because the viewer is seeing for himself and there is suspense. The viewer can become interested in characters. Characters develop. Things happen" (282).

Not surprisingly, several of the documentaries made at that time focused on contests or crisis situations. The idea was that either of these would call for dramatic action, which in turn would provide material for the film. The "crisis model," as it was eventually described, offered a "natural" structure for the documentary. It defined a conflict, established a line of action, and asked for a resolution. Drama was expected to occur effortlessly (Mamber 115–140).

In practice, things did not work exactly this way, for while direct cinema did locate drama in real life, the process of transposing it to the screen was never effortless or transparent. These were clearly delimited narratives in which the promise of resolution also helped define the "message." And the films were, of course, the expression of a particular point of view, even though the filmmakers tried to minimize their own role as mediators in the process of representation.

The "constructedness" of the documentaries is apparent in one particular similarity to the plotting of Hollywood narratives. Most Hollywood films rely on a classical dramatic structure that organizes the story events in three acts, the first serving as a presentation of the narrative's main conflict, the second corresponding to the development of that conflict (a forward march and complications), and the third bringing in the conflict's resolution. Although the crisis documentaries were not designed the same way Hollywood movies are, they, too, seemed to benefit from this narrative structure. Drama, as it existed in real life, was expected to fit into a prefabricated model.

More than simply provide a structuring model for direct cinema, however, the crisis formula actually favored a particular worldview. It submitted the contingency of social reality to a relatively simple plot, in which courage or individual determination served as an engine for real-life events and the protagonists were supposed to meet the obstacles they faced. Even if triumph was less than certain, the value of individual resolve was never questioned.

One of the documentaries that did embrace this formula was revealingly called *Crisis: Behind a Presidential Commitment*. Produced by Drew Associates in 1963 for ABC television, *Crisis* thrives on the promise of dramatic conflict and yields to the need for narrative resolution. The record of an especially tense situation, it has clearly defined characters, a goal that must be accomplished, and difficulties that are likely to delay the achievement of that goal. It also shows us how the classical three-act structure can be used to fulfill the promises of documentary cinema. Much of what we learn from the film depends, of course, on this particular arrangement.

Crisis focuses on a provocative subject matter: the admission of two African American students, Vivian Malone and James Hood, to the University of Alabama. The scenario is easily recognizable to those familiar with the history of the period. On June 11, 1963, Governor George Wallace, a notorious segregationist, tried to stop the two students from entering the university. His gesture defied a federal court order and put the Kennedy administration in a difficult spot. The film follows the efforts of Attorney General Robert Kennedy and his deputy Nicholas Katzenbach as they try to ensure that Hood and Malone are permitted to register. It also shows us Wallace's strategies to resist the pressures from the federal government and prevent integration at the university.

Crisis opens with an introduction to the main characters and locales and a brief explanation of the overall situation. With the aid of voiceover commentary—a device later dismissed by direct cinema filmmakers as a sign of the documentarian's interference—it describes the dispute that we are about to witness and anticipates the dramatic events that will guide the narrative. This quick presentation is followed by a few sequences that concur to make up the first act of the film. We watch Robert Kennedy having breakfast with his family at home in a Virginia suburb and then, in a parallel structure, we see Wallace in the governor's mansion, holding his toddler daughter in his arms. Introducing a pattern that will prove effective throughout the film, the sequence establishes a similarity between the two men while also revealing their differences (Wallace is seen praising Civil War heroes whose portraits hang on the mansion's walls, for example). Later the camera follows both men to work. In his office, Kennedy tries to devise a plan for dealing with the governor. Wallace, meanwhile, prepares a strategy for a possible showdown with the federal government. Here, too, the film's parallel structure allows us to connect two separate situations, thus anticipating the eventual confrontation between the opposing camps.

Although a similar amount of screen time is assigned to each of the main "actors," one of the sides seems to gain prominence in these sequences. From relatively early on, the Kennedy camp takes up a role analogous to that of the protagonist in a fictional narrative. We watch the attorney general and his staff as they try to accomplish a specific goal and tend to see Wallace's gesture merely as a form of resistance to the efforts from the other camp—an obstacle that is at the basis of the dramatic conflict in the film. Kennedy is, in other words, identified with narrative action itself, while Wallace is given the role of antagonist.

What seals this identification between the Kennedy camp and the film's main line of action is a meeting with President John F. Kennedy, from which the attorney general emerges as the main figure in the effort to desegregate the University of Alabama. Shortly after the first scene in his office, we see Robert Kennedy arrive at the White House, pass the gate, and leave the car, the camera tracking him closely as he enters the building. For a few minutes he confers with the president and several staff members about a speech on civil rights, to be delivered by the president himself. Nothing conclusive seems to come out of the meeting. Yet the visit to the White House produces a comforting sense of direction. Toward the end of the sequence, as we see the attorney general walk away from the camera, the voiceover commentary returns: "The president is relying on Robert Kennedy to plan a strategy for gaining the admission of the two students."

This sequence constitutes what theorists and practitioners call a *turning point:* a development that establishes a new course for the narrative action and, in doing so, announces a shift from one of the three acts to another. Robert Kennedy's visit to the president serves this very purpose. Even if no definitive statement can be drawn from the meeting, the idea that the attorney general is now in charge functions as a sort of marker in the narrative, one that brings the first act to an end and points the way to subsequent developments. We already know the characters and the controversy that binds them. We must now find out how that conflict will be played out, what will happen with the students, and how the federal government will deal with Wallace. The aforementioned voiceover commentary gives us a clue as to how these questions will be answered.

Second acts are usually rich in dramatic developments, and the middle portion of *Crisis* is no exception. Here the complications that arise from the initial conflict are expected to test the protagonist's will and determination, eventually proving that all obstacles were hard fought and all achievements—when they do come— well deserved. In the sequences after the White House meeting, the attorney general consults with his staff, discusses possible strategies for the confrontation, and gives a television interview. Wallace, too, speaks with the media. And so do the African American students, whose voices are now heard for the first time in the film. As the deadline approaches—the moment when both plan to enroll in the university—the tension between the opposing camps also rises, calling for an effective response from the actors involved. *Crisis* does a good job of preserving the sense of spontaneity that we expect from a critical situation. But the fact that this material is neatly packed in the middle portion of the film reveals an appreciation of narrative conventions that precede the events captured by the camera. What is exceptional about *Crisis* is the fact that, when the confrontation at the university does take place, it is not Robert Kennedy but his deputy Katzenbach who faces their opponent. Kennedy sends Katzenbach to Alabama to secure the students' admission. To our surprise, Governor Wallace does not bend, and what looked like the final confrontation in the film turns out to be yet another dramatic development, the students walking off to their dormitories with no resolution emerging from the showdown.

A denouement does come, however, a few minutes later, when National Guard troops are sent to the university. This time, the governor has to leave, his pride crushed by a federal order. In the film's final moments, we see separate shots of the students as they walk peacefully on campus. And we witness a last phone call from the attorney general to President Kennedy. For anyone expecting a climactic ending, this might be a somewhat tepid final act. But the sense of closure that it brings to the conflict is indisputable. The Alabama State University system has been desegregated. As would generally be the case in mainstream fiction, here the third act restores an order that was disrupted early on and puts an end to the developments that made up the narrative. Judging from the overall tone of the film, this was, certainly, a happy ending.

Thanks to this particular narrative structure, *Crisis* makes it easy for us to understand the situations portrayed in the film, demonstrating how the crisis formula can serve as a powerful tool in the hands of documentary filmmakers. Yet there are disadvantages, too. Because they use individuated characters and dramatic form as a means of approaching larger issues, crisis films in general and this one in particular tend to limit the scope of worthy documentary subjects. They also reduce the vastness and complexity of those topics to a unidirectional, not to say narrow, set of developments. Compelling as they are, these narratives can thus restrict our perspective on the events represented.

Poetic Experiments

So far, we have been considering documentaries that employ argumentation or dramatic structure to tell their stories. In many ways, these works have been influenced by journalism. They have content they wish to communicate. There are, however, other approaches that are less a communicative act than a poetic form of engagement with the sociohistorical world. Some documentarians use the filmmaking process as a tool to explore personal concerns or aspects of life we often take for granted. They opt for a different kind of formal arrangement in order to provide new insights into the events, situations, or subjects represented. The more unconventional that arrangement appears, the greater the potential to look at the world from a fresh perspective.

These documentaries manage to skirt both narrative and rhetorical conventions by organizing their material around freer associations, sometimes arranging that material in formal patterns, often incorporating aesthetic experimentation and the filmmaker's personal perceptions. In these cases, the record of lived reality exists in dialogue with the desire to explore aesthetic concerns. Poetic constructions prevail over the prosaic quality of storytelling, and formal associations take precedence over well-crafted argumentation.

The use of experimental forms to represent lived reality also goes back to the period of silent cinema. A number of films made at that time combined the impulse to document the historical world with an original approach to the cinematic medium. The so-called "city symphony" films, for example, captured slices of everyday life in modern metropolises, but did so in ways that transformed or enhanced our perception of ordinary reality, usually through nontraditional structures, an inventive editing style, and ingenious cinematography. The result was an image of modernity that had as much to do with the experiences afforded by the film medium as with the referential world.

In *Berlin, Symphony of a Great City/Berlin, die Sinfonie der Grosstadt* (Walther Ruttmann, 1927), this concept of modernity is conveyed through a series of segments that captures various facets of a large European city in the 1920s. At first sight, the film does seem to follow a predictable pattern, offering a "day in the life" sort of narrative bracketed by early morning and late night events. In the beginning, we see shots of a roadside taken from a moving train headed to the German capital. Ruttmann then shows us Berlin's empty streets, which slowly fill up with people as the city prepares for an ordinary workday. From the streets, he takes us to factories, and then to shopping districts, parks, offices, train stations, hotels, restaurants, and so on. In the film's final segment, he focuses on Berlin's nightlife: movie theaters, sports events, music halls, and nightclubs. The passing of time serves as a structuring device in Ruttmann's film. And yet this seemingly neat arrangement turns out to be misleading since each of the film's five segments has a life of its own. Furthermore, the relationship between one segment and others is established less by a sense of narrative development than by the repetition of motifs such as industrial technology, modern means of transportation, and public spaces. The recurrence of these motifs, rather than simply the trajectory from morning to evening, is what allows Ruttmann to create his poetic portrait of a modern metropolis.

A similarly evocative representation of urban life appears in Joris Ivens's *Rain/Regen* (1929), made a couple of years later. At twelve minutes, *Rain* is less than a quarter the length of *Berlin, Symphony of a Great City*. But like Ruttmann's film, it submits the referential aspirations of nonfiction filmmaking to a unique and aesthetically ambitious experience. Here the promise of narrative development is even fainter, the central subject in the film—a rain shower in Amsterdam—offering little more than a pretext for the filmmaker's lyrical impressions of the city. Ivens seems less interested in large events than in the details that make up the fabric of everyday life. Soon after the beginning of the film, the first raindrops start falling on water surfaces, and we begin to observe the changes that a sudden shower brings to an ordinary day. People dash for shelter, open their umbrellas, and cover themselves. Water accumulates on the streets and on the windows of streetcars. All these minor occurrences are, of course, connected to the main topic in the film. But there are no apparent causal relations between the images. While the rain shower itself seems to have a beginning and an end, the experience afforded by *Rain* can never be reduced to a desire for narrative closure. In its loose orchestration of images, the film highlights the significance of each individual shot, each impression left on the filmmaker's eye. As one might expect, *Rain* turned out to be not the record of a single event but, as Ivens himself wrote, the result of footage shot over the course of four months (37).

To be sure, *Rain* does have a formal structure, but it is a structure shaped by

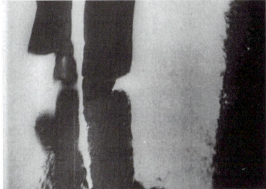

6.5–6.6. Legs of horses in step with legs of pedestrians through a graphic match, in *Rain/Regen* (Joris Ivens, 1929).

poetic associations. Ivens frequently connects separate events by exploring similar visual patterns, producing what David Bordwell and Kristin Thompson call a "graphic match" (221). The view of a flock of birds, for example, is joined to a shot of leaves blown off the ground. There is no narrative correlation between the two occurrences. But the size of the birds and the trajectory of their flight find a visual counterpart in the image of leaves fluttering up. In another occasion, we see an opening umbrella followed by the shot of a closing window. The juxtaposition creates a parallel between the two actions. It also highlights their differences— opening and closing. And it calls to mind the underlying theme in the film, the rainfall, without suggesting any sense of causality between one shot and another.

Both *Rain* and *Berlin, Symphony of a Great City* bear a close relationship to the avant-garde film movements of the first half of the twentieth century. Avant-garde filmmakers saw cinema as an art form in its own right, and their work often pushed the boundaries of film aesthetics beyond the confines of mainstream, narrative filmmaking. When this emphasis on innovation met with documentary's referential aspirations, they ended up with a potentially original perspective both on the film medium and the historical world.

Documentary Essays

In some ways, the meeting between nonfictional representation and experimental aesthetics finds even more complex scenarios in contemporary cinema. Consider the example of ethnographic filmmaking. While traditional ethnographic works tend to perpetuate the cultural hierarchies that separate the filmmaker—usually a white, Western male—from the subjects represented—often non-Western

people or minority groups—some experimental films try to do exactly the opposite. They use aesthetic innovation as a means of questioning those same hierarchies. As Catherine Russell has noted, "experimental ethnography" tries "to
overcome the binary oppositions of us and them, self and other, along with the
tension between the profilmic and the textual operations of aesthetic form" (19).

Trinh T. Minh-hà's *Reassemblage*, examined in chapter 4, is one of those works
in which aesthetic experimentation helps to redefine the idea of ethnographic representation. When asked which genre her work was, experimental or documentary, Trinh replied that she doesn't see them as separate entities at all (Trinh and
Hirshorn 15). *Reassemblage* focuses mainly on rural Senegalese women, subjects
whom we might have encountered in more conventional types of ethnographic
filmmaking. Trinh, however, refuses to see the women as typical ethnographic
subjects or to sanction the traditional role of the ethnographic filmmaker, opt-
ing instead for a kind of documentary that opposes hierarchical distinctions. This
refusal is perhaps most apparent in the way the documentary materials are
organized—the overall structure of the film. *Reassemblage* captures some of the
daily activities of the Senegalese women but does not try to contain or explain
them. We see the women as they work, prepare food, and attend to their children.
Yet these events seem to follow no logical pattern and are best appreciated as
distinct occurrences. Fittingly, Trinh also refrains from offering conclusive statements about the subjects in her film, their way of living, or their culture. *Reassemblage* ends somewhat abruptly, the same way it starts. What stands out is our
momentary engagement with the documentary subjects.

By challenging established aesthetic conventions and filmmaking practices,
Reassemblage redefines the filmmaker's relationship with the documentary subject and, consequently, our understanding of that subject as well.

Such experimental films reveal yet another facet in the filmmaker's relationship
with the referential world. They remind us that this engagement can be personal
and artistic without lacking credibility. A more traditional approach to nonfictional
representation may fault this kind of cinema for its emphasis on the documentarian's subjective viewpoint. But these films can contradict the suspicion that the
convergence of experimental aesthetics and nonfiction cinema threatens the referential quality of documentary filmmaking. They show, instead, that this subjective approach to nonfictional representation involves dialogue with the historical
world, a productive exchange between the filmmakers and their subject matter.

Both formally and ideologically, this scenario finds an inspiring equivalent
in the concept of the filmic essay. As a form of composition, the essay assumes
a comparable dialogue between the subjectivity of the essayist and the themes

discussed. This interaction creates fragmented and multilayered texts, resulting in knowledge that often seems "speculative" and "provisional." Essays thrive not on certainty but on "indeterminacy" (Renov 70). In fact, the term "essay" itself is etymologically related to the idea of tentativeness. In French, the verb *essayer* means to attempt, test, or try. It suggests "an open-ended, evaluative, and specula-tive search" (Alter 18).

How useful is this notion for the discussion of documentary cinema? How can it help us understand the use of poetic or experimental forms in nonfiction film? And what does it say about the way some documentaries arrange and organize factual material? Although it is sometimes hard to pinpoint what constitutes an essay film, there are certain features that can help us work out a definition. We may be able, for instance, to use the notion of the essay to describe documentaries whose structures are dispersed and exploratory, rather than precise and "neatly" arranged. These are films that embrace "digression" in lieu of carefully constructed arguments or well-organized narratives. Rather than declaring their essence at the outset, they tend to draw the spectator in gradually and disclose their direction over the course of the documentary.

By calling some documentaries "essays" we are then thinking not only about their subjective or poetic qualities but also about the impact of these qualities on the epistemological expectations associated with nonfiction cinema. The es-say film contradicts, for example, the assumption that the world can be known in a definitive way. It shifts the focus from the end product of the investigative effort to the process by which knowledge is created. To speak metaphorically, it is the movement, not the destination, that matters the most. Documentaries that embrace this model often suggest important inquiries, but they do not strive to provide comprehensive answers.

Let's look one more time at Joris Ivens's *Rain*. Ivens's response to the situa-tions that unfold in front of his camera encompasses a multiplicity of views, none of which is expected to represent the setting and situation—the city, the sudden downpour—in their entirety. The purpose is to explore the world rather than settle for one perspective or another. Moreover, the film's lyrical qualities situate the encounter between the filmmaker's artistic sensitivities and the sur-rounding environment at the center of the representational process. Finally, while *Rain* does seem to follow a particular event from beginning to end, the apparently centrifugal nature of its design calls to mind the essay's penchant for speculation and digression, as well as its affinity with open-ended structures. *Reassemblage*, too, is open-ended, "headless and bottomless storytelling," in Trinh's own words (*Woman, Native, Other* 43).

In Chris Marker's *Sunless/Sans soleil* (1982), the filmmaker's response to sociohistorical reality goes hand-in-hand with his discontinuous organization of factual material. More exploratory than assertive, *Sunless* is in some ways a travel journal that reflects on the fragmentary nature of memory. It combines footage shot in various locations—Iceland, Japan, Cape Verde, and Guinea Bissau, among others—without pursuing any direct connection between them. Instead, the film offers insights on different ways of living by recording the filmmaker's reactions to these places. The tone is personal, and the way of presenting information defies conventional anticipations.

Already in the first minute of the film we get a sense of the way Marker's evocative impressions will shape the overall structure of his documentary. Over black leader, we hear a woman's voice saying: "The first image he told me about was of three children on the road in Iceland in 1965. He said that for him it was the image of happiness and also that he had tried several times to link it to other images, but it never worked. He wrote me, 'One day I'll have to put it all alone in the beginning of a film, with a long piece of black leader.'" Soon after the narration starts, Marker cuts to a shot of three blond girls timidly glancing at the camera as they walk by an open field. We realize then that the film being referred to by the narrator is precisely the one we are watching. The shot is followed by yet another piece of black leader, which separates it from the rest of the documentary. When Marker finally shows us a new image, an unexpected view of military aircraft, it is only to underscore the singularity of the first one, the impossibility of coherently linking the three girls to any other sight. No specific theme or subject matter is introduced here. Rather, as the narrator explains, the shot exists on its own, as a sliver of memory that embodies a certain ideal of happiness. *Sunless*, we will soon find out, is a film made out of fragmented stories, personal impulses pulled together by the filmmaker's poetic sensibility.

The opening of *Sunless* brings forth the fragmentary nature of the film in yet another way. It establishes a conversational dynamic with an absent male writer whose letters provide the basis for the documentary's voiceover narration. Here as elsewhere in the film, we hear the narrator introduce a new shot by saying, "He said," "He told me," or "He wrote me that. . . ." And we assume that the opinions and observations gathered in the film belong to another person. The narration itself does not provide a cohesive, unified design for the documentary but refers instead to the scattered impressions of that absent author. Each letter can potentially take us in a different direction, introduce a new subject, or offer an opportunity for dispersal. As Nora Alter writes in her study of Marker's work, there is a historical affinity between the epistolary genre and the essay format, which goes back to antiquity and is grounded in the desire for dialogue between the essayist and the world (26). *Sunless* explores this affinity by turning the letters into a structuring device for the documentary.

The letters allow Marker to move swiftly from one continent to another without concern for causal or thematic relations. Early in the film, for example, he cuts from a bar in Japan to a pier on the island of Fogo, in Cape Verde. No transitional device is provided. As we begin to look at the shots taken on the island, we are encouraged to believe that what we see is actually a visual rendition of one of the letters read in the film: "He told me about the jetty in Fogo, in the Cape Verde Islands," says the narrator over images of a crowd gathered along a pier. "How long have they been there waiting for the boat, patient as pebbles but ready to jump?"

This is not the first time Marker uses letters to compose his essays. He does the same thing, for example, in *Letter from Siberia/Lettre de Sibérie*, from 1957. But *Sunless* is peculiar in its engagement with the epistolary form. Sándor Krasna, the author of the letters, is a fictional character, an invention that seems to complicate the distinctions between fiction and nonfiction in the film.

Besides drawing on such genres as the travel journal and the epistolary film, *Sunless* might be seen as an ethnographic documentary (Russell 301–311). Part of its mission is to explore the cultural richness of societies that are foreign to the filmmaker. For example, Marker travels through the streets of Japan, visits department stores, attends ceremonies, and documents the country's fascination with video games. He even invites us to watch Japanese television. All this seems to underscore *Sunless*'s ethnographic aspirations. Yet the film's emphasis on loosely structured impressions works against the notion of a traditional ethnographic documentary. Moreover, like some of the experimental works we have been examining, Marker's poetic film draws attention not only to the reality it documents but also to the subjectivity of the documentary maker, even if that subjectivity often manifests itself through the voice of a fictional character.

The best way to appreciate the relationship between this subjective quality and the essay form may be simply to examine the use of memory as a motif in the film. Memory is a recurrent concern in Marker's oeuvre, a topic addressed in several of his works. Here he uses it in order to mull over the subject of documentary filmmaking itself. "I remember that month of January in Tokyo," says the narrator toward the end of the film. "Or rather, I remember the images I filmed of the month of January in Tokyo. They have substituted themselves for my memory. They *are* my memory." It is not only the mnemonic role of the photographic image, however, that is evoked in the film. Marker's interest in memory recalls the very nature of the essay form—and, in this case, the epistolary genre as well. Memories are personal, fragmentary, and, depending on how we look at them, elusive. Like the essay film, they depend on noncausal associations and tend to escape the necessity for linearity or completion. By choosing the essay form to represent lived reality, Marker offers a parallel between his cinema and the act of remembering.

The analogy seems especially provocative when we contrast the contingent character of memory with the requirements that impinge on official historical accounts. Or when we confront the essay film with documentaries that follow predictable narrative patterns. A film like *Sunless* reminds us that memory can offer an alternative path to past events, just as poetic essays can provide different ways of knowing the historical world. It is not so much that Marker fully dismisses the possibilities of historical narratives. Rather, he turns to the film essay form, with its promises of "dispersion" and "digression," in order to interrogate the limitations of those narratives. As Jonathan Kear puts it, Marker's "questioning of the limits of historical perception reflects less a negation of history as a form of knowledge than a critique of rationalist and teleological versions of history" (58). In *Sunless*, the filmmaker opts for a format that encourages us not so much to find answers as entertain questions.

Database Documentaries

Some recent documentaries take the aspirations of the filmic essay one step further by combining nonfictional representation with the tools afforded by new digital media. What have become known as database documentaries, for example, provide multiple entry points to the historical world without following the logic of linear development or privileging exposition. Here nonfictional material is displayed as individual pieces that can be accessed somewhat randomly on a computer screen.

Lev Manovich describes databases as "collections of items on which the user can perform various operations—view, navigate, search" (219). Structurally, they are closer, say, to a deck of cards than to mainstream films. We engage in the logic of a database whenever we use a CD-ROM, turn to the menu of a DVD, or click on the links of a web site. None of these experiences are comparable to reading a traditional novel or viewing a documentary from beginning to end. While databases may be used to tell stories, or to advance a point of view, they rely on formal principles of their own.

It is not surprising, then, that the database form appears particularly well suited for aesthetic experimentation. Because they avoid the imperative of linear progression, database documentaries do not lead to a conclusion or resolution. There is no teleological trajectory here. There is also no single starting point from which to begin viewing the material, nor any "center." Each fragment is part of the overall design of the documentary, but there is no predetermined order in which to watch those pieces. The selection and combination, the shuffling, so to speak, is up to the user.

When compared to traditional nonfiction films, database documentaries seem inherently incomplete. The users can replay a segment that has already been shown, or they can end the experience at any given point. As was the case with some of the experimental works examined earlier, this incompleteness can make it difficult to establish a single viewpoint on the world. Instead, it encourages the user to explore different angles, make associations, and draw comparisons between subjects. Certain topics and situations seem particularly fit for this kind of documentary. Local histories, for instance, can be documented with material that might be easily arranged as "collections of items," with each new window augmenting our knowledge of the subject without "wrapping up" the issue in one way or another. We can imagine including maps, birth certificates, family photos, school portraits, transit routes, home movies, oral histories, garden plans, and minutes from community meetings. (Rosemary Comella's 2005 *Cultivating Pasadena: From Roses to Redevelopment*, produced by The Labyrinth Project at the University of Southern California, is an interesting illustration of database format local history.) Other themes, such as the ones explored in some of the experimental films discussed in this chapter, can also reveal an affinity with the database format: life in a big city, the effects of a sudden downpour, a series of letters.

Yet even topics that are traditionally associated with narrative progression can find new incarnations in database documentaries. The life of an individual subject, for example, can provide material for a documentary biography in which facts are organized in a cause-effect relationship that implies some form of finality. On the other hand, we can also represent that person's life by giving relative autonomy to specific aspects or segments, treating them as discrete items that are thematically related to one another. *Who Is . . . ?* (Magnus Bärtås and Agence TOPO, 2005) is a nonfictional work about five artists of different nationalities that started as text work, was reconfigured as installation, and was eventually adapted for the web. Bärtås compiled biographical facts about his subjects but did not line them up to create a unidirectional narrative. Instead, the project invites the user to dwell on each item separately or combine them somewhat arbitrarily.

The first thing we see when we enter *Who Is . . . ?* on the computer screen are artfully abbreviated still images of the five artists, sided by their names. Clicking on one, we are transported to another page where we have the option of accessing information under the categories: factual, formal, unexpected, and experienced. Each category is linked to four to seven small windows that in turn load still or moving images of the artist, accompanied by a child's voiceover commentary and a moving print version, visualizing what she says. We watch short clips (less than a minute long) or stills of the subject engaged in prosaic activities and hear somewhat unpredictable comments relating to the artist's life: "He has a dark blue Mercedes that he drives at death-defying speeds," "He was at the front in the war against the Serbs in 1994," "When she lost her travel funds in southern France, she moved to Greece to earn a living picking oranges," and "He says he sometimes sits by himself and laughs." The result is closer to a series of partial portraits than to conventional biographies. We do learn a great deal about situations in the subjects' lives, but there is no suggestion that those lives are constrained by narrative conventions. The fragmentary nature of *Who Is. . . . ?* and the title question's intentional ambiguity provoke consideration of both how we can describe someone and what elements contribute to someone's identity. What is it that defines a person?

Eschewing predefined sequential patterns also suggests that database documentaries can present information in a nonhierarchical fashion, each "item" being in theory as important as the others. *Who Is. . . . ?*, for instance, does not privilege any specific subject or make distinctions between the various aspects of the artists' lives. Rather, it leaves it up to the user to make those distinctions. The "message," as well as any presumption of certainty, will vary according to the patterns that emerge when we access and watch the documentary. Seen this way, database documentaries may afford us an experience that is more open and democratic than what is available in most other types of nonfiction work. Like many new media artifacts, database documentaries are interactive. They depend on direct input from the users.

There is a danger, however, in celebrating this input uncritically, since we can end up overlooking the limitations of the database form. We may want to think that database documentaries provide a potentially infinite pool of information, or that meaning can be in "a constant process of accumulation" (Hudson 90). Most of the time, though, the experience of watching a work of this type is clearly limited by the amount of material recorded and made available for consumption. There are only so many clips available in a documentary like *Who Is . . . ?* And there are only so many windows open at any given moment. The notion of a boundless experience is partly deceptive. The interactive design of database works does assign a new role for the documentary spectator. But as cultural critic Marsha Kinder has argued, "All interactivity is also an illusion because the rules established by the designers of the text necessarily limit the user's options" (4). The data we have at our disposal are limited by the designers of the text as well. If we wish to know more about why "he sometimes sits by himself and laughs," or how "she lost her travel funds," we would have to find it elsewhere. It is not part of the information available in this work.

Still, by drawing attention to the way information is arranged and presented to the user, databases can help us think about the choices involved in the structuring of a documentary. And if there are limitations to the promises of interactivity, there is also the fact that users participate more directly in the process by which that information is communicated. They are, to some degree, coeditors of the documentary. We are faced, once again, with an issue that underlies this entire chapter: different ways of arranging documentary materials allow for different ways of knowing the world.

Additional Filmography

Only the Hours/Rien que les heures (Alberto Cavalcanti, 1926)

On the Subject of Nice/À propos de Nice (Jean Vigo, 1930)

Photo Wallahs (Judith and David MacDougall, 1992)

From the East/D'Est (Chantal Akerman, 1993)

Television and Me/La televisión y yo (Andrés Di Tella, 2002)

The City Beautiful (Rahul Roy, 2003)

The LoveStoryProject (Florian Thalhofer and Mahmoud Hamdy, 2003 and ongoing)

Of Time and the City (Terence Davies, 2008)

Works Cited and Further Reading

Alter, Nora M. *Chris Marker.* Urbana: University of Illinois Press, 2006.

Bordwell, David. *Narration in the Fiction Film.* Madison: University of Wisconsin Press, 1986.

Bordwell, David, and Kristin Thompson. *Film Art: An Introduction.* 8th ed. New York: McGraw-Hill, 2008.

Calder-Marshall, Arthur. *The Innocent Eye: The Life of Robert J. Flaherty.* New York: Harcourt, Brace and World, 1963.

Drew, Robert L. "An Independent with the Networks." In *New Challenges for Documentary*, 2nd ed., ed. Alan Rosenthal and John Corner. Manchester: Manchester University Press, 2005.

Hudson, Dale. "Undisclosed Recipients: Database Documentaries and the Internet." *Studies in Documentary Film* 2.1 (2008).

Ivens, Joris. *The Camera and I.* 1969. Reprint, New York: International Publishers, 1974.

Kear, Jonathan. "The Clothing of Clio: Chris Marker's Poetics and the Politics of Representing History." *Film Studies* 6 (Summer 2005).

Kinder, Marsha. "Hot Spots, Avatars, and Narrative Fields Forever: Buñuel's Legacy for New Digital Media and Interactive Database Narrative." *Film Quarterly* 55.4 (Summer 2002).

Mamber, Stephen. *Cinema Verite in America: Studies in Uncontrolled Documentary.* Cambridge, Mass.: MIT Press, 1974.

Manovich, Lev. *The Language of New Media.* Cambridge, Mass.: MIT Press, 2001.

Nichols, Bill. *Introduction to Documentary.* Bloomington: Indiana University Press, 2001.

O'Connel, P. J. *Robert Drew and the Development of Cinema Verite in America.* Carbondale: Southern Illinois University Press, 1992.

Renov, Michael. "*Lost, Lost, Lost:* Mekas as Essayist." In *The Subject of Documentary.* Minneapolis: University of Minnesota Press, 2004.

Rony, Fatimah Tobing. "Taxidermy and Romantic Ethnography: Robert Flaherty's *Nanook of the North.*" In *The Third Eye: Race, Cinema, and Ethnographic Spectacle.* Durham, N.C.: Duke University Press, 1996.

Rothman, William. "The Filmmaker as Hunter: Robert Flaherty's *Nanook of the North.*" In *Documenting the Documentary: Close Readings of Documentary Film and Video*, ed. Barry Keith Grant and Jeannette Sloniowski. Detroit: Wayne State University Press, 1998.

Russell, Catherine. *Experimental Ethnography: The Work of Film in the Age of Video.* Durham, N.C.: Duke University Press, 1999.

Trinh T. Minh-hà. *Woman, Native, Other: Writing, Postcoloniality and Feminism.* Bloomington: Indiana University Press, 1989.

Trinh T. Minh-hà and Harriet A. Hirshorn. "Interview." *Heresies* 22 6.2 (1987).

PART THREE

Formal Techniques

7

Editing

What do we mean when we say a book is "cinematic"? What is it that reminds us of the movies? Sometimes it might be the vividness of the descriptions. And sometimes it might be the amount of action. But often what we have in mind is the positioning of one part of the narrative next to another, the arrangement of story information, what we would call in film and video making "editing." Alfred Hitchcock once noted: "Cinema is simply pieces of film put together in a manner that creates ideas and emotions" (quoted in Samuels 232). This relates to nonfiction film as well. It is this "putting together of pieces of film" that we discuss in this chapter. The second section of the book already looked at the macro level of these designs, the overall structure of the documentary, the arrangement of information in order to make an argument, forge a dramatic story, or sensuously experiment with form to explore a topic or category. In those chapters, we considered concerns for rhetoric, or dramatic and poetic form, in the sequencing of information. Here we concentrate on the micro level: the placement of one shot or one sequence next to another.

In one sense, editing is simply the joining together of related shots to make a sequence, and the joining together of related sequences to build the film. But editing also reshapes and manipulates material. And when the material is nonfiction, editing can redefine sociohistorical reality. A filmmaker begins by shooting something concrete, a portion of the physical world. That footage, the raw material, takes on a specific meaning when it is placed in a sequence, as it becomes part

161

of a flow of sounds and images. Filmmaker Chantal Akerman comments on this process: "How much time should we take to show this street so that what's happening is something other than a mere piece of information? So that we go from the concrete to the abstract and come back to the concrete" (quoted in Rosen 125). For her, there are innumerable decisions to make as she turns abstract footage into a specific story.

Frederick Wiseman calls editing a "private debate." And he talks about how meaning is created as footage is edited into a story. He contrasts documentary filmmaking with fiction production. With fiction, the writing of the script normally precedes the shooting of the film. In a documentary, however, it is only after editing that the documentarian finds his "script." For Wiseman, the sequences in a documentary are "found" during the shooting process, but he has no idea at the time what shots will make it into the film or what the themes or point of view will be (Wiseman xi). Wiseman calls his films "reality fictions." "The events . . . are all true," he told John Graham, but "they have no meaning except insofar as you impose a form on them, and that form is imposed in large measure, of course, in the editing." "A cut is a judgment . . . the only public trace of a private debate" (quoted in Miller 226). In his first film, *Titicut Follies*, Wiseman spent nearly a month shooting, followed by almost a year of editing. One hundred and fifty thousand feet of film were compressed into little more than three thousand feet for the eighty-four-minute film. In later films, he employed a similar ratio, generally using less than five percent of what he shoots. Yet, when those shots are edited into the final film, they appear as "if no other order were possible" (Wiseman xii). Even editors who work on other people's films claim to have control over content. Sam Pollard, who cut Spike Lee's *4 Little Girls* (1997), told *MovieMaker Magazine* about his early days as a documentary editor: "I was given the responsibility to really direct the material . . . [the producer and director] leave it to you to . . . help build the concept, find the direction, and find the story."

There are some exceptions, of course. Historical documentaries frequently begin with the story they want to tell. The documentarian then looks for evidence and corroboration of that story. As director Jon Else points out, these types of documentary are more popular with funding sources for exactly this reason. The funders "know what they are going to get" (Bernard 281). *Prelude to War*, a film that provides the history of some of the events that led the United States into World War II, began with the story they wanted to tell. They then sought the footage that would support that story. But we have also seen an example of a historical film that was created in the editing room. While making *The River*, Pare Lorentz's camera operators brought back the kinds of shots he wanted (some footage of clouds, of sky, of water, of trees, and so on). It was in the editing that he fashioned these shots into the story of the ecological destruction of the Mississippi River delta. This film, too, gives a historical account. It was scripted, though, in the editing process (Van Dyke 38–56; Snyder 50–78).

Early nonfiction films were generally limited to only one shot. Each shot represented a view that took place in a continuous time and place. But early film companies also sometimes sold different views of the same event separately, suggesting that exhibitors show them one after the other. Historian Stephen Bottomore tells of the Warwick Trading Company's 1897–98 catalogue, which offered eleven views of a Madrid bullfight: "When joined and shown consecutively . . . [they] constitute a thrilling exhibition of 10 minutes duration." He also tells about firms that offered views of the 1897 procession honoring the Jubilee of Queen Victoria taken at various points along the route. Buyers were recommended to purchase several of them, and show them one after the other, combining them in a designated order. Travel films, too, were often sold with an implied sequence. And some producers actually divided a view into several shots. The Edison Manufacturing Company's *Shoot the Chutes* (1899) consisted of three shots of an amusement park ride. By partitioning the scene into multiple shots, the camera operator selected specific points of view to give the audience a better idea of the ride than they would have gotten in a single shot (Bottomore 201–202). While we may not say that these shots were actually edited, some of the principles and functions of the editing process were already present then.

Editing is simply the putting together of pieces of film. But, as we have stated in earlier chapters and explore in more depth here, the sequencing of interdependent shots is part of a film's meaning-making system. We saw this clearly in our discussion of Emile De Antonio and Daniel Talbot's *Point of Order*, the documentary about the 1954 Army-McCarthy hearings. Compiled from television footage of the hearings, the film was edited in a way that impacted the meaning of that footage.

Some documentaries do try to minimize editing, using shots of long duration, sometimes shots that are whole scenes like those in the early films we mentioned above. What we see and hear in these scenes seems closer to our experience of ordinary life, since the passing of time in the film coincides with the passing of time in the physical world. *Lunch with Fela*, Abraham Ravett's 2005 documentary, is a good example. Shooting as he was interacting with his elderly mother in her nursing home, Ravett set up a camera and then joined his mother in the shot. Or he took the camera and recorded the funeral director itemizing the costs of her burial. Or he set up the camera and walked around his mother's apartment enumerating the things he needed to do to empty it out. The camera observes, dutifully, motionless, much like, say, an attendant at the nursing home might observe. And in each shot there is a continuity of time and space.

This is not to say, of course, that the film is free of editorial intervention. But this intervention has more to do with the selection and sequencing of material than the cutting and arranging of shots within a particular scene. In fact, much of the footage never made it into the final cut. Ravett, who was editor as well as director, producer, and camera operator, dispensed with approximately twenty times what he included in his documentary. Whereas the fiction film editor generally discards all but the best of multiple takes, a documentary editor eliminates superfluous footage, footage that is not needed to tell the best story. In *Lunch with Fela*, Abraham Ravett carefully selected and sequenced the material to control the transmission and flow of story information to the viewer, producing a documentary that is at once intimate and unsentimental. "Tomorrow is your mother's birthday," a woman's voice says toward the beginning. "She'd be 92 this year." The use of the past conditional tense clearly establishes Fela's passing. The next image, though, is Fela in the nursing home, a tiny, gray-haired woman eating lunch, with Abraham discussing health insurance matters.

There are six scenes in the nursing facility, each representing time the two spent together. Between them, Ravett edits in carefully framed images of some of Fela's possessions: buttons, a hat pin, change purses, the card of a Brooklyn car service, a scrap of paper with a painter's name and phone number on it, the humble particulars of everyday life. Later, he edits in a Polaroid of Fela in the Massachusetts nursing home; then a hand placing the Polaroid of Fela into the shot. Ravett includes some sequences that were shot earlier as well: Fela standing by the window of her apartment combing her long brown hair, and seated in a park explaining how the Nazis rounded up all the Jewish children of her hometown in 1944. There is also an artist's rendition of the same scene. The filmmaker edits in some still images from Walbrzych, Poland, the town where Fela gave birth to Abraham after the war. He edits in the sounds of people reciting numbers in various Eastern European languages. He edits in a Yiddish language radio broadcast with a running English translation over a black screen. And in the middle of the fifty-nine-minute documentary, he edits in a voice asking some of the questions the viewer might have been asking: How is the camera set up on your shoot? What were you thinking about in the scene when your mother was eating and you were staring off? What are those people saying? Is that your father sitting next to your mother? Some more questions are included again near the end. But no answers are given. Information is left out, and information is vague. Nor is there a simple chronology.

By inference, however, the spectator is able to piece together perhaps not a life but certainly the relationship of the filmmaker to his mother—a woman of multiple languages and many displacements—during the final days of her life. Abraham Ravett edits *Lunch with Fela* in ways that engage the spectator's imagination. The information in each shot, the duration of the shots, and the order in which they are sequenced elucidate and emphasize certain aspects of Abraham's and Fela's lives—and they elicit a certain type of spectatorship. The viewer is actively engaged in conferring meaning and making sense of Ravett's shots.

All documentaries control the order in which information is given, usually through editing sequences together. And a certain degree of inference is a part of any filmgoing experience. But in its avoidance of intra-scene editing, *Lunch with Fela* is unusual. Piecing film together produces cinematic time and space, frequently the illusion of continuous time and contiguous space. Piecing film together can also function to modify or clarify meaning. And piecing film together affects the pace and dramatic tension of a documentary as well. Therefore it is important to understand how editing functions in nonfiction film and video making. In the rest of the chapter, we look more closely at this process. We begin by briefly discussing different ways that shots are joined, and then we elaborate specific strategies for putting sequences together.

Editing to Create Continuity

Each view that the camera takes has spatial and temporal continuity. But putting together different shots also creates cinematic space and time. In Hollywood-style fiction film, "continuity editing" crafts narrative coherence by creating the illusion of continuous time and contiguous space. Say we have a conversation between the leading man and leading woman. The scene would probably begin with an establishing shot, showing the two of them in their setting. Then it would move in closer to a medium or medium close shot of the two leads. Next it would go to an even closer shot of the one who is speaking. Let's pretend it is the man who gets the first word. The subsequent shot would be of the woman reacting (perhaps replying), then the man reacting, and so on. This pattern of the shot of the speaker and then the reverse shot of the other speaker is repeated throughout the conversation. Every once in a while there may be a reestablishing shot to remind us where we are. Although these different shots break time and space into separate units, we have the impression that the images cohere into a smooth flow. That is because the filmmaker utilizes techniques that make the cuts "invisible." For example, while the woman is talking, she is also looking at someone outside the frame. The next image reveals the person she was looking at. And the direction of her gaze connects one shot to the other. By observing such simple strategies, the filmmaker is able to create the illusion of continuity (Bordwell and Thompson 231–238).

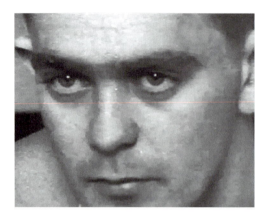

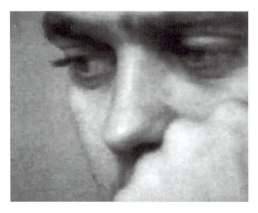

7.1–7.3. A conversation edited in a shot-reverse-shot formation. From *Titicut Follies* (Frederick Wiseman, 1967).

Continuity can be an important part of nonfiction storytelling as well, although we tend to think of documentary as a less controlled representation of the sociohistorical world. And to create continuity, documentaries often employ many of the same storytelling devices and techniques as fiction filmmaking. Take *Titicut Follies*, for instance. In chapter 3 we described a scene early in the film of a conversation between a psychiatrist and his patient. The scene was recorded with one camera and then edited so that closer shots of the two speakers seemingly reacting were intercut in shot-reverse-shot formation—similar to our hypothetical fictional example. This is one of the ways that the film is able to create an intimate connection between the characters and the viewer. The editing pattern repeats itself later, when another patient tries to convince the review panel that he should be released from the institution. We see the patient speaking and two shots of some of the panelists reacting are inserted. Later, after the patient is escorted out of the room, we see a series of tight close shots of the panelists giving their opinions on the case and seemingly reacting to each other.

Wiseman uses straight cuts to join shots in *Titicut Follies*, as does Chantal Akerman in *News from Home* (1976). Her images of New

York City change instantaneously. We are in one shot, say of the interior of a subway car, then, with no fanfare at all (and little regard for continuity), we are in a new shot, in a new space and time. We may not be able to anticipate when the cut will happen. Or what the next shot will be. Yet we know the next transition, whenever it is, will once again be a cut. (We revisit this film in chapters 9 and 10.) The cut is the most common way documentaries move from one shot to the next. (In contrast, the transitions in *Lunch with Fela* are mainly fades. The image gradually appears and disappears. And, as we shall see, some documentaries will occasionally employ dissolves, superimposing one image atop the next one for a moment.)

"Harvest of Shame," too, employs straight cuts. And in "Harvest of Shame" these cuts often construct a space and time that simulates the view of the reporter. When we talked about responsibility, in chapter 4, we looked at a scene in which there is a sort of "eye-line match": David Lowe interviews young Jerome while he is home from school taking care of his three little sisters, and asks him if he has any food to feed them for lunch. After Jerome replies, "Yes," the film, as if mimicking Lowe's visual point of view, shows us a close shot of a pot of beans. The shot of the beans may have been taken three or four hours later, or even earlier, and the pot may have been in the cabin next door; however, the coordination of the two shots in the editing makes the beans seem like a response to Lowe's question. Each of the shots represents a bit of screen time, space, and information. By coordinating the two, time seems to be continuous, and the space seems to be contiguous. This style of editing also helps to put the viewer in Lowe's place. It is as if the viewer sees as Lowe sees and learns as he learns. Earlier in that scene, Lowe asks Jerome his sisters' names. As Jerome lists them, the documentary cuts in closer to his face. And as he says "Lois," it cuts to a shot of Lois, then one of Cathy and Beulah, as he says their names. When Lowe asks, "What happened to your foot, Jerome?" it cuts to a close shot of his foot with a wound on it. The editing has a clear narrational motivation.

In Moscow, in the early 1920s during the foreign blockade of the new Soviet Union, Lev Kuleshov's students learned by experimenting with narrational editing of a different kind. With little new stock, they reedited old films to change their effect, and they created synthetic people and places by editing together parts of different people and different locations taken at different times. They also combined shots from different sources to construct the appearance of causality. By suppressing establishing shots in favor of close shots, they were able to produce the impression of continuity.

Documentaries' adherence to the "unauthored" representation of the referential world makes this kind of synthetic continuity rare. Yet it is not unheard of. At the end of the second section of Dziga Vertov's tripartite film, *Three Songs of Lenin/ Tri pesni o Lenine* (1934), commissioned for the tenth anniversary of Vladimir Ilyich Lenin's death, the sounds and images of ceremonial cannon blasts and rifle shots from around the country, while Lenin lay in state prior to the funeral, are intercut with images of mourners from different regions of the Soviet Union. Diverse shots from different locales are cut together to form an assortment of people and objects that all seem to stop in their tracks, in awe, at the sound of the salvoes. A woman carrying wood on her back pauses mid-frame. A speeding train halts in a freeze frame. A sleigh seems frozen in place. Machines come to a standstill. Soon there is a close shot of a young woman in a headscarf. A few seconds later, we see an old man in sand drifts as he stands listening. Vertov and his editor, Elizaveta Svilova, by combining unrelated shots (differing profilmic realities) have shaped an artificial continuity and portrayed a nation united in respect and sorrow.

In this case, the centrality of editing is tangible. As Vertov explained in a 1935 essay about "[his] latest, many-sided experiment," *Three Songs of Lenin:* "For fifteen years I studied writing in film. To be able to write with a camera and not with a pen. Hindered by the lack of a film alphabet, I attempted to create that alphabet. . . . I learned that at an editing table" (132). V. I. Pudovkin, writing in the early years of the Soviet Union, put it more romantically: "Editing is the basic creative force, by power of which the soulless photographs . . . are engineered into living cinematographic form" (quoted in Bordwell and Thompson 249). For Pudovkin, editing is the essence of cinematic art.

More commonly, however, what we get in nonfiction filmmaking might be closer to the construction of the cinematic space and time that we saw in "Harvest

7.4–7.5. Editing creates the illusion of a citizen listening to the ceremonial cannon blasts, *Three Songs of Lenin/Tri pesni o Lenine* (Dziga Vertov, 1934).

of Shame," an overall pattern that forms a coherent narrative world. One more example from "Harvest of Shame" might illustrate this. Toward the end of the television program, Lowe asks Christine Shack, a teacher in a New Jersey school, whether she believes her migrant students will succeed in their occupational dreams. As she gives her opinion on Laura's and Harriet's ability to enhance their education, a medium close shot of each little girl is inserted. Then, as she discusses the compassion we should have for those who find themselves in such a situation, we again get individual shots of Laura and Otis, another child who, like Laura, had been interviewed previously about his plans for the future. We assume the children are in the same classroom at the same time that the teacher is speaking about them. (The only establishing shot is of the exterior of the school.) But that spatial and temporal connection has been created by the editing. It might be better to say that the editing cues the viewer to *infer* that the children exist in the same space and time as the teacher and the interviewer.

The cuts to Laura, Harriet, and Otis also animate offscreen space. The film frame is finite. Editing, however, can create an expanded space, a space outside the frame, and produce the semblance that that space is continuous with what was in the preceding and subsequent frames.

In "Harvest of Shame," we hear the questions David Lowe asks Laura, Harriet, Otis, Mrs. Shack, and Jerome. In some other documentaries the questions are edited out. In *The Life and Times of Rosie the Riveter*, for example, we do not hear the questions. Nor do we see the interviewer. It appears as if Connie Field's informants happen to be thinking about the issues that she was interested in. This might be a slight exaggeration. Still, the choice of whether or not and how to include the questions posed to informants can be affected not only by ethical concerns (how much you want the audience to know about the filmmaking process) but also by continuity issues (how much you feel you need to generate the appearance of uninterrupted testimony).

Sometimes the testimony we see and hear is a combination of answers to several questions posed at different times. If there is a slight lapse in image, this is frequently covered over by the insertion of a "cutaway," an image from a library of shots the filmmaker collects for exactly this purpose. It may be an image of a stack of books on a windowsill, when the interviewee is a professor, for example. The cutaway may be only tangentially related. Or it may be a significant detail of the speaker, her hands, for instance. A cutaway can help maintain the illusion of clear and continuous action. In fiction film, a cut to a stack of books on a windowsill would likely forecast some future narrative action involving either the books or the window. It would have some relevance to the story's "uncluttered clarity," to use Noël Carroll's words once again. In documentaries, cutaways can be a nonessential digression.

Editing for Graphics, Tempo, and Rhythm

The style of editing that we have been describing creates a continuity of space and time. But sometimes space and time, and sometimes graphics and rhythm, are employed for associations other than those based on spatial and temporal continuity. In the previous chapter, we saw how parts of Joris Ivens's *Rain* were edited based on graphic patterns. Continuities and discontinuities—similarities and contrasts—of light, texture, shape, movement, tone, and direction bind one shot to the next. And the duration of shots is often determined not simply by the amount of information contained in it but by the rhythmic possibilities. (We pay more attention to how music structures the rhythm and pacing of editing in the final chapter of the book.)

Important as pictorial and rhythmic elements are to poetic films, their power has not been ignored in documentaries that are more concerned with an argument or a dramatic story. *The River*, for example, as we saw, builds its argument with aesthetic and formal patterns. A closer look at some of the editing can demonstrate how the film employs graphic similarities, contrasts, and conflicts, as well as rhythm and tempo in order to project its point of view.

The logging sequence, for instance, starts with a close shot of axes chipping away at timber and the voiceover commentary extolling the plenitude of lumber available for the expansion westward. Then, as the commentary stops, there is a long shot of a single tree falling from the left edge of the frame through the diagonal into the right of the frame, then two shots of trees falling in dense forest from the opposite direction, along the other diagonal, from right to left. Then a long shot of a tree again falling from left to right into the river, and the crash of cymbals as it hits the water. A lively rendition of the popular American minstrel tune "Hot Time in the Old Town Tonight" begins, and we see a chute of water and logs flowing down the river away from the viewer from the lower left to upper right of the frame. In the next shot we are closer to the chute. A single log travels along a diagonal from the opposite direction, lower right to upper left. Clearly cut with attention to graphic dynamics, the ensuing shot is much closer, showing a single log once again racing down the chute along a diagonal, this time from the lower right to upper left of the frame. The camera pulls back slightly to show that the single log is followed by many other logs surging down the chute and dropping

7.6–7.7. Graphic contrast in *The River* (Pare Lorentz, 1937).

into the rushing river. As the music picks up speed, the cutting pace increases, and the pattern continues for five more shots, with more and more logs, each time alternating the direction of the diagonal, culminating in a wide shot of the river so full of logs that they are barely moving. The celebration of logging is expressed not only by the lively music but also by the energy created by the tempo of the editing and by joining shots with attention to the graphic conflicts within the frame. The transitions are cuts throughout, punctuating the rhythm with their abrupt breaks. The sequence begins with trees and escalates to several shots of the screen filled with logs, and then three extremely close shots of logs passing through a saw mill, alternating, the first from left to right, the second from right to left, and the third from left to right once again.

Later, as the soil erodes and the musical theme returns with the muted horn, we see water slowly dripping from three small melting icicles and hear the piercing, dissonant chords we spoke about in chapter 5. Then many shots of water coming downhill from the treeless slopes, each shot showing more and more water, as the narrator itemizes the years of flooding: 1903, 1907, 1913, 1916, 1922 . . . until we have the frame overflowing with water. From small to large, from a trickle to a flood, the image is augmented; tension builds, until we feel the force of the deluge, again through the sensitive editing of graphic similarities and dissimilarities. Shots of swollen rivers follow. Once more the editing pattern alternates opposing directions of movement. The images progress to greater and greater ruin. The transitions are cuts, quickly changing the images so that they accumulate and feelings mount. By contrast, in a slower section of the film, after the lumbering, we see a series of sad, somber images: slow panoramic shots over black tree stumps. The narrator once again itemizes the names of the trees, "Black spruce and Norway pine . . . Scarlet oak and shag bark hickory. . . ." Unlike the previous shots, these images are mainly connected by dissolves, their mournfulness being both echoed and created by the starkness of the visuals and the languid overlaps.

Throughout these sequences, space and time are subordinated to compositional considerations. By the joining of different locales and occasions, *The River* disrupts continuity. Yet the emotional and logical relationships become clearer for that very reason. By violating the continuity of time and space, *The River* invites audiences to form emotional and logical connections, making it easier for them to accept the solution to come: the Tennessee Valley Authority's remedial programs.

Editing for Development

Life may sometimes seem like a meaningless string of random incidents going nowhere. Not so in a documentary. Time may be fragmented and reorganized. In fact it usually is. But generally the journey we take moves forward and develops. We have, of course, the film or video's ineluctable movement through time. And we have incidents that are organized to create a sense of forward momentum toward an implied destination. From the time we first get an inkling of what the story is, to the time when the story terminates, we are involved in a chain of events and are prepared to make sense of their unfolding.

Many documentaries plot their events in a linear manner. *Night Mail* (Harry Watt and Basil Wright, 1936), for instance, follows the postal train from its evening departure from Euston Station in London to its morning arrival in Scotland, picking up mail along the way, sorting it, and dropping it off at its destination. Generally historical films such as *Prelude to War, The River*, as well as *Hearts and Minds*, to which we return shortly, also proceed chronologically.

Some stories necessitate entwining two (or more) lines of action that progress in a linear fashion and happen simultaneously. In *Crisis: Behind a Presidential Commitment*, for example, the story of the presidential decision winds around the story of the events taking place in Alabama. Both stories are filmed chronologically from beginning to end and are edited together to alternately present one, then the other. This is a common way to point out parallel happenings.

If *Lunch with Fela* does not develop chronologically, it is for a particular purpose. Ravett organized his documentary in ways that avoid fixed meaning, forcing viewers to create their own spatial and temporal coherence. Fela's displacements find reverberations in the spatial and temporal dimensions of the documentary. Imagine how different the viewing experience would have been if Abraham Ravett had ordered his scenes so that they culminated in Fela's death. Such a linear disposition of the information would be easy to follow, drawing the viewer in with the progression from beginning to end. And, in the case of *Lunch with Fela*, this would forge different kinds of intellectual and emotional involvements.

Danae Elon's *Another Road Home*, on the other hand, progresses in a decidedly linear manner. The relation of one sequence to the next is not at all arbitrary. One incident is connected to another such that each incident seems to throw some light on what we have learned so far and what is to come.

The documentary begins with the filmmaker telling us about and introducing us to (via some 1991 footage) "Moussa," the Palestinian man who helped to raise this Israeli woman. She then introduces us to each of her parents, in their new home in northern Italy, and they each speak about Moussa, his role in her upbringing, and their memories of Moussa's arrival in their home. Her mother, interviewed while cooking and in a manner that is seemingly quite spontaneous, admits that she would have never entrusted her infant daughter to her husband as she did to Moussa. Her father, Amos Elon, a well-known writer on political subjects, displays more experience with and skepticism about the interview process, as well as some discomfort over being interviewed by his own daughter. He is very careful with his words, correcting himself a few times. The documentary also shows Amos and Danae quarreling about whether he should be interviewed while walking through the streets. He would prefer his study.

After her mother mentions that Moussa spent much more time with Danae than with his own children, Danae begins to look for those children. With the money he had earned, Moussa sent his eight sons to the United States to be educated and to keep them from being involved in anti-Israeli violence. In New York City, calling information, Danae tries to find a telephone number for the Abdullah family in Paterson, New Jersey. Unable to find the number, but nowise daunted, she sets out to inquire about them in the Palestinian community in Paterson. As the voiceover tells us some of the history of Paterson, we see images from the point of view of an automobile going over the George Washington Bridge and then general, almost travelogue, footage of Paterson. And as she tells us that Paterson is now the "home of one of the largest Palestinian communities in the United States," we see store signs in Arabic, a license plate reading "Lifta," and the spot of two clocks on a store's wall, one reading "U.S.A." and the other reading "Home." Tellingly, the clock in the second spot is absent. Later, after the suggestion from one of Moussa's sons, Naser, a pharmacist, that she may have had the wrong name, a shot is inserted of his nameplate with the correct spelling. This image both gives us new information and retroactively helps us to understand previous information, and is essential to the development of her story. The nameplate tells us his surname is Obeidallah, not Abdullah. (Earlier we had also learned from another son that Moussa's given name was Mahmoud. His father went by the name of Moussa while working for the Elon family because he thought it would be easier for Israelis to pronounce.) There is no explanation of why Danae did not know his surname. Yet her decision to include this in the documentary speaks poignantly about Israeli-Palestinian relations—and perhaps also about mistress-servant relations. The story builds and so does our understanding of the paradox of her quest.

After Obeidallah arrives in the United States and we see the mutual affection he and Danae have for each other, *Another Road Home* ends with Danae accompanying Obeidallah in his return to the occupied village of Battir, bringing an end to the major part of the narrative. There remains only an epilogue with Danae's parents, now living in New York City, her father no longer seeming to object to the idea of being filmed while walking, wandering along a beach with her mother and ruminating on the idea of "home."

The film starts with a question: What kind of fathering did Danae have? It passes through attempts to answer that question and concludes with the question answered. Each new sequence modifies the meaning of the previous sequences and influences the meaning of later sequences. In this process, our understanding of what Elon is going through in her quest gets progressively fuller. *Another Road Home* is edited so that the forward trajectory of narrative information parallels the cinematic movement forward. The documentary's occurrences are arranged in a linear and causal fashion. The quest—Danae's ongoing struggle—tugs the plot forward.

Contrast and Contradiction

Contrast and contradiction can also serve as a basis for documentary editing. They are sometimes used to provide different opinions on a subject or both sides of an argument, so that the documentary appears to be impartial. But simply giving different sides of an argument does not mean that both sides are received equally. As we have already seen in *The Panama Deception*, the order in which information is given can influence our understanding of it. John Akomfrah's *Handsworth Songs* returns frequently to the racial disturbances, so that we read the instances of optimistic immigrants through the lens of disappointment, disillusion, and worry. By sequencing the information in this way, Akomfrah makes a strong political statement. In *The Life and Times of Rosie the Riveter* the contrasts between the archival footage from World War II and the testimony of the workers in the war plants reveal contradictions between public history and private memories. By combining the two, the documentary deals a forceful blow to the U.S. government's version of the home front. We have spoken above of cutaways that are mere digressions. But cutaways, too, can be used to comment on or undermine the authority of an interview, offering information that contradicts what we hear from the interviewee.

Charles Ferguson's *No End in Sight* (2007) does something slightly different. It uses lengthy interviews with respected informants, and then conflicting excerpts from press conferences held by people in power in the Bush administration, undercutting the authority and dignity of the administration's officials. The precredit sequence opens with a medium close shot of Donald Rumsfeld commending President George W. Bush for his leadership in the "complex" and "little understood" war in Iraq, the "first war of the twenty-first century." After the credits, the film takes us to Baghdad in 2006, showing the damages of war, and proceeds with an editing pattern that is, in the words of critic Stuart Klawans, "almost rhythmic in its regularity." Over location shots from Iraq, the cool voiceover commentary read by actor Campbell Scott describes the chronology of what has taken place: "On May 1st, 2003, President George W. Bush declared an end to major combat operations in Iraq. . . ." Scott's description of Bush's speech is followed by images, often split-screen, of absolute devastation. We get quiet anger from informants (close and medium shots of talking heads), sober statistics from Scott over brutal footage of wreckage and desolation in Iraq, casket after casket, then, to borrow again from Klawans, "a punch line of utter obliviousness" from Bush's foreign policy inner circle: Rumsfeld, Dick Cheney, Paul Wolfowitz, and Condoleezza Rice in press conferences. For instance, after Marc Garlasco, senior Iraq analyst for the Defense Intelligence Agency, testifies that his group could find no relationship between Saddam Hussein and al-Qaeda, we see Cheney standing before several American flags announcing: "[Saddam's] regime aids and protects terrorists, including members of al-Qaeda." After a number of government officials, a marine lieutenant, and several journalists talk about the Pentagon's lack of planning and refusal to declare martial law after the fall of Baghdad (so that nothing was being done to stop the looting and large-scale destruction, which quickly transformed into violent lawlessness), we see Rumsfeld saying, "Stuff happens." Ferguson and editors Chad Beck and Cindy Lee have cut the film in an order that emphasizes the contradictions, inviting the spectator to judge the validity of what has been said.

Toward the beginning of *4 Little Girls*, a film about the 1963 murder of four children when a bomb blasted "the Sunday School quiet" of a church basement in Birmingham, Alabama (see Paule Marshall, *Praisesong for the Widow* 31), Circuit Judge Arthur Hanes Jr., a white man, looks back and pronounces Birmingham in the 1950s a wonderful place to live and raise a family. Then after vintage footage of lynchings, Ku Klux Klan parades, and water fountains marked "white" and "colored," Queen Nunn, a neighbor of Denise McNair, one of the little girls killed, remembers having to tell her seven-year-old son that he was not allowed to drink from the "white" fountain: "It was an awful time. It was an awful time for young people to grow up in this city." The disagreement is never stated directly. The contradiction is meant to be understood ironically. It is an oblique way to say this white man has a limited view of Birmingham. Here, too, the contrasts and contradictions provoke the spectator to interpret—and to form an opinion.

Peter Davis's *Hearts and Minds* (1974) offers a more sustained use of this editing strategy. Any documentary dealing with history is faced with too much data and needs to be selective in choosing material to use (Rosenstone 13). *Hearts and Minds* is no different. It introduces us to compelling individuals who are able to give the audience firsthand accounts of the U.S. war against the Vietnamese people and occasionally employs archival footage to illustrate their words. But one noteworthy thing that this feature-length documentary does is to comment on the opinions expressed in the interviews via the way the film is edited. By taking advantage of the fact that each new segment affects the way we understand previous and future segments, *Hearts and Minds* is able to lead the viewer's impression of the material presented.

The film never pretends to be objective. Like *4 Little Girls* and *No End in Sight, Hearts and Minds* frankly and clearly acknowledges its perspective. And the film demonstrates that editing is never a transparent or neutral carrier of meaning. The documentary treats the structure of a film not only as a tool for reporting but also as a means of persuasion. The problem that Peter Davis—or his editors, Lynzee Klingman and Susan Martin—faced was how to fashion the social world into a form that might incline the public to reach the filmmakers' desired opinion, to accept the documentary's well-informed engagement with pressing issues. It is worth pausing here for a moment to look at some specific sequences that illustrate how the film does this.

Hearts and Minds begins with Vietnamese music over a shot of a horse-drawn cart, children running with book satchels, then several shots of peasants in what a title tells us is Hung Dihn Village Northwest of Saigon. The village seems to be living a fairly bucolic existence. Then a long shot of women working in a field is jarred by a soldier walking across the foreground carrying an assault rifle. Then another shot of several more soldiers with weapons slung over their shoulders. The camera moves slightly and we see, once again, the soldiers' proximity to the women in the field. After another long shot of the women stopping for a break, the camera pulls back, the music fades, and we cut to a medium shot of Clark Clifford (identified in the title as "Aide to President Truman, 1946–50") seated in the quiet refinement of a Georgian interior, presumably in the United States, talking about U.S. political and military power after World War II.

The film begins by setting up three clear and affecting contrasts: Vietnamese pastoral life, the war, and the distinguished diplomat knowledgeable about U.S. dominance. The relation of one to another is indicated by the sequencing of the information. We cannot help but understand Clark Clifford's setting and the information he gives us through the context of the previous images of Vietnamese village life and the war.

This kind of editing is not uncommon. More unusual is the way the film takes advantage of the possibility that a sequence can affect how we understand new material in order to radically call into question testimony *as we are hearing it*. The documentary has damning evidence. But how can it present it so that it instills outrage in its viewers? *Hearts and Minds* does this aggressively. With no voiceover commentary at all, it uses editing to guide the viewer's interpretation so that rage can be coupled with the pleasure of knowing. In a strongly articulated and sincere, principled stance, the film condemns the war. And it does so by using contradiction to point to the ethical consequences of the hostilities. Toward the end of the film, for example, there is a scene in which a rural North Vietnamese man talks about his losses. "Talks about" is not strong enough. The man is devastated. He points to where his mother and three-year-old son died, and to where his young daughter was killed. "She was feeding the pigs. She was so sweet." "No targets here. Only rice fields and houses." "I'll give you my daughter's beautiful shirt. Take it back to the United States. Tell them what happened here. My daughter is dead. She will never wear the shirt again. Throw this shirt in [President] Nixon's face. Tell him she was only a little schoolgirl." The film then cuts to a sequence in the South Vietnamese National Cemetery, in which we see a woman so overcome with emotion that she tries to climb into the grave. We also watch a small boy dressed in ceremonial white, sobbing at the picture of his father atop a mound. Then there is a shot of General William Westmoreland, calmly sitting under a tree by a pond, seemingly in a thoughtful mood, slowly nodding his head in the affirmative, explaining that "the Oriental does not put the same high price on life as the Westerner. Life is plentiful; life is cheap. . . . As the philosophy of the Orient expresses it, life is not important." This is followed by a handheld shot of bombing and the sound of a low-flying plane.

Because the editors place Westmoreland's testimony *after* the scenes of distraught Vietnamese—the heartbroken father who mourns his daughter, the woman who tries to join her loved one in the grave, and the boy who wails at the loss of his father—we watch and listen to him with our knowledge of evidence to the contrary. The meaning of all these sequences must be inferred by the spectators, but their inferences are guided by the editing. Such an ironic frame may seem imprecise and ambiguous. Yet the arrangement of the material, the juxtaposition of Westmoreland's pious certainties with contrary evidence, and the concomitant implication that attitudes such as this are responsible for the bombing destruction of Vietnamese life lead concerned viewers to a searing indictment. It may inflame pro-war viewers, too, but not so much at the absurdity of Westmoreland's remarks as at the "unfairness" of the editing.

Remember Bill Nichols's concept of "the voice of documentary," which came up in chapter 3? "We may think that we hear history or reality speaking to us through a film, but what we actually hear is the voice of the text, even when that voice tries to efface itself" (21). The voice of this documentary shares our standards of judgment. Undeniably, Peter Davis is critical of what General Westmoreland says; but more than that, the voice of the text points out the moral stupidity of what Westmoreland says by first letting the spectators share scenes of mourning, so *they* become critical of what comes next. In *Hearts and Minds*, the voice of the documentary is apparent even though we don't see and seldom hear an author. It is the controlling voice, the voice that gives us images of all-American cheerleaders just before we see GIs with Vietnamese prostitutes. It is the voice of the text that shows Colonel George S. Patton III describing the look of both determination and reverence on the faces of the GIs at a memorial service for four fallen comrades ("my feeling for America just soared") and, with a smile, praising those soldiers as "a bloody good bunch of killers," then follows it with a football team's prayer service and scenes from a game. It is the voice of the text that gives us images of Vietnamese schoolchildren while an ex-GI talks about the thrill you get seeing a bomb explode. It is the voice of the text that follows a Concord, Massachusetts, father discussing with pride the death of his eldest son (a pilot who died in Vietnam) as a worthwhile sacrifice with a Saigon father's grief as he points to the tiny coffins he is hammering together and says, "Many have died here." He himself lost seven children. "But it is nothing like in the countryside." And he details the effect of the planes' daily spraying of the defoliant Agent Orange on rural children.

The voice of this text, its "social point of view," to quote Nichols again, makes its message understandable; it answers its own questions. And it does this through the editing of its material. Some films—Marker's *Sunless*, for example—overflow with meanings. Not so with *Hearts and Minds*. It is a beautifully complicated work. Its meanings, however, are quite clear. In its own way, it is a very didactic film.

Editing for Clarification

There are times when a documentary needs to illustrate or clarify what is said. Inserting a shot or two can help to do this. In *Halving the Bones*, the filmmaker's mother looks into the tea tin containing her mother's bones and smiles with surprise at their beauty. As she comments that they look as if they had been painted, a close shot of the pink and white bones appears, supplementing her description. In this case, the quick shot of the bones helps the audience to know what the woman is talking about. Here the connection between shots is fairly obvious. It seems quite natural to look inside the tin as she does. In other examples, however, making the connection requires more effort on the part of the spectator. And there are instances in which making the connections between shots reminds us that a filmmaker is responsible for creating the sequence.

Let's return to the unusual example of editing in *Titicut Follies* that we discussed in chapter 3: the flash-forward from the force-feeding of a patient to the mortician preparing the body for burial. In the midst of the scene, images from a different time and space are edited in. Gradually, perhaps drawing on our experience outside the film, we come to understand the causal relations of the flash-forward to the "present" event. By violating the continuity of time and space, this sequence of *Titicut Follies*, like some in *The River* and *Hearts and Minds*, invites audiences to make emotional and logical connections. Joining the two sequences in this way may weaken spatiotemporal continuity but clarify meaning. (See figures 3.2 and 3.3.)

This clarification, of course, requires a certain amount of work from the spectator. Documentary film and video makers often ask us to make associations that might not be as direct as what we saw in *Halving the Bones*. When Alan Berliner edits in footage of a house falling off its foundation into the teeming waters while we hear his father discussing his divorce from Alan's mother (*Nobody's Business*, 1996), he is employing a sort of symbolic displacement. He is implying a comparison. We see the image of one tragedy and are supposed to connect it to another, which is not pictured. The house is metaphoric for something the filmmaker does not depict. He also uses shots of a boxing ring as a metaphor to make clear how he felt when his father and his mother fought—or later, during the filming of the documentary, when he and his father argued. And we know that it is the film-maker, Alan Berliner, not his father, who is making that symbolic displacement. It can be seen as a distinctly authorial intervention.

In order to allude to that which is not visible or audible, documentary makers often make use of figures of speech, rhetorical tropes. Berliner's editing sets up unexpected similarities. His metaphors are rhetorical tactics to elucidate meaning. We can also describe them as hyperbole, an exaggeration to emphasize a point. This is a kind of extravagance we do not expect from the sober stance of most documentaries.

Yet hyperbole is an essential part of most verbal communication, as is metaphor. Hyperbole is an overstatement that is meant to make a strong impression. Metaphor draws upon a familiar set of meanings to explain another set of meanings that are less familiar—or less tangible. Neither is intended to be taken literally.

In documentaries, too, they are not intended to be taken literally. Documentaries present concrete sounds and concrete images. Many expect viewers to infer more abstract concepts. Berliner, for example, magically reunited his parents by editing in the sound of his mother singing "The Nearness of You" over the sound and image of his father singing the same song. In the case of this miraculous duet, or the shot of the house washed off its foundation, or the image of the boxing ring, the filmmaker is asking spectators to imagine what his parents' broken marriage meant to him. Those feelings may not be possible to picture or even to articulate directly. Instead, by editing in these sounds and images, he uses rhetorical tropes to illustrate them. These tropes disrupt any spatial or temporal continuity the film might have had. But they symbolically express a deeper or larger reality that is more difficult to portray.

Documentaries can use metonymy as well. An attribute is substituted for the thing itself. How often have you seen an inserted image of the White House when the documentary was discussing the U.S. presidency? Or the Capitol building for the U.S. federal government? And any documentary is in itself synecdochical. Since they can only re-present a fragment of the sociohistorical world, all documentaries are a part that stands in for the absent whole that cannot be re-created. When we first spoke of *The Life and Times of Rosie the Riveter*, we noted that it was implied that the five "Rosies" interviewed stood in for the experiences of many more women—three million, some say. Seen this way, "Lola" embodies—or portrays—both that feisty woman from Brooklyn who worked as a welder and dreamed of making an ornamental gate, and other women who worked in the war industries and also had dreams. The stories she tells, then, can take on other meanings, transcendent meanings, as they point to broader associations. In fact, showing the subject in all its partiality can enhance the documentary's value, perhaps even its aura of "realness." That fragment becomes special because it represents the larger world.

Montage

The word montage comes from the French word *monter*, "to assemble." In many ways, any edited film or video is a montage. Indeed, the word is sometimes used as a synonym for editing. The French call a film editor a "monteur." In Spanish and Portuguese the film editor is a "montador" or, frequently, a "montadora." And the Italians use the word "montaggio" for film editing. But such a broad definition is not too useful for us here. We limit our discussion of montage to documentaries or sequences in documentaries in which archival footage is cut up and reassembled; time and space are fractured and then sutured together to create different connotations. Images, once removed from their historical setting, are reactivated by their inclusion in a montage with other images.

We have already discussed *Point of Order*, a film composed entirely of a montage made from existing sources. This kind of compilation film has a long and luminous history. In 1927, for the tenth anniversary of the Russian Revolution, Esfir Shub created *The Fall of the Romanov Dynasty/Padenie dinastii Romanovykh*, a film made out of both archival footage and the Romanov family's home movies. And the form remains popular. In 1995, with the help of selected songs, prayers, poems, legends, and added background sounds, Vincent Monnikendam turned silent footage shot by colonial officials of the Dutch East Indies from 1912 to 1933 into *Mother Dao—the Turtlelike/Moeder Dao—de schildpadgelijkende*, a story of the colonization and exploitation of the people we now know as Indonesians. Thom Andersen's *Los Angeles Plays Itself* (2003) dismantles nearly two hundred films to show how LA has appeared as background, character, subject, and symbol in Hollywood movies. By reframing existing material, these filmmakers astonish us with new meanings.

Santiago Álvarez made numerous compilation films as head of the newsreel and short film departments at the Instituto Cubano del Arte e Industria Cinematográficos/Cuban Institute of Cinematographic Art and Industry, a state-run agency created within months of the 1959 Revolution taking power. With a mandate to keep the Cuban populace informed about current events at home and abroad, his work was meant for local consumption. His 1968 film *LBJ* is a sharp attack on U.S. president Lyndon Baines Johnson. Built from found footage and still photographs, the seventeen-minute satire is accompanied by evocative music, including Miriam Makeba, Nina Simone, Carl Orff, Leo Brouwer, circus music, and beer hall ditties. The film animates photographs of Luci Baines Johnson's wedding, images from *Playboy* magazine, cartoons, newspaper clippings, and collages. It also excerpts moving images from newsreels, as well as Hollywood gangster films, war films, and westerns. Some images of President Kennedy in the Dallas motorcade are followed by a "reverse shot," a clip from a Hollywood film of a knight aiming a crossbow from behind a tree. Then there is a movement in on a set of crosshairs superimposed on an image of the back of Kennedy's head, then the knight firing the weapon, some quick cutting, and a still image of LBJ taking the oath of office. In another sequence, footage of riot police in helmets, soldiers in helmets, and a Hollywood epic of medieval knights in helmets, as well as a collage of LBJ in a knight's helmet, are intercut to the music of Orff's *Carmina Burana*.

7.8. Lyndon Baines Johnson in the documentary *LBJ* (Santiago Álvarez, 1968).

Álvarez employs no voiceover commentary. The only voices in the film come from footage of Stokely Carmichael, over a minute long, calling for black Americans to come together in solidarity and charging white America with brutality and racism, and from Martin Luther King's "I Have a Dream" speech, interrupted by footage of rifles firing. The film ends with a series of images of LBJ amusing his young grandson. Playing on the sound track is Pablo Milanés's "Yo vi la sangre de un niño brotar" (I saw the blood of a child flowing) about napalm and children dying. The final image is well-known footage of a Vietnamese child on fire. Álvarez's dynamic montage of images, music, and sound effects presents a stringent and emotional condemnation of Johnson and his "cowboy" foreign and domestic policy.

Alan Berliner's *The Family Album* (1986) is a montage of unidentified 16mm silent black-and-white home movies he purchased and borrowed from several sources. They picture infants, babies walking, birthday parties, parades, graduations, weddings, pets, outings to the beach, vacations . . . , happy moments from the mid-1920s through the late 1940s that people treasured. The images are organized from birth to old age. The sound track is partially from found sources, home recordings, people playing with tape recorders, oral histories, and interviews with members of his own family. Interestingly, much of the audio montage contradicts the joyful times pictured in the image track. According to Berliner, the sound track "is a subversion of the implicit lie of home movies—that life is all leisure and no struggle." He wanted to reveal the realities hidden beneath the surface of the movies by progressively introducing such factors as alcoholism, arguments, suicide, and divorce. In Berliner's words, "As the anonymous characters grow older, the issues the film introduces grow more complicated" (MacDonald 165).

By and large, though, montage is used for short sequences in larger films that are made from a variety of materials. And as such, it performs a special service: a series of shots are edited into a sequence, condensing filmic time and space, for a heightened expressive effect. Whereas most film and video makers subordinate their editing strategies to a tight rhetorical or dramatic logic, in montage sequences they can enjoy increased editorial freedom. Other elements, such as the sensuous play of light and dark, or graphic similarities, can come into prominence, an explicit rupture with the realist traditions of much documentation. These shots are generally bound together by the music, a voiceover commentary, and/or tempo and rhythm. Optical effects like dissolves and other means of layering images sometimes form the transitions. From time to time documentaries even use spatial montage within the frame, as we saw in *No End in Sight*. In these, split screens, back projections, electronic keying or mixing, or digital composites allow different images to coexist in the same frame simultaneously, creating a dense visual space. Separate realities become a part of a single image.

Montage sequences are often employed in documentaries to give a quick history of the subject under investigation. The title of *4 Little Girls* is white letters over a black-and-white traveling shot of a cemetery. Then after a long dissolve, a pattern of alternation begins: a montage of vintage black-and-white images, both moving and still, of civil rights demonstrations in the U.S. South during the late 1950s and early 1960s, and color shots, both moving and static, of a cemetery and individual gravestones with keyed portraits of the little girl buried there. Throughout the sequence Joan Baez sings Richard Farina's "Birmingham Sunday," with the repeated refrain "and the choir kept singing of freedom." Later, when the filmmaker wants to draw our attention to the history of race relations in Birmingham, he, or editor

Sam Pollard, composes a montage of still photos of lynchings and other aggressions. Howell Raines, a journalist for the *New York Times*, is interviewed. Raines explains that Birmingham was a blue-collar town where belligerence against union members and other workers was condoned by police and industry: "You have a tradition of violence flowing out of an industrial setting, with the overlay of rural racism coming in from the countryside, traditional Old South racism." As he says this, his image changes to the montage. The same logic that allows the character "Lola" in *The Life and Times of Rosie the Riveter* to represent both herself, a particular woman, and a whole class of other women allows still images from a lynching to represent the particular tortured and murdered individual as well as racial violence in the southern United States. It is this generalizability that allows such images to be used without identification in documentary montages.

But montage sequences in documentaries are seldom like the kind of close, rapidly edited sequences cut to music that you see in today's fiction films. Such editing obliges the viewer, in order to experience the exhilaration of the action, to assemble discrete pieces of visual detail. That kind of fast cutting of images taken from many angles, where shots are sometimes only a few frames long, is more unusual in nonfiction film precisely because it is aimed more toward visual and aural excitement than toward conveying information.

Whereas interviews and testimony are familiar forms (from courtrooms and conversations, for example), montage sequences are supremely cinematic. Taking place over time, yet compressing time and space in expressive ways, montage sequences—and, according to some, editing in general—are unique to cinema. In that same 1935 text on *Three Songs of Lenin*, Vertov complained, "Some are still unaware of what it means to write a full-length film in film shots. They still confuse films translated from the theatrical and literary language with film-originals, with work by a film author" (137). Film differs from theater and literature in its editing and the way its incidents and events are recorded by the camera. We turn to camerawork next.

Additional Filmography

Victory at Sea (M. Clay Adams, 1952–1953)

Now! (Santiago Álvarez, 1965)

Woodstock (Michael Wadleigh, 1970)

Oración/Prayer for Marilyn Monroe (Miriam Talavera and Marisol Trujillo, 1984)

Introduction to the End of an Argument (Jayce Salloum and Elia Suleiman, 1990)

The Gringo in Mañanaland (DeeDee Halleck, 1995)

Artist (Tracey Moffatt, 2000)

Iraqi Short Films (Mauro Andrizzi, 2008)

Works Cited and Further Reading

Arthur, Paul. "The Moving Picture Cure: Self-Therapy Documentaries." *Psycho-analytic Review* 94.6 (2007).

Bernard, Sheila Curran. *Documentary Storytelling*, 2nd ed. Burlington, Mass.: Focal Press, 2007.

Bordwell, David, and Kristin Thompson. *Film Art: An Introduction*, 8th ed. New York: McGraw-Hill, 2008.

Bottomore, Stephen. "Shots in the Dark: The Real Origins of Film Editing." *Sight and Sound* 57.3 (Summer 1988).

Carroll, Noël. *Mystifying Movies: Fads and Fallacies in Contemporary Film Theory.* New York: Columbia University Press, 1988.

Chanan, Michael. "The Revolution in the Documentary." In *Cuban Cinema.* Minneapolis: University of Minnesota Press, 2004.

Dancyger, Ken. *The Technique of Film and Video Editing*, 4th ed. Woburn, Mass.: Focal Press, 2006.

Graham, John. "'There Are No Simple Solutions': Wiseman on Film Making and Viewing." In *Frederick Wiseman*, ed. Thomas Atkins. New York: Simon and Schuster, 1976.

Klawans, Stuart. Review of *No End in Sight. The Nation*, August 13/20, 2007.

Kuleshov, Lev. *Kuleshov on Film.* Trans. and ed. Ronald Levaco. Berkeley: University of California Press, 1974.

Levin, G. Roy. *Documentary Explorations: Fifteen Interviews with Filmmakers.* Garden City, N.Y.: Doubleday, 1971.

Leyda, Jay. *Kino: A History of the Russian and Soviet Film.* London: Allen and Unwin, 1960.

MacDonald, Scott. "Interview with Alan Berliner." In *A Critical Cinema 5.* Berkeley: University of California Press, 2006.

Marshall, Paule. *Praisesong for the Widow.* New York: Penguin, 1983.

Miller, Toby. *Technologies of Truth: Cultural Citizenship and the Popular Media.* Minneapolis: University of Minnesota Press, 1998.

Musser, Charles. "The Travel Genre in 1903–1904: Moving Towards Fictional Narrative." In *Early Cinema: Space, Frame, Narrative*, ed. Thomas Elsaesser. London: BFI: 1990.

Nichols, Bill. "The Voice of Documentary." In *New Challenges for Documentary,*

2nd ed., ed. Alan Rosenthal and John Corner. Manchester: Manchester University Press, 2005.

Pudovkin, V. I. *Film Technique and Film Acting.* Trans. and ed. Ivor Montagu. New York: Grove Press, 1978.

Reisz, Karel, and Gavin Miller. *The Technique of Film Editing.* 1969. Reprint, Woburn, Mass.: Focal Press, 2002.

Rosen, Miriam. "In Her Own Time." Interview with Chantal Akerman. *Artforum* (April 2004).

Rosenstone, Robert A. "History, Memory, Documentary: A Critique of *The Good Fight.*" *Cineaste* 17.1 (1989).

Samuels, Charles Thomas. "Interview with Alfred Hitchcock, 2/28/72." In *Encountering Directors.* New York: Capricorn, 1972.

Snyder, Robert L. "The River." In *Pare Lorentz and the Documentary Film.* Norman: University of Oklahoma Press, 1968.

Van Dyke, Willard. "Letters from 'The River.'" *Film Comment* 3.2 (Spring 1965).

Vertov, Dziga. "My Latest Experiment." In *Kino-eye: The Writings of Dziga Vertov,* ed. Annette Michelson, trans. Kevin O'Brien. Berkeley: University of California Press, 1984.

Wiseman, Frederick. "Foreword." In *Five Films by Frederick Wiseman,* by Barry Keith Grant. Berkeley: University of California Press, 2006.

Wood, Jennifer M. "Life With Spike: Moviemaker Sam Pollard Puts His Money Where His Mouth Is." *MovieMaker Magazine.* http://www.moviemaker.com/articles/item/life_with_spike_2689. Accessed October 3, 2007.

8

Camerawork

In the first minutes of *Born into Brothels* (Ross Kauffman and Zana Briski, 2004), we hear a voiceover saying: "It's almost impossible to photograph in the red light district. Everyone is terrified of the camera. They are frightened of being found out. Everything is illegal." The comments play over black-and-white still photographs of prostitutes in north Calcutta, India. And the voice we hear is that of photographer Zana Briski, who managed to earn the trust of the sex workers in order to take their pictures. In these opening lines, Briski reminds us of the problems that sometimes arise when we try to document the lives of others, a predicament that is familiar from some of the documentaries already discussed in this book. She also acknowledges a more widely understood sentiment. We all seem to attribute a special power to the camera. We know that, when the subject documented is actuality, the photographic image has the capacity to reveal as well as condemn aspects of the sociohistorical world that might otherwise remain unremarked. And, indeed, *Born into Brothels* exposes—and denounces—the miserable conditions in that red light district of north Calcutta.

When you first try to recall a particular scene in a documentary, or any film for that matter, it is a visual memory that often comes to mind. It is the authority of the moving image that leaves the first and, sometimes, most lasting impression on us. Surely sound, too, plays a key role in the process through which documentaries represent sociohistorical reality. In fact, as we will have a chance to discuss in the final chapter, the use of sound in nonfiction films can anchor or alter the meaning of any given image. But even if we know that the visuals can never fully account for the "message" in the film, we seem to find comfort in the apparent immediacy of the photographic record. *Born into Brothels* is a film that might impress us in many ways. Chief amongst them is the power of the still and moving images used in the documentary.

This chapter focuses on the role of camerawork in the process of nonfictional representation. It examines the way documentary makers and camera operators look at lived reality, the options they have when they point their cameras toward a particular subject, and how their view influences the spectator's. More generally, it asks: How does camerawork "translate" lived reality into documentary images?

Film theorist Siegfried Kracauer might have been contemplating this question when he wrote about the documentary *Housing Problems* (Edgar Anstey and Arthur Elton, 1935) five decades ago. "Cinematically," he noted, "this report is anything but exciting, for it confines itself to photographic statements which could not be plainer." There is, according to Kracauer, a general lack of aesthetic ambition in the film's visual treatment of reality. As he sees them, however, these modest "statements" do not really constitute a problem since the documentary's "plainness is in harmony with the whole character of the film. . . . The thing that matters is veracity; and it is precisely the snapshot quality of the pictures which makes them appear as authentic documents" (202). As he discusses the role of the camerawork in *Housing Problems*, Kracauer looks not for virtuosity but for a self-effacing quality that legitimizes the documentary record.

This argument relies on a simple and familiar equation. It aligns documentary authenticity with aesthetic restraint. But is the "plainness" of the image all we look for when we think of the camerawork in a documentary? And more importantly, is this really what most documentaries have to offer? Attractive as it may appear, the equation that connects visual restraint and authenticity can only provide a limited assessment of the options available for nonfiction filmmakers. Many documentaries rely on stylistic choices that depart from the stoic realism of *Housing Problems*. They use the camera imaginatively in order to inform or persuade, move or entertain their audiences—and to establish the veracity that Kracauer saw in *Housing Problems*.

Framing

We see what the camera sees. But we also see what the camera operator wants us to see. Objects or people can go in and out of focus for dramatic emphasis. Or they can be framed in a particular way to make a point. In the field, the selection process begins when the camera operator decides how to look at something. This is important because the way the cameraperson pictures the subject helps determine how the audience perceives that subject. It also defines what is and is not relevant, what should be excluded from the screen space, how much of the world the documentary may reveal, and what aspects of reality need to be accentuated.

While the choices available to documentary filmmakers are similar to those that we find in fiction films, their use and implications tend to be different when we think of visual recording in nonfiction cinema. We can start with the size of the subject within the frame. Scale is associated with the distance between the camera and what it photographs. The smaller the subject, the farther away the camera seems to be. In long shots, for instance, the camera appears to be at considerable distance from the subject and we get a general sense of the setting without privileging any particular detail. Close shots, by contrast, are likely to isolate a specific subject and assign importance to it. They can also indicate familiarity with and proximity to that subject; or they may suggest curiosity and even intrusiveness, depending on the context in which the shot is included. In nonfiction cinema these decisions about where to place the camera usually follow conventionalized procedures that are typical of the documentary form. Consider a common example: the documentary interview. Most interviews shot in a studio use medium close shots, a polite distance that allows us a good look at the interviewee's face, without taking us too close to the subject. We should be able to recognize the interviewee and even notice significant facial expressions. We should also feel somewhat comfortable with the person in front of the camera, as if we had been granted privileged access to a worthy informant. Studio interviews in general, however, are formal occasions. And the camera usually observes this formality by maintaining a certain remove from the subject. We normally see the interviewee's face and upper body, as if we were watching from a couple of feet away. Any significant change in the frame or scale of the subject is likely to alter that sense of formality and create a different rapport between the audience and the interviewee.

This happens, for example, in Mindy Faber's *Delirium*. The camera seems at times too close to the person in front of it, producing an unexpected sense of intimacy with the interviewee. The first thing we notice when the interview starts is the framing itself. The interviewee's face fills up the entire screen. *Delirium* explores women's mental illnesses, and the subject interviewed is the video maker's mother, a woman with a history of nervous breakdowns. The conventional medium close-up of the interview subject might have been an effective way of introducing Patricia Jane Faber to the audience. The video maker, however, opts for a shot that seems tighter than usual. Given the nature of the subject matter—

8.1. Close shot of Patricia Jane Faber: "My mind just froze; it was just paralyzed." From *Delirium* (Mindy Faber, 1993).

Mrs. Faber is talking about her first nervous breakdown—the tight close-up can make us feel slightly uncomfortable. Yet it is helpful as a means of underlining the personal implications of the mother's story. It also works as an indicator of the closeness and trust between daughter and mother.

Because they look so unconventional, extreme close-ups can be a compelling tool of communication. Remember the shots of the tape recorder in the final moments of *The Thin Blue Line*? As the testimony recorded in the tape begins to disclose evidence about the murder case examined in the film, the shots become increasingly tighter. (See figure 2.3.) The extreme close-ups correlate the size of the object photographed with the importance of the information we hear from the tape recorder.

Between an extreme long shot and an extreme close-up, there is a vast range of options that determine the scale of the subject matter within the frame. Choosing one or another is a decision often based on how much information one wants to include in the shot, what piece of information should be privileged, and what kind of rapport with the viewer one wants to pursue.

Besides the scale of the subject photographed, other factors contribute to our perception of what we see in the frame. The camera angle, for example, helps define the position of the subject within the shot as well as the way that subject appears to the viewer. Do we look straight at it? Do we see it from above or from below? And what kind of image results from these different angles? Film aesthetic textbooks normally point out that the angle and height of the camera are not necessarily related. A camera may stand above the subject without looking down at it. Or it can sit below and face it straight on, privileging the lower part of the subject. Most of the time, though, height and angle are correlated concepts, as the technical terminology already suggests. We call it a *high* angle, for instance, when the camera captures the subject from above, looking down at it.

Colloquially speaking, the words "angle" and "perspective" are used interchangeably, implying that choosing an angle is equal to taking a particular point of view. The same is true when we talk about camerawork. More so than decisions about scale, the angle brings forth the idea that the camera offers a situated perspective on reality. Filmmakers normally place their cameras at a height and angle that emulate our ordinary viewing experiences, as if to suggest that we are looking straight at the subject. "Eye-level shots," as they are sometimes called, seem natural and inconspicuous; for that reason, they also encourage the belief in the transparency of the filming process. Stylized angles, by contrast, can create dramatic effects and function as markers of authorial intervention, especially since the optical properties of the lens tend to distort the natural shape of things. Anyone who has used a still camera may remember that high angle shots produce an image in which the subject photographed appears smaller than usual. The opposite happens when the camera looks up at the subject, from a low angle position, as is the case in Leni Riefenstahl's *Olympia/Olympiad* about the 1936 Berlin Olympic Games. In the beginning of the film, we see a series of shots that feature a discus thrower framed from below. The low angle magnifies the stature of his body and highlights the ideal of physical "perfection" endorsed by the documentary.

Sometimes it is the nature of the event documented that determines the choice of a conspicuous or dramatic angle. There is a shot in *Primary* (Drew Associates, 1960) in which the cameraperson follows John F. Kennedy, then a young senator from Massachusetts, as he enters a crowded building in Milwaukee. The camera is placed above Kennedy's head, literally looking down at the scene. Rather than simply lowering the stature of the documentary subject, though, this high angle shot is meant to create a broader and richer perspective than would have been possible if the camera were looking straight at the senator. We see not only Kennedy but also the multitude of supporters gathered around him. Framing from above turned out to be the most effective way of giving the viewer a general sense of the enormity of the event. We will come back to this shot shortly.

The height and angle of the camera can also establish spatial relations by connecting distinct points of view. In the previous chapter, we talked about how editing is capable of creating continuity between different spaces. And we noted that one way to do this is through point-of-view shots. In mainstream fiction films, this procedure can produce tightly knit spatial arrangements, which reinforce the apparent autonomy of the fictional world. Documentaries seldom give this impression. Still, by associating the camera angle with a specific point of view, nonfiction filmmakers are able to situate one subject in relation to another. Think, for example, of the way concert performances are commonly rendered. When recording these performances, documentary makers employ several cameras, capturing images both of the stage and the audience. The shots of the audience are conventionally taken from above in a high angle, whereas the performer is normally photographed from below, with the camera looking up. The edited film alternates between the stage and the audience, and the placement of the camera helps us figure out where one stands with respect to the other.

Camera and Lens Movement

The frame normally changes every time there is a new shot. The second image is either a reframing of the same subject or shows us something different. Yet we need not have editing in order to alter the frame. Camera movements can serve a similar purpose. They can expand or reduce the area covered by the frame, shift the perspective on the subject photographed, or direct our attention to a new subject.

Oftentimes, a movement is motivated by an occurrence within or around the profilmic space. For example, if the main subject starts to move, the camera most likely follows, keeping that subject in focus while changing the view of the surrounding environment. Camera movements can also be prompted by a sudden disclosure of relevant information or a need to draw attention to a specific detail within the frame. Imagine a shot in which we see two people having a conversation. If a third party starts to contribute from outside the frame, the cameraperson will probably adjust the visual field to include that new speaker.

In Alain Resnais's *All the Memory in the World/Toute la mémoire du monde* (1956), the camera does not follow any particular subject. Neither does it respond spontaneously to unpredictable events. Instead, it travels through the rooms and corridors of the National Library in Paris. Ghislain Cloquet, the cinematographer, uses a series of tracking shots, smooth movements for which the camera is normally mounted on a dolly, in order to explore the building's interior. He also moves the camera around a fixed axis in long sinuous pans that turn from one side to another, or diagonally. And he tilts the camera up and down. Unlike what happens in the situations described above, the movements in this film are clearly premeditated and carefully executed. The idea is not so much to react immediately to an unknown event but to investigate a setting that seems remarkable to the filmmaker. *All the Memory in the World* shows the vastness of the spaces in the National Library and the massive number of books and documents housed in the building. As a means of gathering information, the camera movements help establish the nature and scale of the subject represented. Had the filmmaker decided to change the frame by cutting from one space to another, he might still have been able to compose a convincing picture of the library's interior. But we would have missed the sense of magnitude that the uninterrupted movements manage to convey.

Deciding on whether to plan shots carefully or react on the spot to a particular situation frequently goes hand in hand with the type of subject represented and the film's attitude toward it. Both options can prove useful; however, they are likely to suggest different stances regarding the historical world. Likewise, the decision to employ a static camera or a moving shot may communicate a specific attitude toward the profilmic situation. Kamal Aljafari's *The Roof/Alsateh* (2006) tells the story of his Palestinian family's dwelling. Displaced when their home became part of the modern state of Israel in 1948, and resettled in the unfinished quarters of a family who had fled, they resist completing the top floor of "something that doesn't belong to us." Our understanding of the "physical and psychic" terrain in which the family is living is greatly influenced by Aljafari's selection of a static camera to shoot the interiors of the home and traveling shots to survey the ruins of the Palestinian neighborhood ("First Person Films").

Practical concerns can also determine the nature of the camera movements. Tracking shots demand some preparation and offer less flexibility than may be required from the makers of a film. For that reason, documentarians might choose, instead, to carry the cameras in their hands. While not as elegant as tracking shots, handheld movements can provide a more effective response to unplanned events. And because they are determined less by premeditated design than by the contingencies of the situations documented, they can also help to authenticate the process of representation. In fact, there is such strong association between handheld movements and documentary aesthetics that fiction filmmakers have sometimes used them just to add a realistic quality to their images. For instance, handheld shots help to give a "documentary look" to *The Battle of Algiers*, a film that was entirely staged, even though it was based on actual historical events.

Abrupt zooms give a similar impression, underscoring the priority of the subject matter and the spontaneous nature of the shooting process. A zoom is not really a camera movement but a modification in the scale of the subject through the gradual change of lens focal length. The camera itself does not move, although we may experience a greater sense of closeness or distance. Zooming in, for example, can quickly single out a certain detail or capture a sudden change in the profilmic space. The cameraperson does not need to approach the documentary subject; instead, that subject is enlarged for the viewer.

To the untrained eye, a zoom can sometimes appear like a tracking shot. Yet there are both functional and formal differences between them. When recording unstaged material, zooms might be more convenient than camera movements. They are also, on the other hand, a little mechanical, less graceful. A zoom flattens space, never really exploring its depth, and therefore tends to imply a less direct assessment of the space photographed.

But there can be other reasons besides convenience to use a zoom. In Claude Lanzmann's *Shoah*, the camera is mounted on a train locomotive, traveling toward the entrance gate of Auschwitz. Then, as we are about to enter the gate, there is a cut to an interview with a survivor from the concentration camp. When we return to Auschwitz, the shot of the gate changes to a zoom, bringing us closer, allowing us to visually cross the threshold, without going in. The filmmaker has made a moral choice not to enter that space. In Fred Camper's words, because of Lanzmann's "profound respect" for the dead, he holds back, never moving physically through the gates, acknowledging that neither he nor the audience members can ever "recover lost time," come close to understanding what the inmates experienced, or "live their loss" (106).

Camerawork may cast an expressive and openly opinionated look at the subject matter in the film. Or it may suggest a more self-effacing attitude toward historical reality. In the next two sections, we discuss these different approaches.

Observing and Interpreting

Observing reality is part of the effort to document the sociohistorical world. All camera operators must observe what they shoot. And yet, when we refer to a documentary as "observational," we usually have something more precise in mind. An observational film is not simply a film that involves an effort to look attentively at a particular subject. Most often, the term is used to designate a type of documentary filmmaking. Bill Nichols describes observational documentaries as those that "[stress] the nonintervention of the filmmaker," and which are expected to "cede 'control' over the events that occur in front of the camera more than any other mode [of documentary]" (*Representing Reality* 38). Observational filmmakers, in other words, try not to interfere in what they see. They play the role of onlooker or bystander, rather than the part of provocateur or participant in the profilmic situation.

Historically, the term observational documentary also has a specific meaning; it refers to a particular set of developments in the history and technology of nonfiction film, when lightweight filming equipment, refined by the military during World War II, became more easily available. Combined with portable synchronized sound equipment, powered by batteries, the apparatus could be operated by a smaller crew, enabling documentaries to be made quicker (and at lower cost) with increased flexibility. This also allowed documentary filmmakers to shoot less conspicuously. As a result, when we watch an observational film, we may get the impression we are looking closely at the documentary subjects without being noticed by them. In the United States, the concept of observational documentary is generally associated with the term *direct cinema*, which we examined briefly when we discussed authority and in more depth in our discussion of dramatic structure. *Crisis: Behind a Presidential Commitment* is an example of observational filmmaking.

What first stands out when we talk about observational documentaries is thus a certain attitude toward the documentary subject, a particular sense of ethics. To observe reality—rather than, say, to impose the filmmaker's will on the situations in front of the camera—is to define a particular set of protocols, to determine what can or cannot be done to the documentary subject. It is also to establish some form of relationship with the audience, a rapport through which the filmmaker assures the spectator that the world documented was not altered to meet the needs of the film. Just as important as these ethical attributes, however, are the aesthetic implications of the observational format. Here the idea of watching attentively finds a formal equivalent in the appearance of the film. Since what counts is the subject observed, the camerawork should be inconspicuous or subdued, much as it is in the example used by Kracauer. Additionally, the shots can be unusually lengthy, as if the camera were waiting for something to occur. Even if not very much happens, this prolonged view allows for a strong sense of intimacy with the material documented. And that, along with the ethical principles that give support to observational film, serves as a way of authenticating the representational process.

Titicut Follies, for instance, has a number of scenes in which the camera patiently watches the events in front of it without making much of a statement about them. The film, as you may recall, explores the daily events in a psychiatric hospital for incarcerated criminals in Massachusetts. Frederick Wiseman, the filmmaker, examines the lives of different inmates, hoping to put together a portrait of the institution. At one moment, we see an elderly man in the hospital's exercise yard, giving a lengthy and frantic speech about war and politics. The camera lingers on the subject well past the moment in which the idea of his insanity registers in the viewer's mind. As an attentive observer, the camera refuses to move away or interrupt the subject. We end up thinking that it is not the filmmaker but the event that determines the length and nature of the shot.

Yet observational camerawork need not be artless. In fact, one of the advantages of shooting with lightweight equipment was the increased mobility enjoyed by the cameraperson, which sometimes resulted in very elaborate shots. Enhanced mobility expands the visual field. But at the same time it can make the camerawork appear more conspicuous. While the subject matter may still anchor the act of filming, the virtuosity of the camerawork clearly molds the experience made available by the film.

One of the celebrated images in direct cinema is, indeed, Albert Maysles's handheld "tracking" shot of JFK, discussed briefly above. *Primary* is one of the films that set the standards for observational documentaries in the United States, and it combines imaginative shooting with an effort to create the impression of witnessing events *as they happened*. Made for television, the film documents the 1960 Democratic presidential primary elections in Wisconsin, with Kennedy running against Senator Hubert Humphrey of Minnesota. Like other observational films, it offers ample opportunity to scrutinize the documentary subjects. But few images create such a strong feeling of proximity vis-à-vis the profilmic event or reveal such ingenious camerawork as Maysles's "tracking" shot of JFK's entrance.

The shot, which lasts over one minute, starts as Kennedy is moving through a throng of bystanders inside the building. Maysles follows him closely as he shakes hands with people on both sides, walks up a set of stairs, and enters the auditorium where he is to deliver a speech. For the most part, the camera is placed behind and above the subject's head, in a high angle that allows us to see both the senator and the people around him. Kennedy moves steadily through the crowd, looking alternately toward his left and right. The camera trails right behind him, only briefly panning away from the senator in order to give us a wider view of the enthusiastic supporters gathered in the building. We, of course, move along as well, sharing the experience of being there, in the moment of shooting.

8.2. Albert Maysles's shot of John F. Kennedy entering a campaign rally. From *Primary* (Drew Associates, 1960).

Adding to the sense of immediacy is the wobbliness of the handheld movement. Instead of a smooth shot, what we see is an image that trembles a bit on the edges. As Maysles walks behind the senator, the camera shakes slightly, giving us the impression that the camerawork itself is spontaneous, crafted on the spot. In a different context, this shakiness might indicate lack of technical polish. But here it suggests a different scenario, implying that the camera, too, is caught in the middle of the event. Like the senator, Maysles is struggling to get through, the unsteadiness of the image functioning as an indexical sign of his presence amidst the mob. The cameraman is responding directly to a situation that is not really scripted, even if it follows a somewhat predictable protocol.

One way to look at this shot is thus to think about how it meets the aspirations of observational cinema. Because the camera seems to connect us closely to the event on the screen, the role of the mediating apparatus recedes, paradoxically, to the background. We have the feeling, once again, that the camera does not control the event documented. And we are tempted to accept the transparency of the image, as if we, too, were there, witnessing the situation firsthand.

There is, however, another way to make sense of this image. Although it does invite us to focus on the "immediacy" of the event, the handheld shot can just as easily be read as an artificial construct. In this case, the shakiness of the camera brings to light the nature of the mediating process, drawing attention to the fact that what we are watching is a photographic record of a given occurrence, not the occurrence itself. When we look at the shot more closely, we discover still other signs of artifice. The image of Kennedy's back, for example, corresponds to no one's point of view. Rather, it reveals the lens's unique perspective on the event recorded. Moreover, in this shot Maysles uses a wide-angle lens that augments the visual field. Wide-angle lenses normally expand the area covered by the camera from one side of the frame to the other. As a result, and even though Maysles remains close to Kennedy, we are able to see not only the senator but also the surrounding context, the admiring supporters.

What the shot offers, then, is not simply the feeling of being one with the crowd but the experience of looking at the scene as a privileged observer. The camera can see more than any of the "participants" in the event. And we, by virtue of sharing its point of view, are allowed to do the same. By choosing to shoot the scene as he did, Maysles did convey the impression of *being there.* But he also drew upon specific cinematic tools—lens and camera angle—to produce an experience that "enhanced" our perspective on the actual situation.

Choosing what to shoot and how to shoot involves, of course, production issues such as budget, available equipment, access to the documentary subject, and so on. In fact, documentary filmmaking manuals frequently suggest that filmmakers plan their shoots carefully, so they can minimize production risks and also take advantage of spontaneous occurrences when these happen to arise. Besides these practical considerations, and perhaps more significantly, filmmakers and cinematographers make their choices based on their interpretation of the material they intend to shoot. Even when they try to minimize the impact of preconceived ideas on the making of their films, a certain level of interpretation is part of the shooting process. As Willard Van Dyke explains: "In the course of making a documentary film, a cameraman must be eternally alert to grasp the significance of some bit of unplanned action and decide whether it is important to the basic script plan; if it is, he must capture it on film" (407). Responding on the spot to ongoing action thus already implies that a decision must be made regarding what to film and how to film it. Van Dyke wrote these notes more than a decade prior to the advent of direct cinema. But the idea was not lost to the observational documentarists of the sixties, as Robert Drew reminds us: "There is a tremendous effort that goes into being in the right place at the right time—understanding what's about to happen, understanding what we have to get as it happens, and being ready and sensitive to get it at the time of happening" (Mekas 15).

Let's go back to *Primary*. In the sequence that follows the lengthy handheld shot described above, we find an image that exemplifies how interpreting factual material contributes to the shooting process. It is a close-up of a pair of hands in white gloves, a small detail in what seems otherwise like an important event. After Kennedy moves past the crowd, he enters a packed auditorium and takes a place next to his wife on the stage. We then see a series of relatively brief shots that alternately show the candidate and his wife on one side and the audience singing and cheering on the other. Then comes the shot of that pair of gloved hands against what seems to be a woman's back, and the sound of a woman speaking. The white gloves contrast sharply with the dark attire she is wearing. But it is the movement of her fingers that really catches our eye. Touching at the tips, the fingers keep fidgeting, suggesting a little bit of nervousness. The frame remains steady for approximately ten seconds. Then the camera tilts up to reveal the back of a woman's head, a cut to her profile in front of a microphone, and it is confirmed: the hands we are looking at are those of Jacqueline Kennedy as she delivers a brief speech to her husband's supporters.

This minute detail might not add much to the event in the auditorium. By choosing to frame it, though, the camera operator switches the focus from Jackie Kennedy's public image to her private emotions. This choice involves a certain interpretation of the event documented, which in turn is likely to affect the way we perceive the overall situation.

The Camera as an Expressive Tool

The shot of Jackie Kennedy's hands is meaningful in yet another way. It demonstrates that, even when recording factual material, the camera has an expressive potential. It may single out a particular occurrence, direct our attention toward a given object, or give visual configuration to a certain idea. It can also express an emotional state related to the subject matter, the filmmaker, or the act of filming itself.

Think, for instance, of the way Nathaniel Kahn's *My Architect* (2003) introduces us to the Salk Institute for Biological Studies in La Jolla, California. The building is one of the best-known pieces by the world-famous architect Louis Kahn, the filmmaker's late father. Nathaniel visits the place with a mixture of curiosity, admiration, and filial devotion, as if he were trying to invoke the father's presence through his work. All this is conveyed through the camerawork, which highlights the imposing and, at the same time, serene and spacious features of the building complex.

My Architect is in part an autobiographical documentary. When Louis Kahn died, Nathaniel was only eleven years old and had known his father in somewhat unusual circumstances. Louis was married to another woman when he met the filmmaker's mother and remained so until his death. Nathaniel, who never lived with his father, recalls seeing him only once a week. To the young son, the renowned architect remained a somewhat mysterious figure. The film tries to unravel the mystery through a series of interviews with people who knew Louis Kahn personally and professionally. But it is in the shots of the buildings that Nathaniel's feelings find their most vivid manifestation.

In the sequence at the Salk Institute, we see the building complex as a sort of ceremonial plaza. Kahn starts the sequence with a smooth tracking shot that leads to an open area, sided by buildings on the right and left. Then there is a cut to a long shot that reveals the entire space, with structures on both sides and the horizon in the background. Framed in a low angle, the Salk Institute appears grand, solemn, almost otherworldly.

8.3. The Salk Institute's stately plaza in *My Architect* (Nathaniel Kahn, 2003).

Later in the sequence, Kahn notes in a voiceover narration: "There is something spiritual about this space. For the first time since he died, I felt that I was getting closer to my father." Spirituality is not a concrete attribute. And it may therefore be hard to translate it into images. But that's exactly what this shot communicates. The static frame, with all the structures pointing toward the horizon, makes the space look ethereal.

A similarly majestic and reverential atmosphere characterizes some of the closer shots of the Salk Institute. Following the beginning of the sequence, we see specific details of the façade, as the camera moves slowly over the walls and windows. One of these shots, taken from a steep low angle, magnifies the height of the building so as to make it look like a tower. Other shots give the structure a totemic quality, with the buildings, framed once again from a low angle, contrasting with the blue sky above the Pacific Ocean. At a certain point, Kahn returns to that initial view of the Salk Institute, the open plaza with the horizon in the background. On this occasion, through time-lapse photography, he also captures the passing of time.

8.4. Low-angle shot of Louis Kahn's Salk Institute in *My Architect* (Nathaniel Kahn, 2003).

As the clouds move by and day turns into night, the framing remains unchanged. So does the space, a perennial site that is expected to "stand the test of time," as we heard earlier from the architect I. M. Pei, one of the interviewees in the film.

There is a distinctly personal feeling in the shots of Louis Kahn's buildings. It is not only the architect's work that stands out but the artistry of the cinematography as well. Compared to the plainness of the images described by Kracauer in the quote we used earlier, in which "veracity" is the only thing that matters, these shots do look studied and meticulously designed. It is, however, precisely this aesthetic treatment of reality that secures the film's veracity. Its stylized cinematography expresses a particular kind of sentiment, which in turn authenticates the autobiographical nature of the documentary.

Documentary filmmakers who use the camera as an expressive tool encourage us to see the world anew. Their images may portray familiar subjects from unusual angles or magnify certain attributes. In doing so, they can both broaden and deepen our understanding of reality: a certain degree of stylization can help filmmakers retrieve or preserve an aspect of the world that could otherwise be lost in the process of representation.

Werner Herzog's *Lessons of Darkness/Lektionen in Finsternis* (1992) does exactly that. It shows how visuals can help us to reach a more profound awareness of historical reality. Shot in Kuwait, the film focuses on the devastation that resulted from what is now referred to as the First Gulf War. It has little of the rhetoric that we expect from traditional documentaries, very few interviews, and a solemn but parsimonious voiceover narration. It does not have a conventional structure, either. Instead, Herzog arranges his shots within thematic blocks that have titles such as "Satan's National Park," "And a Smoke Arose Like the Smoke from a Furnace," and "Protuberances." In each block, it is the images—shots of burning oil fields, damaged buildings, and debris—that tell us the tale of destruction.

How can we turn into images the colossal damage caused by the war, in particular the damage caused to the natural environment? And what kind of camerawork may endow those images with the weight and intensity suitable to the subject matter in the film? Herzog answers these questions with dramatic tracking shots in which he scans the desolate postwar landscape. In one of these shots, he takes us on the road to show the rubble accumulated along a vast stretch of land. The shot is captured from a moving vehicle, with the camera pointing to the roadside. Against a pale, sandy landscape, we see the carcasses of abandoned cars and trucks, the most noticeable vestige of human existence passing before the camera's eye. The shot continues for over one minute, but the landscape does not change. The farther the camera goes, the more wreckage there is to film. In postwar Kuwait, Herzog seems to be telling us, there is no end to the destruction.

Other shots are taken from an aircraft and allow us to see even vaster stretches of devastation. "This was once a forest," he says in voiceover commentary, "before it was covered with oil." We see dark reflecting surfaces that could be mistaken for a series of lakes. Everything that looks like water, however, is in fact oil. "The oil," Herzog continues, "is trying to disguise itself as water." Flying low, the camera now passes by half-flooded, crumbling buildings that echo the devastation we saw along the road. Later the aircraft travels over burning oil fields. One after the other, fires indicate that the destruction continues even after the war has ended. At one moment, we are able to make out a few workers trying to put out flames. But what stands out is the fire itself. *Lessons of Darkness* opens with a disturbing epigraph: "The collapse of the stellar universe will occur like creation—in grandiose splendor." The shots of the burning fields bring to mind the power of this opening line. Herzog's alarming prophecy materializes on the screen as dark clouds of smoke envelop the land.

The film's treatment of historical reality can be overwhelming sometimes. But the eloquence of the camerawork never betrays the mandate of documentary cinema. As with *My Architect*, the images lend emotional intensity to the documentary, and that intensity helps shape our "path" to the historical world.

This notion that the camera can provide a unique perspective on reality is not, of course, unique to contemporary documentaries. We can trace its roots to the scientific spirit that inspired the invention of motion picture photography in the 1800s. We can also think of the fascination that the medium exerted over the artistic avant-gardes of the first half of the twentieth century. Filmmakers at the time explored the idea that the camera's eye can exceed the constraints of ordinary vision by expanding our perception of the physical world. Early experimental documentaries like Walther Ruttmann's *Berlin, Symphony of a Great City*, discussed in chapter 6, transposed this belief to the realm of nonfiction filmmaking. In Ruttmann's film, the camera travels on trains and in airplanes, observes the city from above and below, and watches ordinary people from afar and nearby. The numerous shots, the variety of angles, and the expressiveness of the camera movements create a portrait of the city that finds no precise equivalent in the perception of an ordinary observer.

Within the context of early avant-garde filmmaking, the documentary that best exemplifies the camera's capacity to reveal the world anew is probably Dziga Vertov's *Man with a Movie Camera/Chelovek s kino-apparatom* (1929). Like Ruttmann's city symphony, *Man with a Movie Camera* captures some of the everyday occurrences in a metropolis. And here, too, the virtuosity of the camerawork helps characterize the film as an experiment in documentary cinema. Mikhail Kaufman, the chief cameraman, uses dynamic shots and inventive compositions to sweep through multiple sites and events, bringing about a startling, sometimes exhilarating vision of modern life.

Importantly, this ability to generate a variety of perspectives on the referential world also appears as a theme in *Man with a Movie Camera*. Vertov's film consciously analyzes the power of the camera as a recording apparatus. It shows us not only the results of the filming process but also the process itself. We see, for instance, a shot of a train speeding toward us. A few seconds later, we watch the train from below, as if it were passing above our heads. This last shot is special; it offers a point of view virtually impossible to achieve under ordinary conditions. We may wonder how the cameraman produced such an image. Vertov chooses to satisfy our curiosity toward the end of the sequence, when we see a hole dug

under the tracks. We assume now that the camera was placed in the hole, pointing up at the moving train. Disclosing information about the filming process is
a pattern that repeats itself throughout the film; first the resulting image, as film
scholar Annette Michelson has observed, then the means by which that result has
been achieved.

Vertov himself wrote enthusiastically about the promises of what he called
"kino-eye"—the eye of cinema. In a tone that seems reminiscent of a political
manifesto, he proclaimed: "Kino-eye is understood as 'that which the eye doesn't
see,' as the microscope and telescope of time, . . . as the possibility of seeing without limits and distances, as the remote control of movie cameras, as tele-eye, as
X-ray eye, as 'life caught unawares,' etc., etc." (41). As he saw them, these technical capacities were directly associated with the social purpose of nonfiction filmmaking. Vertov's cinema was an intellectual cinema, a cinema aimed at creating
awareness and helping audiences "understand the phenomena of life around
them" (49). In *Man with a Movie Camera*, this awareness involved a more acute
knowledge of daily reality as well as an understanding of how that knowledge was
created through the film medium.

While not the only tool that stands out in Vertov's work, the camera clearly
plays a key role in this effort to help us see the world "without limits and distances." The mechanical eye seems capable of being in all places at any time—
not only underneath but also on top of moving trains, planted on sidewalks and
standing between cable cars, panning from one side to the other, tilting up and
down, moving diagonally, and so on. Indeed, the film may be justly described
as "visual pyrotechnics," as it places the supple artistry of the camerawork at the
center of the documentary process. We also see superimposition of images, slow
and fast motion photography, and freeze frames.

Ironically, Vertov repeatedly spoke against dramatic uses of the film medium
and believed that artistic excess compromised the mission of the filmmaker. *Man
with a Movie Camera*, however, is infinitely rich in aesthetic qualities. And it is its
ambitious visual aesthetics that grants us multiple viewpoints on the historical
world.

Point of View

We have already explored the correlation between the camerawork and the way
a documentary looks at lived reality. The notion of point of view, nonetheless,
deserves closer attention. Overall, this is a concept that exceeds the domain of

camerawork. In fiction cinema, it intersects with the process by which the plot communicates story information—the film's narration, as David Bordwell and Kristin Thompson put it. While analyzing the plot of a narrative film, we may ask, for example, if it offers an omniscient point of view on the story events or if we have access only to what one particular character knows about those events. Does the film grant us the position of an all-knowing spectator or does it restrict our perspective? We may also think about whether that point of view is objective or subjective, that is to say, whether or not it reflects anyone's opinions, attitude, or sentiments (88–94). These questions pertain to documentary cinema as well, although they take on a more specific form in the context of nonfiction filmmaking. Let's turn one last time to Bill Nichols's notion of the "voice of documentary," the way a documentary "speaks" or "how it [organizes] the materials it [presents] to us" ("Voice of Documentary" 18–19). Implicit in a documentary's voice, as we noted earlier, is a given perspective on the historical world. Films like *Prelude to War*, for instance, arrange their materials in a way that suggests an omniscient standpoint. Even if we recognize its biases, we cannot connect its "voice" with a specific "speaking" agency. Rather, it appears to us as if the world could "speak" for itself in a decisive and absolute manner. Other documentaries, such as *Delirium*, allow for a more limited and subjective view. We recognize the voice of the video maker—a young, feminist artist. What we learn from the video—and how we learn it—results from her individual perspective.

To be sure, the idea that a documentary can ever delineate an all-encompassing point of view on any event or situation is as questionable as the often-criticized presumption of documentary objectivity. When we watch a nonfiction film, we already know that the historical world exceeds the parameters of what we see and hear. In a fictional work, as filmmaker and scholar Michael Chanan has argued, "nothing that is not contained within the film, directly or by allusion, has any relevance. . . . In documentary [however] there is in principle no such self-enclosure" (109). This does not mean, of course, that we should plainly dismiss the aspirations of films like *Prelude to War*. Understanding how a documentary establishes a point of view can tell us a great deal about its role as a nonfictional text and the way it addresses its audience. *Prelude to War* is a propaganda film. Lest it lose its efficacy or fail to serve its purpose, it must, at least in theory, present a seemingly unanimous, totalizing view of reality.

A number of elements, other than the overall design of the film, can help to shape a documentary's point of view. Voiceover narrations, for example, may establish or direct a documentary's approach to its subject matter. (Think of the differences between the disembodied commentary in *Prelude to War* and the video maker's voice in *Delirium.*) The arrangement of the shots, too, can guide our attention to a particular piece of information or even support the development of an argument, as we saw in our discussion of editing. It is the camera, though, that provides the most direct translation for the concept of point of view because it organizes the visual field in a way that implies a standpoint on reality. We literally share the experience of viewing the world from a particular angle or perspective. An instructive example of how the camera establishes a point of view for the spectator would be the shot of Jackie Kennedy's hands.

Film theorists use the term "point-of-view shot" to designate an image in which the framing coincides with what is viewed by someone within the film. A character looks down from a window and then we cut to a high angle shot of what he or she sees, say, a busy street framed from above. The second image is interpreted as being equivalent to the viewing experience of the character in the first shot. Point-of-view shots, however, only partly explain the role of the camera as a means of organizing information. Furthermore, they are relatively rare in documentaries. Most of the time, we identify not with the viewpoint of an individual within the screen but with what the camera sees in general, the perspective brought forward by the frame at any given moment in the film.

In *The Roof*, the camera quietly watches what happens or passes before it. It records a few conversations with Aljafari's family members, captures quotidian events in the family's home, and travels through the landscape in Ramle and Jaffa, old Palestinian cities that are now part of Israel. The sober, restrained quality of the camerawork results in a contemplative mood that sometimes recalls the aesthetics of observational cinema. *The Roof*, however, is deeply affective and clearly partial in its account of reality. And the camera does more than simply amass visual information; it forges a close connection with its subjects and offers a distinctively personal viewpoint on what it documents.

The title of the documentary evokes the history of the house to which the filmmaker's family moved after the displacement of the Palestinian population as a consequence of the Arab-Israeli war. "The people who remained," explains the director in voiceover, "were forced to live in one neighborhood, and they were given the houses of other Palestinians." In 1948 the owners of what became his father's family home in Ramle were still building the second floor. "Today the house is still the same: my parents live on the first floor and the past lives above them." As a leitmotif in the film, the roof symbolizes this history of displacement. The camerawork, accordingly, helps bring forth the meanings that concepts such as home and homeland have for the Arab population living in Israel.

Not surprisingly, several of the sequences in *The Roof* focus on domestic spaces.

In one of them, we look at the interior of the filmmaker's family house and see a quiet, modestly furnished room captured with a wide-angle lens. We notice his father sitting on a couch, smoking and watching TV. Then, in a shot taken from a different angle, we glimpse one of his sisters and their mother as they prepare food, with the television on. Next, from still another angle, we observe the family gathered around the dining table, sharing a meal, the TV in the background. The shots are generally uneventful; the scenes seem predictably ordinary; and the camerawork by Diego Martínez Vignatti strikes us as austere and unremarkable. The simplicity of these images could almost be read as a sign of indifference. In fact, the opposite turns out to be true. The camerawork creates a strong connection with the room, representing it as a hospitable and familiar environment. The stillness of the frame (there is only one camera movement in this sequence) and the relatively long duration of the shots keep our eyes fixed on the domestic space as we slowly become accustomed to the things and people in it. It is not distance but intimacy that is communicated by these images.

8.5. The father of the family watching television. From *The Roof/Alsateh* (Kamal Aljafari, 2006).

The same impression crops up in the close shots of objects in the house: a clock hanging on the wall; bottles of perfume, nail polish, and cosmetics on top of a dresser; draped windows; a bird cage. The camera also shows a series of family pictures, snapshots and portraits, which connect us to the people in the house even before we see them gathered at the dining table. Later, when the filmmaker

8.6. Objects on the dresser in the house in Ramle. From *The Roof/Alsateh* (Kamal Aljafari, 2006). 8.7. Family photos in the house in Ramle. From *The Roof/Alsateh* (Kamal Aljafari, 2006).

visits his uncle's place in Jaffa, we are introduced to yet another set of photos. These are close, static shots as well, which give us a glimpse of the family's past and its different generations. In all these images, the framing functions as an informed but partial guide to the referential world, putting into effect the notion that the history to which the documentary refers has deeply impacted the lives of the people in the film.

By contrast, many of the exterior shots are fluid, moving shots that do not follow any particular subject but, instead, affectionately inspect the landscape of crumbling walls, remains of buildings, weeds and broken fragments in decay, anonymous barrenness. Several images are accompanied by natural location sound—near silence. But in one, toward the beginning of the film, soon after a passage from Anton Shammas ("And you know perfectly well that we don't ever leave home, we simply drag it behind us wherever we go, walls, roof and all"), the camera tracks along empty shells of dwellings and we hear a 1942 Egyptian love song, a tango of longing, Asmahan's "Ya Habibi Taala." A traveling shot always erases its past. Most importantly, like the other tracking shots that haunt *The Roof*, this shot conveys a sense of the presence of an absence, an absence located outside the time and space of the image, an absence that cannot be represented concretely. While recording the actual, the tracking shot arouses our wonder for the potential, the endless world that exists beyond the borders of the frame, beyond the borders of its historical limits.

All documentaries present us with a point of view from which we are invited to enter the historical world. *The Roof* turns that point of view into one of the film's most significant features. It is because we can look into the private world of the filmmaker's family (as they are today, as they were, as they might have been), because of the film's personal interpretation of history, that the documentary leaves such a strong impression.

Digital Technology and the Documentary Image

One key factor in the shaping of this type of personal documentary has been the development of recording technologies that have simplified the shooting process. Smaller, lighter, and more affordable cameras have made it easier for individuals to work on their own and create documentaries that focus on their lived experiences. Michael Renov has argued that the advent of portable video equipment, with its embedded promise of instant replay, has been particularly fitting to confessional modes of documentary. "It is the systematic solipsism and 'immediacy' of video . . . that suit it so well to the confessional impulse. No technician need see or hear the secrets confided to tape" (198). We can apply a similar argument even to videos in which the video maker and the individual in front of the camera are not the same person. In *Delirium* the intimacy conveyed by the visual treatment of the subject derives partly from the nature of the medium.

This is not to say, of course, that technology is fate. Changes in cultural and social attitudes have also greatly contributed to the development of novel approaches to nonfiction. Personal documentaries find support, for instance, in the idea that private lives constitute a legitimate locus of interpretation for public history. This was the case with several nonfiction films made in the 1970s, as we noted in the second chapter, especially those that dealt with minority subjects. Individual circumstances, too, play an important role. And so does the nature of the subject represented.

Even so, new technology does enable documentary makers to explore different shooting methods, which in turn have influenced the objectives and aesthetics of their work. Consider what digital technology has done for documentaries in recent years. Because digital equipment is usually less expensive than traditional film equipment, access to the means of production is more easily available, too. Digital cameras also affect the production process by encouraging closer and seemingly more immediate scrutiny of the documentary subject. In some ways, digital recording recalls the "revolution" ushered in by the introduction of portable film equipment after World War II, when technological innovations helped launch the movements known as direct cinema and *cinéma vérité*. In other ways, it benefits from some of the features already found in earlier video making, such as instant viewing of the material recorded. Digital video, however, has the advantage of meeting the standards of theatrical exhibition more easily, opening a traditionally independent mode of production to mainstream audiences.

Abbas Kiarostami's *ABC Africa* (2001), a documentary that looks at the impact of AIDS on the lives of children in Uganda, was shot entirely with digital cameras. Kiarostami first brought two small cameras to Africa in order to take "pictorial notes" that could serve as the basis for a future film. The idea was to return later and shoot with 35mm equipment. When he looked at the original material, though, he realized that much of the spontaneity contained in it would be lost in a film shot with heavier, more cumbersome equipment. The "pictorial notes" became, then, the documentary that we know as *ABC Africa* (explained in Abbas Kiarostami's *10 on Ten*, 2004). The spontaneous quality that impressed Kiarostami can be detected both in the shooting style and in the actions recorded.

The camera moves freely among the documentary subjects, changing angles and location effortlessly. The orphaned children, too, react comfortably to the act of being filmed, often treating the camera as a playful object rather than an intimidating technology. They dance for the cameras, smile, wave, clap hands, jump up and down, hop, and make funny faces, and then crowd around to look at themselves in the camera's LCD screen.

But shooting with digital cameras is only part of the way new technologies have impacted documentary filmmaking. Sometimes, when we talk about digital images, we are referring not to images recorded by the camera but to those generated by a computer. The focus shifts from production to postproduction—and from the profilmic event to the artifice of the technological process. This adds an interesting twist to the discussion of documentary cinema because, as we noted in chapter 1, the technology compromises the indexicality of the representation. An image generated by a computer does not constitute a record of an actual event. Do we still believe in what we see when we know that it has been produced—or at least manipulated—by a computer?

We can begin to answer this question by reminding ourselves once again that, in fact, every aspect in the documentary process involves some degree of artificiality. The photographic image itself is artificially created, even if it retains an indexical relationship to that which is photographed. Computer images exacerbate this artificial quality. And because they can sever the indexical bond with the historical world, they force us to think of trustworthiness in different terms.

One area in which computer graphics have proved particularly useful is documentary animation. Although it is conventionally associated with fantasy and entertainment, animation has a long tradition in the history of nonfictional representation. Winsor McCay's *The Sinking of the Lusitania* (1918), for example, already showed "how an animated work can be used to visualize an historic episode" (Strøm 49). Documentaries that rely entirely on animated images may be somewhat rare, but the use of animation in individual sequences is not. We can think about how the Disney-made animated maps function as visual aids in *Prelude to War*, or about the way animated diagrams can serve a similarly didactic purpose.

Because it successfully evades the documentary's commitment to the indexicality of the image, the use of animation seems like a perfect fit for experiences of which there is no historical record. Animated sequences work as a sort of reconstruction, the re-creation of events that are no longer available for documentation. Ari Folman's *Waltz with Bashir* (2008), for instance, uses animation as an alternative to live action footage and as a means of reflecting on the nature of memory.

The film collects various testimonies from individuals who were involved in Israel's 1982 military offensive against Lebanon. Folman chooses to animate the stories in a dreamlike way that represents the subjective character of the recollections and phantasmagoric dimension of the war experience. *Diary Film—I was 12 in '56/Naplófilm—12 voltam 56'-ban* (Boglárka Edvy, animator, and Sándor Silló, 2006) layers images from a twelve-year-old boy's diary begun during the Hungarian uprising of 1956 with archival footage, reconstructions, children's drawings, and animation in order to evoke both the gravity of the events and the fact that the story is told from a child's point of view. And we saw how Lin Tay-jou used animation along with enacted live action scenes in *The Secret in the Satchel* in order to safeguard the identity of his informants.

Compared to traditional animation, computer graphics can appear particularly realistic, providing remarkably compelling simulations of the physical world. There are different techniques that normally fall under the category of digital animation. Some involve the manipulation of photographic images for which there exists an actual referent in the physical world. We still see the record of an actual situation, although that situation no longer appears in its original form. Others generate wholly artificial realities, pure simulations, which may allude to actual places, objects, lives, or events without bearing any indexical relation to them. As Craig Hight writes, "At one pole of a continuum of techniques is the computer mediation of images (CMI), which positions elements of the indexical and photographic within animation and morphing sequences during post-production. At the other pole are entirely computer-generated images (CGI), derived from the many advances towards synthetic realism achieved in fictional film-making" (3).

Animation in general and computer graphics in particular contradict the notion that a documentary can only fulfill its purpose when the camera records a profilmic reality. As an alternative or a complement to the photographic record, animation draws attention to aesthetic codes; the formal aspects stand out since what we see unequivocally presumes some form of fabrication. Interestingly, though, even when we look at live action, the profilmic event is never entirely free of aesthetic considerations. Animation may render those aesthetic considerations more obvious, but the profilmic reality is also part of the process by which documentary films give form to the world. We look at the contribution of the profilmic to the aesthetics of documentary in our next chapter.

Additional Filmography

A Happy Mother's Day (Joyce Chopra and Richard Leacock, 1963)
Hatsu Yume (First Dream) (Bill Viola, 1981)

Koyaanisqatsi (Godfrey Reggio, 1983)

The Gleaners and I/Les Glaneurs et la glaneuse (Agnés Varda, 2000)

Swivel (Oliver Husain, 2003–05)

13 Lakes (James Benning, 2004)

Fifty Minutes of Women/Nüren wushi fenzhong (Shi Tou, 2005)

Works Cited and Further Reading

Beattie, Keith. *Documentary Display: Re-viewing Nonfiction Film and Video.* London: Wallflower Press, 2008.

Bordwell, David, and Kristin Thompson. *Film Art: An Introduction.* 8th ed. New York: McGraw-Hill, 2008.

Camper, Fred. "*Shoah's* Absence." In *Claude Lanzmann's "Shoah": Key Essays,* ed. Stuart Liebman. New York: Oxford University Press, 2007.

Chanan, Michael. *The Politics of Documentary.* London: British Film Institute, 2007.

"First Person Films/Birinci Sahis Filmleri." Symposium, May 29–31, 2009, Istanbul Modern, Istanbul, Turkey, Program Notes.

Hight, Craig. "Primetime Digital Documentary Animation: The Photographic and the Graphic within Play." *Studies in Documentary Film* 2.1 (February 2008).

Kracauer, Siegfried. *Theory of Film: The Redemption of Physical Reality.* 1960. Reprint, Oxford: Oxford University Press, 1978.

Landesman, Ohad. "In and Out of This World: Digital Video and the Aesthetics of Realism in the New Hybrid Documentary." *Studies in Documentary Film* 2.1 (February 2008).

Mamber, Stephen. "*Primary.*" In *Cinema Verite in America: Studies in Uncontrolled Documentary.* Cambridge, Mass.: MIT Press, 1974.

Mekas, Jonas. "The Frontiers of Realist Cinema: The Work of Ricky Leacock (from an Interview conducted by Gideon Bachmann)." *Film Culture,* nos. 22–23 (Summer 1961).

Michelson, Annette. "From Magician to Epistemologist: Vertov's *The Man with a Movie Camera.*" In *The Essential Cinema,* vol. 1, 2nd ed., ed. P. Adams Sitney. New York: Film Culture and Anthology Film Archives, 1989.

Moran, James M. "A Bone of Contention: Documenting the Prehistoric Subject." In *Collecting Visible Evidence,* ed. Jane M. Gaines and Michael Renov. Minneapolis: University of Minnesota Press, 1999.

Nichols, Bill. *Representing Reality: Issues and Concepts in Documentary.* Bloomington: Indiana University Press, 1991.

———. "The Voice of Documentary." In *New Challenges for Documentary*, 2nd ed., ed. Alan Rosenthal and John Corner. Manchester: Manchester University Press, 2005.

Renov, Michael. "Video Confessions." In *The Subject of Documentary*. Minneapolis: University of Minnesota Press, 2004.

Strøm, Gunnar. "The Animated Documentary." *Animation Journal* 11 (2003).

Vertov, Dziga. *Kino-eye: The Writings of Dziga Vertov.* Ed. Annette Michelson. Berkeley: University of California Press, 1984.

Van Dyke, Willard. "The Interpretive Camera in Documentary Films." *Hollywood Quarterly* 1.4 (July 1946).

9

The Profilmic

We have already explored the ways filmmakers position fragments of lived reality through editing. And we know that camerawork can add to or subtract from the events or situations documented. But we haven't discussed how the profilmic environment—that which the camera records—contributes to the making of a documentary. Nonfiction filmmakers often draw on settings and lighting to communicate information and characterize specific situations. They also commonly enlist the "collaboration" of people in front of the camera in order to further their stories or arguments. While we may be tempted to draw a line between the act of filming and the material recorded, that line is usually fuzzy. The profilmic is in fact an integral part of the re-presentation process.

The handling of the profilmic environment is generally known as the *mise-en-scène.* The term comes from theater. A literal translation from the French would be "put into the scene." Because it is associated with theatricality and fiction, *mise-en-scène* seems to contradict the very notion of documentary. It implies that the situations captured on film are arranged for the camera. And it assumes a large measure of creative control over the profilmic material. In nonfiction cinema, as Bill Nichols notes, "[the profilmic] and the historical referent are taken to be congruent with one another." We presume that what is recorded "remains identical to the actual event that we could have ourselves witnessed in the historical world" (*Representing Reality* 25). Interfering in what happens in front of the camera could seemingly upset this equation.

In practice, the treatment of the profilmic in nonfiction cinema involves a more complicated scenario. Documentary makers frequently intercede in the events recorded. The subjects in the films, too, participate in this process by responding to the presence of the camera, taking up a role comparable to that of an actor. They are performers of some sort. As we shall see, however, neither situation necessarily poses a threat to the authenticity of the historical referent. Rather, they are part of the conventions of documentary cinema.

The difficulties posed by the concept of *mise-en-scène* may be partly understood as reluctance to embrace the idea of aesthetics in nonfiction filmmaking. As we noted in the book's introduction, absence of style in documentary often imparts a greater sense of credibility (Corner 96). Aesthetic "flourishes," by contrast, might appear to distort the material available for documentation or even distract us from the subject in the film. While this attitude can guide our appreciation of all aspects in the documentary process, it is the profilmic that seems most resistant to aesthetic consideration. From the profilmic we expect not *form* but *content.*

The problem with this argument is that it confines documentary filmmaking to a very limited set of procedures. It also overlooks the exchanges that take place between the documentarian and the referential world, and it diminishes the significance of the *mise-en-scène* as a means of addressing historical reality. As Keith Beattie has recently argued, critics have repeatedly neglected the power of what he calls "visual display" in nonfiction cinema, despite evidence that documentaries rely heavily on visual aesthetics to produce knowledge (3–5). The creative treatment of profilmic reality is one important way in which visual display can be used in order to generate meaning. Only within certain film movements or historical contexts—the direct cinema documentaries that we discussed in the last chapter, for example—have filmmakers openly resisted creative intervention in the profilmic. But even in these cases the suggestion that the documentary can record completely uncontrolled events has come under critical scrutiny.

Documentary filmmakers intervene creatively in the profilmic not only by staging events but also by assigning meaning to situations or settings that already exist in the historical world. That is to say, they select and organize the material available for shooting, including the subjects who appear in their films. This chapter focuses on the way documentarians treat profilmic reality. More specifically, it discusses how settings can be used in documentaries, and how nonfictional performers, now and then the documentary makers themselves, contribute to the documentary's meanings.

Reenactments

One way to start this discussion is to revisit the notion of reenactment in documentaries. A reenactment is the repetition of an action—or series of actions—that has already taken place. It is a staged event, not an "original" occurrence. A documentary about the American Revolutionary War, for example, can rely on various forms of evidence as well as on expert testimonies to examine the history of the period. But because there is no cinematic record of it, the filmmaker would have to resort to a reenactment in order to represent any specific action. Reenactments can provide reliable representations of the historical world. Yet they never coincide with the earlier event. They are "[copies] of what has already happened once and for all" (Nichols, "'Getting to Know You'" 176). And, as we have seen in previous chapters, imagination may be a part of the reenactment. So what we notice is the artificial character of the scene.

It is precisely because reenactments are staged events, however, that they can inspire us to think about how documentary makers in general approach *mise-en-scène*. While many documentaries conceal the intervention of the filmmaker in the sociohistorical world, those that employ reenactments foreground the means by which lived reality is translated into what we see onscreen. Documentaries always involve some form of planning, even when they eschew elaborately staged action. But we frequently fail to notice these strategies. Looking at documentary reenactments is a way of bringing them to the surface.

Reenactments were fairly common in the pre–World War II era, in part because of technical limitations that made the filming process comparatively cumbersome and laborious. Before lightweight equipment became standard in nonfiction filmmaking, the recording apparatus allowed only for limited mobility. Documentary filmmakers, as a result, had to plan their scenes meticulously, staging even ordinary or habitual actions.

Night Mail's train cars, for example, were constructed on a set. The original postal carriages were too small and dark for the 1930s cameras to shoot in. Moreover, the train's movement caused some blurry shots. In order to simulate the sway inside the car, some objects were manipulated by hand from offscreen. The real mail sorters performed their usual activities in a mock-up carriage in the studio (Winston 129). Their actions were intercut with location footage of the real train as it sped through the countryside, passed through stations, and dropped off mailbags. Spontaneity was in part compromised by the technical requirements of the medium, but the staging itself was not looked upon with suspicion. Instead, it was accepted as a legitimate convention of nonfiction filmmaking.

Some contemporary film and video makers, however, treat reenactments not as substitutes for actual events but rather as incursions into the nature of nonfictional representation. They look at the staged scenes less as a means "to authenticate the past than [a way] to stress the variability of its interpretation" (Nichols, "'Getting to Know You'" 178). Reenacting prior events becomes an occasion to reflect on the relationship between the representation and the represented; more specifically, it allows us to think about how documentaries creatively use cinematic codes that we normally place under the rubric of *mise-en-scène*.

Take Jill Godmilow's *Far from Poland* (1984), for example. Because the reenacted scenes in this work do not exactly "fill in" for past events, they highlight the way the filmmaker utilizes acting and décor to represent the historical world. The situations look more contrived than they normally would in traditional documentaries. But these same scenes also expand our understanding of nonfictional representation by emphasizing a distinctively creative and clearly interpretive dimension in the filmmaking process. As Godmilow herself has noted, *Far from Poland* is a "post-realist nonfiction film" that frees the documentarian from the obligation to "shoot the 'real thing' as it's happening" (quoted in MacDonald 132–133).

The film opens with a brief prelude in which the filmmaker appears on camera to explain how the project came about. Godmilow happened to be in Poland in the late summer of 1980, when the workers at the Lenin shipyards, in the port city of Gdansk, went on strike demanding a series of reforms from the government as well as the right to organize independent trade unions. In a few weeks, the workers' actions gave birth to the Solidarity movement. Godmilow rushed back to the United States, raised money to make a documentary about Solidarity, and bought a plane ticket to Warsaw, only to find out that the Polish government had denied her a visa to enter the country. Barred from making the documentary she had planned, she followed what was happening in Poland through the nightly broadcasts on American television.

What looked like an insurmountable obstacle, though, turned out to be a catalyst for a provocative experiment in documentary filmmaking. Several of the scenes in the film are reenactments of situations that took place in Poland, to which the filmmaker had no direct access. In one of them, Godmilow stages an interview with a crane operator named Anna Walentynowicz, who was a pivotal figure in the process that led to the formation of Solidarity. The reenactment was based on an actual interview with Walentynowicz. But what we watch in the film is an actress, Ruth Maleczech, playing the role of the crane operator. Godmilow also re-creates the office space in which the original interview took place, using a sparsely furnished setting decorated with a Solidarity banner on the wall to represent the Polish location. We understand that this is not the original site, just as we know that Maleczech is not Walentynowicz. Yet it is not this discrepancy that stands out but the emotional impact of the scene, especially the affective quality of the performance delivered by Maleczech, which invites sympathy and emotional identification with the interviewee. Her calm and modulated speech, her calculated pauses, and the sudden changes in the intensity of her voice, all contribute to the way we perceive the original event.

By reenacting the interview, Godmilow adds her voice to the experiences represented in the film and draws attention to her role as mediator between the spectator and the historical world. While the documentary does show us footage shipped from Poland—some of which was shot by members of the Solidarity movement—it is through the staged scenes that the film speaks most eloquently about the events of 1980.

Other documentaries resort to even less orthodox techniques in order to re-create lived reality. We saw in the previous chapter how Ari Folman's *Waltz with Bashir* deploys animation to re-create memories of Israel's 1982 military offensive against Lebanon. Jessica Yu's *Protagonist* (2006) relies on similarly inventive procedures. It uses puppet theater in its reenactments, forfeiting not only the indexical bond with the original events but also the traditional aesthetics of documentary cinema.

The film focuses on the lives of four men whose stories involve different forms of "obsession": a former terrorist, a bank robber turned journalist, a gay man who used his religious ministry to preach against homosexuality, and a writer whose fixation with martial arts helped define his adolescent identity. Yu interviews all four at length and has them talk about their childhoods, the motivations that led them to live unconventional lives, and how they eventually "escaped" their particular obsessions. Much of the information we receive comes from these interviews. Records of the situations described by the documentary subjects are also used in the film. But some of the key events—a bank robbery, a church sermon in Malaysia—can only be represented through reenactments. The puppets illustrate what we hear in the testimonies. More importantly, because of the apparent incongruity between the puppet show and the conventional format of the testimonies, the reenactments also highlight the distance that separates the documentary interviews from the events to which they refer. As Robert Rosenstone points out, for certain events in the past, "literalism" may evoke "a feeling of normality," whereas the true feelings we wish to convey "might call out for 'facts' delivered through an expressionist or surrealist mode of presentation" (836).

The use of puppets in *Protagonist* deserves attention for yet another reason. While the puppets are made to look like the actual documentary subjects, they are not dressed in contemporary costumes but appear instead as characters from ancient Greek theater. Yu's initial motivation for the documentary was the work of Euripides, the Greek tragedian from the fifth century B.C.E., known for having introduced psychological complexity and personal motivation to the classical stage. The reenactments in the film draw on this legacy. Not only does Yu dress the puppets as ancient characters, she also intersperses the various episodes narrated by the documentary subjects with titles such as "turning point," "catharsis," and "reversal," suggesting a strong parallel between life and theater, and reminding us that documentaries as well employ dramatic forms to communicate information.

More than simply flaunt the artifice of their reenactments, films like *Far from Poland* and *Protagonist* raise fundamental questions about documentary in general. They shed light on the way other documentarians, too, rely on representational strategies that can include premeditated use of settings, expressive performances, artificial lighting, and so on.

Our task in the rest of the chapter is to look more closely at the ways the documentary maker treats the profilmic event. We will start by discussing the settings and how they are used in documentaries. What do filmmakers do with the spaces, sites, or locations where the actions and events represented in their documentaries take place?

Settings

Settings can be simple and subdued, like the studio backdrops commonly used in documentary interviews. Or they can be complex and rich in information, as when people are interviewed in their homes, surrounded by their belongings. In each case, the setting does not just materialize in front of the camera; it is part of decision-making processes that enable documentary filmmakers—and sometimes their subjects—to "speak about" the world. A studio backdrop may not provide much information, but it can create a sober atmosphere. Actual locations, in turn, may offer not only atmosphere but also insight into the interviewees' relationship with their immediate environment.

The term "location shooting" normally refers to filming that happens in an actual locale, as opposed to shooting that takes place in a studio. Chris Marker's *Sunless*, for example, was shot on location in several countries, including Japan, Cape Verde, and Guinea-Bissau. The buildings and streets that we see were not created for the film; they existed prior to the making of the documentary. But location shooting does not always imply that the filming occurred in the exact place "where the story is set" (Pramaggiore and Wallis 91). Some of the scenes in *Far from Poland* were shot on location in the United States, while the situations they depict took place in Europe. In this case, there is no direct connection between the shots in the film and the setting of the original event.

There is good reason, though, for nonfiction filmmakers to shoot at the exact location in which events occur. Observing the integrity of the relationship with the original context usually lends credibility to the documentary because it strengthens the indexical bond with the actual occurrence. While we may accept the settings in *Far from Poland* as analogous to the original locations, we know all along that we are not looking at the "real thing." Shooting at the place "where the story is set" nourishes our desire for immediacy and encourages the belief, illusory as it may be, that documentaries can provide direct access to "the real."

Constructed sets do exactly the opposite. They widen the gap between the film and the original locale. A constructed set in a documentary implies that even the physical aspects of the historical world may be subject to manipulation. The filmmaker's choices are more apparent; so are the stylistic qualities of the scenes. As a result, the effort to authenticate the process of representation can also become more complicated, requiring that we look beyond the indexicality of the situations represented.

As we have seen, Errol Morris's *The Thin Blue Line* turns this apparent difficulty into an asset as it substitutes actual locations with fabricated environments. Morris understands that drawing attention to the artificial character of the settings goes against the yearning to capture the immediate presence of the referential world. Yet in *The Thin Blue Line* he manages to use this artifice to develop a specific point. Because some of the settings in the film look highly stylized and noticeably fake, the desire for an indexical bond with the actual event never arises. Instead, we become aware of its absence, conscious of the impossibility of witnessing the scene of the crime that stands at the center of the story. The deliberately artificial settings, in other words, call upon us to take into consideration the uncertainties that permeate the murder case examined in the film.

The Setting as a Source of Meaning

Settings, as David Bordwell and Kristin Thompson note, "need not be only a container for human events but can dynamically enter the narrative action" (115).

The statement refers primarily to fiction films. But it can be legitimately applied to nonfictional narratives as well. Documentary settings provide information. They can also function to organize that information in a manner that guides the viewer's interpretation of the world represented. In *Up the Yangtze* (Yung Chang, 2007), for example, the vanishing landscape along the Yangtze River allows the filmmaker to issue a poignant statement about contemporary life in China. Here the setting simultaneously establishes a context for the events in the documentary and helps us understand how those events relate to Chinese society in general.

The longest river in Asia, the Yangtze is the site of an ambitious and controversial engineering project: the Three Gorges Dam. By the time it is completed, in 2011, the dam will have forced approximately two million people, many of them peasants living on the riverbanks, out of their homes. Chang's documentary captures these developments as it follows two Chinese youths employed on a luxury cruise ship up the Yangtze: Chen Bo Yu, a blustering young man who dreams of becoming rich, and Yu Shui, a peasant girl whose family's modest farmhouse is swallowed by the rising waters of the Yangtze during the shooting of the film. Contrasting with the humble peasant dwellings are the showy, rapidly developing cities along the Yangtze, which are also used as settings in the documentary. Yung Chang explores this contrast in order to represent the dramatic changes that have spread over various parts of China in the past few decades. Not everyone has benefited equally from the country's impressive economic development, he reminds us. And the locations used in the film are there to demonstrate it.

Up the Yangtze treats the sites along the river as metonymic extensions of China's social problems. What we see are specific places on the riverbanks. But their role in the film exceeds their literal meaning. Chang uses location shooting to articulate a particular view of the world.

9.1. "Nanook's harsh environment." From *Nanook of the North* (Robert Flaherty, 1922).

Documentary settings can also motivate the situations that take place in front of the camera. In *Nanook of the North*, the arctic landscape both encompasses and prompts the events represented, functioning not simply as backdrop for the situations depicted by Flaherty but also as a living force within the story.

Nanook's efforts to secure the survival of his family coincide with his struggle against the elements of his environment. Will he win over the indomitable forces of nature or will he be overpowered by them? Flaherty shows us a snowy landscape that looks at once treacherous and majestic, and locates in that setting the very obstacles that motivate Nanook's actions. Walking through vast ice fields, Nanook seems diminutive by comparison, his figure contrasting with the immensity of the arctic scenery.

Nanook of the North also illustrates how documentary settings may be utilized to characterize individual subjects. Throughout the film, Nanook is seen as intrepid, inventive, and resourceful, and it is his relationship with the natural elements that creates this impression. We think of him as ingenious when we watch him build an igloo; we acknowledge his tenacity when we see his tug of war with an arctic seal; and we admire his bravery when we follow him and his comrades on a walrus hunt. Each scene integrates setting and action in order to portray a subject whose distinctive attributes overlap, not by accident, with Flaherty's romantic view of the Inuit people.

Even though few documentaries draw so emphatically on the relationship between the subject and the landscape, the association of settings and individuals is not uncommon in nonfiction cinema. In fact, settings often serve as an eloquent indicator of a person's characteristic attributes. They may establish the subjects' ethnic backgrounds, social status, and professional affiliations, or even characterize their individual personalities. Think, for example, of the settings conventionally used in documentary interviews. Writers are habitually framed alongside bookshelves; farmers, standing in a field; teachers, in front of a blackboard. While the content of the interviews may bear no direct relation to the visual elements in the frame, the use of recognizable settings helps distinguish the interviewee from other subjects in the film. It functions much like the caption that normally identifies the person on camera.

More unusual, but equally significant, is the use of nonfictional settings as a way of defining the filmmaker's authorial position. If certain documentaries attempt to associate the "characters" represented with the surrounding world, others highlight the relationship between the filmmaker and the sites or locations depicted. This response to nonfictional settings is at the center of Chantal Akerman's *News from Home*, a film that has a strong autobiographical component. *News from Home* is composed of lengthy, uneventful shots that show anonymous subjects and nondescript locations in New York City. In some of them we watch empty streets without being able to recognize the sites; in others we see people gather on sidewalks or stand in subway cars, occasionally acknowledging the presence of the camera. The simplicity of the images suggests a realistic style that is typical of documentary filmmaking. Yet, even at its most subdued, the use of location shooting strikes us as deeply personal. The general impression is one of loneliness and disconnection from the world on the screen. Akerman's compositions privilege no individual object or profilmic element, no details in the cityscape, and no outstanding event. As a result, we find it difficult to engage with the places that we see. We look at the city without knowing what to look for.

One shot displays the interior of a deserted diner. The camera stays put and the composition never changes. Nor does any part of the setting solicit our attention. We observe the counter and stools; we scan the scene hoping to find something of interest. But our gaze is met with indifference. In its lifeless appearance, Akerman's interior communicates a sense of detachment that prevents us from ever connecting with the space on the screen. The next shot, not surprisingly, produces a similar impression. We now see the exterior of a donut shop, framed in a long shot that includes the street in the foreground. The brightness of the shop window stands out from the rest of the setting, but the shop itself remains distant, a flashy but stubbornly remote site that we will never know very well. Like the cars passing in front, it never speaks to us. And even when it holds our attention, it cannot reveal anything other than its impersonal façade, drenched in bright light and adorned with neon signs.

9.2. Interior of a diner in *News from Home* (Chantal Akerman, 1976).

9.3. Exterior of a donut shop in *News from Home* (Chantal Akerman, 1976).

This apparent distance from the surrounding world is certainly not accidental. The overarching theme in this film is the experience of displacement, the condition of being away from home. Born in Belgium, Akerman lived in New York City in the early seventies. Every store and street corner in her film becomes the embodiment of her separation from home and family. Reinforcing this overall impression is a voiceover narration in which the filmmaker reads letters from her mother. At first, the narration seems unrelated to the settings. But we soon realize that they refer to the same experience; they both evoke the feeling of being a foreigner.

Akerman's views of New York recall Siegfried Kracauer's notion of the street as "a center of fleeting impressions," "a region where the accidental prevails over the providential" (62). The locations in *News from Home* are such places: they are sites of chance occurrences and haphazard events. Akerman depicts them as they are, and the authenticity of the settings gives credibility to her representation of the referential world. But Akerman also shows us that settings are more than physical spaces, and that acknowledging their material existence does not fully account for their role in the process of representation. By exploring their banality, their lack of distinctiveness, Akerman manages, paradoxically, to endow them with a unique expressive quality.

Lighting

Like the setting, lighting may help characterize the profilmic situation by literally giving shape to the world depicted in the film. Moreover, the differences between actual sites and constructed sets find parallels in the distinctions between natural and artificial lighting. Because natural lighting seems to escape the control of the filmmaker, we tend to overlook its significance in the filming process. Controlled or artificial lighting, on the other hand, indicates that a particular environment has been altered or created specifically for the purposes of the film. Much like a constructed set, it underscores the filmmaker's intervention in the world of lived experience.

The analogy between nonfictional settings and the way lighting is used in documentaries, of course, has some limitations. Artificial sources sometimes simulate natural conditions. And that, in turn, can make it hard for viewers to tell whether or not they are looking at a controlled environment. Even though we can make a similar argument in relation to constructed sets—which may stand for an actual location—the implications are different in each case. Because the setting is normally perceived as part of the documentary's subject matter, mistaking a constructed set for an actual site can jeopardize the credibility of the film. This is less likely to happen when we confuse artificial and natural sources of lighting, since neither has an ontological status comparable to that of nonfictional settings.

Overall, though, the choice of lighting says a great deal about the way filmmakers use their settings.

Documentary makers may combine different types of lighting for technical reasons. Having abundant natural light at one's disposal, for instance, does not exclude the use of artificial sources, which can simplify the shooting process by making the profilmic situation more predictable. And a certain level of control over the lighting conditions may in fact be necessary in order to create a "natural" look. An otherwise important object, for example, can lose its distinctiveness against a background that offers little contrast, as Rudolf Arnheim taught us over half a century ago (15–16). When this happens, filmmakers may use artificial lighting precisely to render the object photographed more easily recognizable. Because an image is never really a replica of the real thing, relying on natural sources alone does not automatically secure the verisimilitude of the representation.

Lighting can affect our perception of the profilmic event in myriad ways. It may underline the role of a particular element in the setting or, conversely, downplay its relevance. It can also define the mood of a scene or give character to a particular locale. Documentaries regularly juxtapose images shot in unrelated sites, and the way the settings are lit helps distinguish one from another. In *The 11th Hour* (Leila Conners Petersen and Nadia Conners, 2007), for instance, the filmmakers interview writers, journalists, and activists about current threats against the environment. The interviews are conducted in a studio and have an orderly, almost ceremonial quality. Appropriately, the lighting—the conventional three-point technique that many fiction films use, contouring the figure and separating it from the background—matches the overall formality of the situation, differentiating it from the environmental catastrophes depicted elsewhere in the film.

Similarly, in *Man on Wire* changes in lighting technique and style help separate reenactments from original events. The documentary relies on a variety of materials—interviews, still photographs, footage shot by other filmmakers—in order to revisit Philippe Petit's 1974 high-wire walk between New York's Twin Towers. But the reenactments of the clandestine preparations inside one of the buildings stand out from the rest. Director James Marsh opts for a kind of lighting that accentuates the contrast between bright and dark areas within the frame, a stylistic choice that is further emphasized by the use of black-and-white photography. The resulting scenes look eerily contrived, unlike other situations included in *Man on Wire*. Lighting functions as a way of encoding a specific message. In this context, it informs us about the nature of the scenes we are watching.

Marsh's lighting style serves yet another purpose in these scenes. It produces an ambience that boosts our interest in the story events. *Man on Wire* is a sort of heist movie, as the filmmaker himself has claimed publicly, and the peculiar, unnatural atmosphere of the reenactments brings a suspenseful and at times comical note to Petit's adventure. Marsh gives us only a partial rendition of Petit's preparations, the action itself often alluded to but not always depicted in the film. To a large extent, it is the atmosphere created by the contrasts between dark and bright areas that secures the dramatic effect produced here. In the absence of a full reenactment, the lighting style seems to make up for what we cannot see.

The other settings in the film are lit in a clearly different manner, and the result also differs from what we find in the reenacted scenes. Exterior shots, often taken from footage of Petit and his entourage shot earlier, tend to rely on natural sources, which, as expected, encourage us to believe that we are looking at uncontrolled environments. The film's studio interviews, by contrast, appear studied and artificial, with soft shadows that add volume to the interviewees' faces and produce a calm ambience reminiscent of a formal portrait. Even though the interviews utilize artificial sources of light, they never aim at creating the dramatic impact of the reenactments.

Nonfictional Performances

Man on Wire impresses not only because of its reenactments but also thanks to the lively, intense testimonies recorded by the filmmaker. The people in the profilmic space share with us both their experiences and their perspective on the events that took place in 1974. These responses to the filming process are different from the acts performed in the reconstructed scenes, but they are no less relevant as examples of performance in documentary.

Performance is a notoriously complicated issue for documentary scholarship because the idea of *acting* is often associated with artifice and pretense, attributes that seem more suitable to fantasy and entertainment genres than to serious representations of the historical world. Performing, however, is by no means foreign to nonfictional representation. In fact, it has a long history in documentary cinema. *Nanook of the North*, for example, includes deliberate acts from its protagonist, who literally collaborated with Flaherty in (re)creating the situations depicted in the film. Reenacted scenes in *Night Mail* and other documentaries from the first half of the twentieth century also involve performances from the people in front of the camera. And the rich exchanges between the filmmakers and the documentary subjects in a film like *Chronicle of a Summer*, discussed in chapter 4, can be described as performances as well. The idea that the subject might be putting on

an act for the camera does seem to contradict the promise of unobtrusive shooting taken up by direct cinema filmmakers in the 1960s. But that attitude has had
limited reverberations beyond its specific context. Moreover, as we shall see in
our discussion of *Don't Look Back* (a prominent direct cinema documentary),
nonfiction subjects may be performing even when they do not explicitly address
the camera. Every time they respond to the filming process, the subjects engage
in some kind of performance, even if all that is involved in this performance is the
act of "playing oneself" (Waugh 66–74).

Bill Nichols has used the term "social actors" to designate the subjects who
appear as themselves in documentary films ("The Documentary Film and Principles of Exposition" 184). Social actors are players who, by virtue of their existence in the historical world, permit some form of access to the events and situations represented. The mail sorters in *Night Mail* are social actors. They portray
themselves performing their real job. More than just providing "material" for the
documentary, social actors participate in the filming process, as their lives overlap
in part with the making of the film.

Some filmmakers take a less orthodox approach to documentary acting. They
cast performers—professional or not—to play roles that are unrelated, or only
partly related, to their actual lives. This is often the case with films that depend
heavily on staged material, as we saw in *Far from Poland*. It is also the case in films
such as *Jaguar* (1954–1967) and *I, a Black Man/ Moi, un noir* (1958), both made
by Jean Rouch, in which the players assume semi-fictional roles in order to address general aspects of ordinary life in western Africa during the 1950s. Because
the overlap between the players' lives and their roles is not as obvious in these
examples, the connection with the historical world may also take a more subtle,
oblique, or complicated form.

Most documentaries discussed in this book, however, feature individual subjects who play themselves—people who lend not only their faces and bodies but
also their histories, opinions, and experiences to the making of nonfiction films.
The dual status of these subjects, at the same time actual referents and discursive agents, is what makes them worthy of attention. Here we shall refer to them
not only as social actors—borrowing Nichols's term—but also as "nonfictional
performers." And we use the phrase "nonfictional performance" to identify their
contribution to the making of the film.

In João Moreira Salles's *Santiago* (2007), an elderly man plays himself for
the camera and agrees to answer a series of questions posed by the filmmaker.
Interviewed in his small apartment in Rio de Janeiro, Santiago Badariotti Merlo,
the colorful subject after whom the film is named, speaks eloquently about his

life in Argentina, Italy, and Brazil, about the time when he worked as a butler for the filmmaker's family, and, above all, about his lasting devotion to researching the history of the world's nobility. A fascinatingly complicated character, he is an ideal subject for a portrait film. But it is his active engagement with the camera—his performance—that accounts for the power of his screen presence. Santiago knows that he is being filmed and reacts accordingly.

In still another respect the documentary stands out as a character study and an example of the significance of nonfictional performance. While interviewing Santiago, Salles tries not just to delve into the "character's" personality but also to explore the relationship between the filmmaker and the subject in front of the camera. As the director put it, this is "a film about an encounter, my encounter with a character" (in Dieleke and Nouzeilles 143).

Salles shot the interviews in the early 1990s, but the film was only completed more than a decade later, a few years after Santiago's death. The finished documentary provokes the audience to reflect upon Salles's dialogue with his former servant, to mull over the filmmaker's directorial interventions, and to examine Santiago's part in the film. We can hear it, for example, when Salles asks Santiago to repeat his stories and deliver the same lines again and again. What might have elsewhere looked like a "clean" and straightforward interview appears here as a laborious negotiation between filmmaker and performer. As a result, we take Santiago's screen appearance for what it is: a conscious act staged for the camera. And we think of the shooting process as a series of exchanges in which we hear the voices of both the filmmaker and his subject.

Not all performances look like Santiago's, though. Interviews and personal testimonies offer recognizable examples of nonfictional performance because we quickly understand that the documentary subject is responding to the presence of the filmmaker and the camera. But oftentimes this interaction is veiled by the performance style itself. Nonfictional subjects may consent to being filmed without overtly acknowledging the camera. When this happens, the action recorded appears as if it had nothing to do with the making of the documentary. That's what the phrase "acting naturally" usually implies.

Thomas Waugh has drawn on the notions of "presentational" and "representational" performances to distinguish between these two types of response to the filming process (68). Presentational performances are those in which the interactions between the subject and the filmmaker are apparent in the subject's poses, gestures, or speeches. As Waugh explains, the subjects reveal their awareness of the camera. This is evident with Santiago, but also happens in more traditional documentary interviews. Representational performances, on the other hand, tend to give the impression that the subject is oblivious to the filmmaker's presence, or that the camera did not interfere in life's ordinary events. In *Nanook of the North*, the subjects rarely address the camera directly. Yet we know that their actions were planned and executed for the sake of the film. Representational performances invite us to believe that we are looking at a world untouched by the filmmaker, when that is not the case at all. They emulate both the casualness of ordinary life and the codes of fiction cinema. And the "message" seems to be conveyed effortlessly, as if no one were trying to impose it on the audience. Representational performances depend less on the promise of assertiveness than on the impression of slackened control, of spontaneity.

9.4. Bob Dylan displays an awareness of the camera in the pre-title sequence of *Don't Look Back* (D. A. Pennebaker, 1967).

A useful example of the differences between presentational and representational performances can be found in D. A. Pennebaker's *Don't Look Back* (1967), a documentary filmed during Bob Dylan's 1965 concert tour of the United Kingdom. In the pre-title segment, a single shot of over two minutes, we see the singer in an alley holding up handwritten cards displaying the lyrics of the song "Subterranean Homesick Blues," which is playing on the sound track. Dylan stands at the right of the frame, in a medium long shot, and alternates between glancing at the camera and looking at the cards, which he drops one by one as the song continues. We know that Dylan is putting on an act because of his presentational style. The segment, which was his own idea, self-consciously and playfully mocks his reputation for unintelligible lyrics in his concert and record performances.

9.5. Representational performance style in *Don't Look Back* (D. A. Pennebaker, 1967).

In most other scenes, however, the camera seems to observe him unnoticed. We watch Dylan sing and play guitar in his hotel room, read the newspaper and use a typewriter, argue with a journalist and chat with various interlocutors. The focus is on ordinary actions that may have little significance by themselves but which together give us insight into the behavior and personality of the documentary subject. Pennebaker's observational approach would seem to favor these unstudied moments. Yet, even in these ostensibly spontaneous situations, the closeness between Dylan and the camera—in cars, backstage, or hotel rooms—makes it hard for us to believe that he is not directly engaging in the filming process. Furthermore, Dylan's behavior in these private moments conforms to his public image in such a way that we wonder if he is not inspired by the camera. Dylan seems to be playing a role, enacting his persona through much of the film. But in lieu of the presentational assertiveness we saw in the pre-title segment, we have the apparent spontaneity of a representational performance.

Interviews and Performance

Interviews often appear as ritualized, artificial "events." Most are staged proceedings with a clearly defined presentational quality, in which the filmmaker solicits responses from a performing subject and, to a certain extent, directs the scene that takes place in front of the camera. Documentary makers, not surprisingly, tend to choose their interviewees based not only on their representativeness and credibility but also on their charm, their capacity to perform. We saw the care that Connie Field took in casting *The Life and Times of Rosie the Riveter.*

At their most formal, interviews do seem stylistically predictable and aesthetically repetitive. The exchanges between the filmmakers and their subjects are molded into easily recognizable patterns that privilege the screen presence of the interviewees (frequently alone in the frame) but limit their performances to established norms. In these cases, the subject's talk follows a conventional model and the pose struck for the camera is restrained by the specifics of the interview situation. As Nichols explains, "The common interview normally requires subjects to provide a frontal view of themselves and generally discipline their bodies to oblige the camera's requirements regarding depth of field and angle of view" (*Representing Reality* 53). In addition to simply meeting a technical obligation, this traditional format serves in fact to reinforce the seriousness of nonfiction film discourse, thus helping legitimize the interviewee's testimony.

There are examples, however, in which the interview can be more than a tool for gathering information or recording testimonies from authorized informants. In Eduardo Coutinho's *The End and the Beginning/O fim e o princípio* (2005), the predictability of the encounter described above gives way to exchanges that exceed the normative function of the documentary interview and contradict the customary stiffness of the subject in front of the camera. Most of the subjects in *The End and the Beginning* are senior citizens from a rural community in the *sertão*, the arid lands in the northeast of Brazil, who speak generously about their past, their families, and their feelings for each other. More conversational than inquisitorial, the filmmaker and his crew, including Rosa, a young woman from the area who acts as a liaison, spent a few weeks visiting the community: sitting on the veranda of a house with multiple generations chatting about their way of life; talking with an elderly woman in a rocking chair who flings her arms around, gestures wildly, and yells at Coutinho when he doesn't understand her; or listening to a bare-chested man with few teeth who leans out a window and covers half his face with his elegant, worn, long-fingered hands. There are sometimes several people in the shot, talking, listening, and reacting to what is being said. But sometimes the interviewee is alone, the younger generation having left the *sertão*. We observe Coutinho consulting with Rosa; we observe the still photographer wandering around in the background; we observe informants acknowledging the camera and filmmakers; and we observe Rosa explaining what they are doing. The interviewees interact freely with the crew and with each other. And the dialogical nature of these encounters is key to how the documentary communicates with the audience.

Because of this conversational approach to the interview process, *The End and the Beginning* offers an opportunity to look not only at the interviewees' lives but also at their social and cultural milieu. Many of the interactions between the filmmaker and his subjects seem to go on for "too long," stretching the temporal boundaries of the interview format and allowing us time for a close look at the world surrounding the interviewees. Coutinho shot all his scenes on location. More precisely, he chose to meet his subjects in their homes and ranches, interrupting them in their daily activities, showing us both where they live and how they live. Even though class and cultural background are not always addressed in these conversations, the lengthy exchanges with the camera clearly reveal that these are people of modest means, accustomed to hardship, and attached to their traditional culture and religion. As an entry point to the sociohistorical world, the interviews end up connecting setting and performance, helping to define a collective identity for these profilmic subjects.

Giving the interviewees a chance to speak their minds freely also increases their contribution to the making of the documentary. It expands the significance of their performances, allowing them greater control over their screen acts. This is important because their credibility and status in the film depend partly on how they appear before the audience. Documentary subjects can use the interview situation as a means of fashioning their public images. Most commonly, they rely on speech and behavior to do that. But self-presentation can also include elements that we normally associate with fictional *mise-en-scène*, such as the way the subjects have dressed and coiffed themselves, and perhaps even applied makeup.

Let's look again at Shirley Clarke's 1967 *Portrait of Jason*, a documentary in which the act of self-presentation helps establish both the player's identity and his contribution to the making of the film. Focusing on one single subject, an African American gay man who calls himself Jason Holiday, Clarke's documentary has little to show other than the encounter between that subject and the camera. Jason sees the profilmic space as a sort of stage from where he can address an imaginary audience, using the film as an opportunity to interfere in the way he might be perceived by the public.

Already in the first minutes of the film, we realize that Jason is indeed putting on an act. Dressed in a dark jacket and a light shirt that befit Clarke's black-and-white photography, and wearing a pair of horn-rimmed glasses that give him a vaguely studious appearance, he delivers a performance that combines anecdotes, personal recollections, and role-playing—all in a conversational tone that strikes us as reminiscent of standup comedy. We hear about his bohemian life style, his stints as a houseboy and prostitute, and his troubled relationships with his friends. We also learn something about class differences, race relations, and sexual discrimination in 1960s America. Throughout the film, Jason comes across as adventurous, unconventional, and carefree. Moreover, he appears articulate, witty, and acutely aware of his status as a minority subject. All this is, of course, conveyed to us through his performance: his flamboyant demeanor, his lengthy and humorous speeches, his ironic comments, his histrionic gestures, and so on. In his interactions with the camera, Jason manages to (re)invent himself as a character, thus determining, in part at least, how we should get to know him.

The prominence of Jason's performance is explicitly acknowledged toward the end of the film, when Clarke tries to look beyond the surface of his act. It is as if, at that point, she had decided that his performance compromised the credibility of her documentary. "Did you ever do anything really bad?" she asks offscreen, suggesting that Jason may be hiding one secret or two. Clarke's intervention is soon followed by questions from a second offscreen interlocutor, who appears just as determined to lift Jason's "mask." For a brief moment, they seem to succeed as Jason's attitude changes from self-confident to emotionally distraught. Clearly upset, he breaks into tears, his transfigured face captured in a lengthy and merciless close-up.

This episode recalls the suspicion that acting is anathema to documentary representation. Can we trust Jason's previous act? Judging from this particular scene, the answer might be no. There is more to this brief exchange, though, than a move to secure the authenticity of the profilmic situation. Behind the attempt to strip Jason of his performance is an effort to take charge of what happens in front of the camera, a shift toward redefining the terms by which the documentary subject appears on the screen. As Lauren Rabinovitz asks, is it Clarke or Holiday who controls the profilmic (137)?

Dismissing the notion of performance as a threat to documentary authenticity may be a frustrating project because we cannot always draw a clear line between performance and ordinary behavior. Jason himself never fully disengages from the filming process and seems to connect with the camera even in his most vulnerable moments. But the most compelling reason to embrace the role of social actors may simply be that nonfictional players can wrest some of the authority normally held by the filmmaker. This was the case with Miyuki Takeda in *Extreme Private Eros: Love Song 1974*, as we saw in chapter 3. It is one of Jason Holiday's most remarkable achievements as well. Clarke's encounter with her subject does recall the popular belief that acting is synonymous with pretense. But ultimately her film takes us beyond this faulty equation, placing the notions of performance and self-presentation at the center of the exchanges between the documentary subject and the filmmaker.

The Filmmaker as Performer

What happens, though, when the performance staged for the camera overlaps with the act of filming, or when the documentarians themselves appear as performers? How do we relate to documentaries in which the filmmakers play themselves to the audience? And how does that change our understanding of the profilmic situation?

One way a filmmaker-performer can intercede in the protocols of documentary filmmaking is by drawing attention to the subjective and partial nature of that process. Think, for example, of the role played by Ruth Ozeki Lounsbury in *Halving the Bones*, which we discussed in the first chapter. The granddaughter of Japanese immigrants, Lounsbury uses her film as an opportunity to revisit her family's history. Yet *Halving the Bones* is no ordinary family album. The focus here is as much on her ancestors as on the filmmaker herself. We see Lounsbury on the screen and listen to her voiceover narration as she examines family photographs, interviews her mother, or reminisces about her grandmother's personality. Being part of the family, Lounsbury is, of course, a natural subject for her film. But it is her role as storyteller and filmmaker that stands out in *Halving the Bones*. Lounsbury reminds us that filmmakers are individuals with particular histories, interests, and aspirations, and that the making of a documentary may involve not only material evidence but also personal relationships.

Because they expose the role of the filmmaker—the agent who normally hides behind the camera or sound apparatus—documentaries that feature filmmaker-performers tend to have a strong reflexive component. But this is a particular kind of reflexive film. We watch the filmmakers as they enact the very process by which knowledge is acquired and made available to the audience. Because of that, we also perceive that knowledge to be contingent upon a particular set of circumstances. Omniscience gives way to a more limited perspective on reality, which finds validation not in the promise of objectivity but in the filmmaker's personal relationship with the subject matter in the film. As Nichols has put it, knowledge is represented as situated rather than omniscient: the "local [takes precedence] over the global, the specific over the general, the concrete over the abstract" ("Embodied Knowledge" 6).

Another way to approach the filmmaker's screen act is to look at how it can revitalize existing documentary techniques. In this case, the outcome of the performance will have less to do with reflexivity and demystification than with the reinvention of nonfiction film conventions. Let's return one last time to another familiar example, the screen performances of filmmaker Michael Moore. In *Roger and Me*, Moore relies on a number of recognizable techniques in order to make his case against the corporate policies that left thousands of workers unemployed in Flint, Michigan. These techniques, however, are so overpowered by his act that we can easily miss the lineage that connects them to traditional documentary practices. As happens in other documentaries, his voiceover narration does serve clearly as an explanatory device. But in *Roger and Me* it also works as a means of constructing a character and enlisting support for the filmmaker's mission: his campaign against General Motors and his efforts to interview the company's then CEO, Roger Smith. "As soon as I could," we hear Moore say while we watch him walk toward the GM building, "I headed down to Detroit, to Roger's office, where I was determined this time to get onto the fourteenth floor." When we can trace their source to a character, as happens in this film, voiceover commentaries sound less official and intimidating than the detached godlike voice of classical documentary.

Similarly, Moore's interviews routinely bypass standard protocols and are best described as interactions in which the filmmaker's role is no less important than the interviewee's. In his conversations with the woman who makes a living selling rabbits for pets or meat, the usual procedure gives way to a seemingly unstructured situation that does as much to build Moore's character as provide information about rabbit raising. "Now *you* know what I'm talkin' about," she tells him, assuring the viewer that Moore has experience with her kind of situation.

By incorporating recognizable conventions to his performance, the filmmaker breathes new life into familiar practices. This, in turn, accounts for the freshness of his films. To paraphrase Paul Arthur, Moore subjects documentary's conventionalized procedures to the appearance of spontaneity and immediacy that we expect from observational films like *Don't Look Back* (128).

The impression of looking at an artless, innocent, spontaneous act is, of course, misleading. Documentary makers work hard at creating their screen roles, and those roles function as mediators between the audience and the sociohistorical world. We may see filmmaker-performers as diligent investigative reporters and committed social activists. Or we may look at them simply as plain ordinary people. Oftentimes these roles coalesce to create a sort of persona, a public image that stands for the maker of the film, in the case of Moore, a slightly overweight fellow in a baseball or trucker cap who couples anti-intellectualism and disrespect for authority with innate wisdom and moral fiber. It is to this image as a pugnacious and populist adventurer, rather than the actual individual behind the making of the documentary, that we normally relate as spectators.

Michael Moore's films may offer the most recognizable example of how a filmmaker's public image can contribute to the process of representation. But Moore is hardly alone in his effort to create a distinctive persona. Nick Broomfield's documentaries of the past two decades, for instance, are similarly centered on the filmmaker's enacted self. As Stella Bruzzi has written, "Nick Broomfield the documentary filmmaker is not synonymous with 'Nick Broomfield' the charming man with Mickey Mouse earphones and boom who extracts information from [the people in his films]" (208). It is, however, this beguiling and apparently imperturbable fellow—Broomfield's enacted self—who helps define the way we look at the subjects and events in his documentaries. In *Tracking Down Maggie* (1994), for example, his persona acts as a foil for the film's elusive subject, former British prime minister Margaret Thatcher. Broomfield follows Thatcher tirelessly from Britain to the United States but never manages to talk to her. As happens in *Roger and Me*, the focus quickly shifts from the film's presumed subject—the prime minister—to the filmmaker's performance, his theatrical efforts to interview her. Broomfield comes across as a well-meaning, earnest, and politically conscious (if also somewhat naïve) individual, while Thatcher appears as an arrogant, coldhearted, and untrustworthy politician.

The presence of the filmmaker as public figure, performer, or entertainer has become common enough to suggest the emergence of a subgenre in contemporary nonfiction cinema. Michael Chanan speaks about "a mode of political reportage in which the filmmaker's personality invades the film," usually adopting "a satirical and ironic stance." Some of these films seem to parody the figure of the television reporter, offering an alternative to mainstream news presentation (12–13). But even at its most satirical or self-deprecating, the screen presence of the filmmaker continues to lure us with a promise of reassurance. While they make no claims to objectivity, these films satisfy our desire for certainty by giving us, in lieu of carefully constructed arguments, the familiar presence of legitimate and trustworthy characters.

In this context, a documentary like Tony Buba's *Lightning Over Braddock: A Rust Bowl Fantasy* (1988) stands out precisely because it challenges this promise of reassurance. *Lightning Over Braddock* couples the interest in forging a screen persona with a more reflexive attitude on the part of the filmmaker. Like Michael Moore, Buba comes from a working-class family. And like *Roger and Me*, *Lightning Over Braddock* deals with the unemployment caused by plant closings in the filmmaker's hometown (Braddock, Pennsylvania), as well as the unresponsiveness of large corporations to the lives of the workers. Buba's humor, like Moore's, engages the viewer. But Buba also encourages us to reflect upon the nature and suppositions of documentary representation. His character's critical wariness calls into question the stability of the filmmaker's persona and interrogates the adequacy of documentary's potential to capture lived reality.

Lightning Over Braddock is a more complex film than the examples discussed earlier as it combines seemingly disparate materials such as footage of Braddock's abandoned steel mills, testimonies of steelworkers, television news, comic fantasy scenes, and clips from Buba's earlier independent shorts. At the center of this multifaceted approach to the historical world is, once again, the filmmaker's performance. Buba's screen act reveals a disarmingly complicated character. He plays himself not only as a local celebrity but also as a self-doubting independent filmmaker. He mentions, for example, that he has made his mark chronicling the demise of Braddock's steel industry: "[A]s Braddock . . . declined, my fortunes increased. Dying mill towns are a hot media subject. My exposure on TV was directly proportional to the number of layoffs." He wonders if his films are doing any good; he worries about offending potential funders at a party; and when Sweet Sal, a small-time hoodlum who appeared in several of Buba's previous works, quits with the film only three-quarters finished, Buba admits that not only does he no longer have a lead, with several more sequences left to film, but he is also out of grant money. Finally, in one of *Lightning Over Braddock*'s most memorable scenes, Buba appears before a fake priest and, in a mock confession, admits that he doesn't want to make social documentaries anymore. Instead, he wants to make a Hollywood musical.

In lieu of a reassuring performance, what we have is an act that fails to create a fully coherent or unambiguous subject. Even if that act invites parallels with the performances of celebrity documentarians like Michael Moore, Buba's persona calls for a different kind of relationship with the audience. Like other reflexive documentaries, *Lightning Over Braddock* uses the filmmaker's voiceover and screen appearance as a way of interrogating both the filmmaker's status and the role of documentary cinema in general. Whereas Michael Moore relies on humor and irony to make fun of authority, never questioning his own, Tony Buba's more distanced and sardonic approach takes apart and examines the issue of authority, where its power comes from, and how it is related to the viewing audience.

Different as they may be, these screen acts underline some of the key points in this chapter. They help us think of what happens in front of the camera as part of the processes through which nonfiction films speak to us. In the next chapter, we continue to examine the means by which documentaries speak to their audiences, this time (quite literally) by discussing the use of sound in nonfiction filmmaking.

Additional Filmography

Farrebique (Georges Rouquier, 1946)

The Sorrow and the Pity/Le chagrin et la pitié (Marcel Ophüls, 1970)

Sherman's March (Ross McElwee, 1986)

Broken Noses (Bruce Weber, 1987)

Super Size Me (Morgan Spurlock, 2003)

The Blonds/Los rubios (Albertina Carri, 2003)

Tarnation (Jonathan Caouette, 2003)

Encounters at the End of the World (Werner Herzog, 2007)

Works Cited and Further Reading

Arnheim, Rudolf. *Film as Art.* Berkeley: University of California Press, 1957.

Arthur, Paul. "Jargons of Authenticity (Three American Moments)." In *Theorizing Documentary*, ed. Michael Renov. New York: Routledge, 1993.

Beattie, Keith. *Documentary Display: Re-viewing Nonfiction Film and Video.* London: Wallflower, 2008.

Bordwell, David, and Kristin Thompson. *Film Art: An Introduction.* 8th ed. New York: McGraw-Hill, 2008.

Bruzzi, Stella. *New Documentary.* 2nd ed. New York: Routledge, 2006.

Chanan, Michael. *The Politics of Documentary.* London: British Film Institute, 2007.

Corner, John. "Television, Documentary and the Category of the Aesthetic." *Screen* 44.1 (Spring 2003).

Dieleke, Edgardo, and Gabriela Nouzeilles. "The Spiral of the Snail: Searching for the Documentary, an Interview with João Moreira Salles." *Journal of Latin American Cultural Studies* 17.2 (August 2008).

Kracauer, Siegfried. *Theory of Film: The Redemption of Physical Reality.* Oxford: Oxford University Press, 1960.

Leacock, Richard. "For an Uncontrolled Cinema." *Film Culture* 22–23 (Summer 1961).

MacDonald, Scott. "Jill Godmilow (and Harun Farocki)." In *A Critical Cinema 4: Interviews with Independent Filmmakers.* Berkeley: University of California Press, 2005.

Margulies, Ivone. *Nothing Happens: Chantal Akerman's Hyperrealist Everyday.* Durham, N.C.: Duke University Press, 1996.

Nichols, Bill. "The Documentary Film and Principles of Exposition." In *Ideology and the Image: Social Representation in the Cinema and Other Media.* Bloomington: Indiana University Press, 1981.

———. "Embodied Knowledge and the Politics of Location: An Evocation." In *Blurred Boundaries: Questions of Meaning in Contemporary Culture.* Bloomington: Indiana University Press, 1994.

———. "'Getting to Know You . . .': Knowledge, Power, and the Body." In *Theorizing Documentary*, ed. Michael Renov. New York: Routledge, 1993.

———. *Representing Reality: Issues and Concepts in Documentary.* Bloomington: Indiana University Press, 1991.

Pramaggiore, Maria, and Tom Wallis. *Film: A Critical Introduction.* 2nd ed. Boston: Pearson, 2008.

Rabinovitz, Lauren. "Shirley Clarke and the Expansion of American Independent Cinema." In *Points of Resistance: Women, Power, and Politics in the New York Avant-garde Cinema, 1943–71.* Urbana: University of Illinois Press, 1991.

Rosenstone, Robert A. "Revisioning History: Contemporary Filmmakers and the Construction of the Past." *Comparative Studies in Society and History* 32.4 (October 1990).

Waugh, Thomas. "'Acting to Play Oneself': Notes on Performance in Documentary." In *Making Visible the Invisible: An Anthology of Original Essays on Film Acting,* ed. Carole Zucker. Metuchen, N.J.: Scarecrow Press, 1990.

Winston, Brian. *Claiming the Real II: Documentary: Grierson and Beyond.* London: British Film Institute; New York: Palgrave Macmillan, 2008.

10

Sounds

Coauthored with Carl Lewis

S ound! We have looked at several films made in the silent period. Few of them, of course, were shown without sound; some early films were presented by lecturers and many were accompanied by live music. But for a long time now recorded sound has been a major part of documentaries—especially the information conveyed through voiceover commentary and interviews. Words often link together the images and carry much of the argument. Speech, however, is only part of the way that documentaries use sound. They also frequently use music, effects, and ambient sound (the background noises that emanate from the world pictured). Think again of *The River*. The voiceover commentary imposes a particular form of organization on seemingly scattered visual material. The music does, too. And so does the sound of the factory whistles and the flood warning horns. It is the combination of visual, verbal, and sonic discourses that shapes the film into the story about the Mississippi.

We have already discussed how *Night Mail's* carriage interiors were built on a set for adequate space and light, with workers re-creating their nightly routines. As in *The River*, the crew also had to shoot silent and add the sound afterward. But this was not a disadvantage. In fact, under Alberto Cavalcanti's sound direction, the simple story of an overnight postal train is crafted into a complex assemblage of speech, music, noises, and poetry.

Over brief opening credits, trumpet fanfares jolt the viewer to attention. The short musical excerpt quickly establishes what is to come. Agitated, repeated ascending notes suggest a forward, climbing and repetitive motion. And indeed, much of the film illustrates movement, speed, and urgency with shots of the train wheels churning round and round, the sound of train whistles, rattling tracks, hissing steam, the clang of metal, the thump of leather mail pouches, and the whoosh of the wind created by the train's velocity.

The musical score quickly disappears from the film, not returning until the closing sequence. A voiceover, an invisible male voice with a carefully constructed nondescript professional quality, speaking in short sentences, explains the technical aspects of the traveling post office, its route, functions, and mechanisms. Sometimes it gives details of what is in the images; at other times it gives information that is not available visually. There are also snatches of overheard conversations. Conversations of the English and Scottish workers were recorded separately and then carefully matched with the location shooting. And then at the end, we hear a poem written for the film by W. H. Auden together with music composed for the film by Benjamin Britten. It is only after the story has been told—when we have learned everything the filmmakers want us to learn about the night mail delivery system—that we are escorted back into the world of "artificial" sound. As we see a long shot of the train traveling through the Scottish countryside, the rhythmic percussive sound, almost a repetition of the rumbling and clanging we have heard at other points in the film, commences. The recitation also begins rhythmically, with a strong 4/4 meter:

> This is the Night Mail crossing the border,
> Bringing the cheque and the postal order,
> Letters for the rich, letters for the poor,
> The shop at the corner and the girl next door.
> Pulling up Beattock, a steady climb:
> The gradient's against her, but she's on time.

The poem is not sung or spoken, but intoned on a single vocal note. It doubly emphasizes the strong meter of this part of the score, the voice functioning as the lead instrument over the orchestra, a vocal punctuation to the beat that the orchestra is accentuating. The voice then drops out for another repetition of the relentless orchestral rhythm, reentering with a slightly more insistent tonal quality as the poem honoring—almost eulogizing—the night mail service continues.

Suddenly, the mood of the music changes, and trumpets, like the ones heard at the start of the film, are heard again in a similar fanfare. Wind instruments reintroduce the agitated music previously played and aurally paint a rushing sensation.

There is a slight ethereal quality to this short section of the score, and the words of the text seem to take on more importance than the meter previously established. The rhythm then returns to prominence, and as the train finally begins to reduce speed and pull into the station that is its final destination, the trumpet fanfare sounds five times before the rhythm slows, simultaneously recalling our attention and signifying that the journey is ending. The final sequence of the film does not serve to advance the "story" as much as it canonizes the story already told. The carefully explicated account of how the mail is transported is now virtually enshrined as a ritual important to us all.

Night Mail uses a variety of sounds: words, music, and effects. This complex arrangement of sounds plays a role that exceeds the need to simply record and transmit information aurally. Like all other formal aspects in a documentary, sound helps shape the spectator's experience. *Night Mail* does not merely teach us about the British postal service; it exalts its efficacy as a *public* service. It does so by exploring rhythmic elements that, as we noted earlier, evoke the notions of speed and recurrence. Even a seemingly straightforward feature such as a voice-over narration, which is common to many other documentaries, deserves attention beyond the strict level of content information. (We may think, for example, of the timbre of the voice, the volume and rhythm of the speech, as well as its accents and inflections.)

In this final chapter, we are concerned with how sound serves as a resource for documentary film and video makers. And we will be discussing not only voice-overs but also speech in interviews, the role of music in nonfiction films, and, briefly, the way documentaries deal with ambient noises and sound effects.

Direct and Prerecorded Sound

Before we pay closer attention to these different forms of sound, though, we need to consider an important distinction. As happens in any other kind of film, the sound in a documentary can be directly recorded on location or edited into the film after the shooting. Sound recorded on location normally carries a special type of authority. We think of it as evidential material, a trace of the physical world captured by the microphone. What we hear is what was there to be heard at the moment of recording. Sound that comes from a different source, on the other hand, is indicative of the creative intervention of the filmmaker. It draws our attention not to the event recorded but to the way that event is shaped through the filmmaking process.

In practice, this distinction can get fuzzy since sound recorded on location can be easily manipulated, and sound added later can be matched so that it appears to come from the documentary space. But the distinction has both historical and critical relevance, and it allows us to better understand different approaches to documentary filmmaking.

The recording technologies available to Cavalcanti in 1936 did not hinder *Night Mail*'s creativity or expression. But the apparatus was cumbersome. This changed soon after World War II, with the popularization of the new recording technology—lightweight 16mm cameras capable of shooting in synchronization with portable tape recorders—that we read about in chapter 8. With the technological means for synchronous sound recording on location, filmmakers were excited about the idea that this less intrusive type of filmmaking would make it possible to observe things *as* they were happening. With no need for staging or re-creation, or post-dubbing, which were common in 35mm films like *Night Mail*, the new equipment seemed to ensure a greater fidelity to the aural pandemonium of the real world, even if the less than optimal conditions that sometimes come with minimal control over the profilmic produced a certain lack of clarity on the sound track. Keeping with the idea of "pure observation," many of the films made in the United States in the early 1960s use little explanatory voiceover commentary or added music, but exude a lavish mixture of everyday sounds— especially talk. Observational filmmakers felt that to record speech live was to discover something about the way people really were. Richard Leacock, one of the camera operators on Drew Associates' 1963 *Crisis: Behind a Presidential Commitment*, stated in an interview soon after the film was made, "The only way you can [capture life as it really is] with human beings is to record the way they communicate, that is, talking" (246). People have their own manners of expressing themselves. Indeed, we hear a wide diversity of idioms and inflections in *Crisis*, as well as in the conversational passages of Frederick Wiseman's 1967 *Titicut Follies*, another film recorded with synchronized sound. We also hear differing volumes, tones, and pitches. Conversations trail off or digress. People interrupt each other and speak at the same time. The sound is sometimes muddled. This is spoken language in all its richness, recorded as it happens.

This same type of equipment, lightweight camera and synchronous sound recording, allowed National Film Board of Canada directors Wolf Koenig and Roman Kroitor to follow Canadian teen idol Paul Anka on a tour of New York and New Jersey. *Lonely Boy* (1962) begins with traveling shots of roadside billboards announcing Anka's Atlantic City Steel Pier concerts. The song "Lonely Boy" plays as background music on the track. The end of the song coincides with a cut to

Anka finishing the ballad on stage. The film includes many of the singer's most popular tunes, both performed in concert and overlaying other scenes. But, more than his music, it is really the vocal interactions between Anka and his fans, his manager, his support personnel, and a nightclub owner that most interest Koenig and Kroitor.

In contrast with the principles of U.S. observational cinema that we read about in chapter 3, some of these interactions also involve the crew. The filmmakers are not really unobtrusive and certainly not invisible. At one point, for example, Anka enters his dressing room, briefly glances at the camera, and comments, "Oh fellows, of all days to do this. . . ." Shortly afterward, when a still photographer asks if he is in the way, the singer tells him not to pay attention to the men and their equipment: "Just forget they are even there." In a nightclub, the crew is asked if they would like to have the waiters circulate a bit. Later, Anka holds up a portrait of himself so the camera can record it. And an offscreen voice asks for a kiss to be repeated because the camera moved during the first one. All this is included in the release print. It is as if the fact that the filmmakers are not inconspicuous was an important part of the truth-telling process. They do listen in on Anka's seemingly unrehearsed exchanges with Irvin Feld, his manager, and with Jules Podell, owner of the Copacabana. Most importantly, they record apparently spur-of-the-moment exchanges with his unnamed young female fans. But they also ask Anka and his manager questions and document their answers.

Although these vocal interactions seem more revealing than the concerts, there is one performance in which the use of sound is noteworthy. Toward the end of the film, at Freedomland Amusement Park, in the middle of "Put Your Head on My Shoulder," we hear Paul Anka crooning and we see close shots of teens screaming. But we do not hear their shrieks. This tangling of action and stillness, this soundlessness, comes as a surprise in a film that has celebrated the possibility of live sound recording. When the sound of the teens drops out, the silence deafens into a roar. The very lack of sound accentuates their rapture. Wolf Koenig, Roman Kroitor, and their sound editor Kathleen Shannon seem to be calling our attention to the interrelation of stardom and fandom. Just as Anka is performing his contractual role for the concert audiences—and the filmmakers—these adoring teens are performing their expected roles as well. The passage suggests that the ecstasy and desire of teenage girls, their admiration and their need to be heard, are not only the performance of femininity, the grand and pleasurable reenactment of stereotypical behavior, as Jane Gaines (arguing from Linda Williams) claims, but also the basis of Paul Anka's stardom (116). And this suggestion is largely accomplished through the manipulation of location recording.

Some documentaries use direct recording to emphasize not speech but ambient sound. Ertuğrul Karslıoğlu's *Sweat and Felt/Keçenin teri* (1988), a documentary on felt rug makers in Şanlıurfa, Turkey, makes good use, for example, of the pounding and grunting of the master and his apprentice as they "cook" the folded felt with their chests in a steam room and beat the nearly finished rug with their hands and feet. We also hear the extraneous noises that fill their world as they pray, lunch, play dominos, release their pigeons, and watch the manufacture of machine-pounded felt. Talking, too, is treated as ambient sound. There are no interviews or voiceover commentary—until the very end of the twenty-four-minute film, when an anonymous voice tells us that the sixty-two-year-old master felt maker now produces his felt by machine and his young aide works in an office. One of the men depicted, however, was still making felt by traditional methods. In Karslıoğlu's portrait of the rug makers, while the men go about their ordinary activities, the microphone, like the camera, observes the supple pulse of daily life. But by limiting the sounds, the filmmaker and his sound team—Erol Yazıcı, Ömer Demirci, Ali Komser, and Yılmaz Karadoğan—amplify them, making audience members aware of their cadences and reverberations, endowing them with special resonance and importance.

Even with the capability to record sound on location, however, documentary makers may choose, instead, to use sound effects. Jalal Toufic's *Saving Face* (2003), taped during the 2000 parliamentary campaign in Lebanon, is a series of head shots, posters of candidates; first huge faces on buildings, then smaller, life-sized ones on walls, then faces being removed from walls, peeled off with a small metal scraper, and finally faces piled up as paper scraps, with one of the men who did the scraping sitting proudly on the heap in front of the near-naked wall. The sound design, by Nadim Mishlawi, includes no music or dialogue. The first sounds we hear seem like natural street noises. Later, as the visuals change to still images of the pentimento of partially peeled faces, the street noises and the sounds of the metal implement and tearing paper turn into an abstract symphony of effects. Noises that sound like the slow click of a single lens reflex camera, then ripping sounds, then voices, laughing, breaking glass, airport noises, crushed cigarette packets, then seemingly ambient street noises again, but this time clearly manipulated, form a waterfall of noise. Cut to the rhythm of the changing images, the lush blend of sounds builds on itself to convey a sense of both familiarity and excess.

Nobody's Business also employs an abundance of sound effects. In this case, however, they are used to underscore the meaning of many scenes. Like the documentary's metaphorical images, some of these noises are key elements of the film's humorous hyperbole. Toward the beginning, as it visually counts down from 8, we hear the ticking of a kitchen timer. When we would have seen "0," instead, we hear the "bing" of the timer as the seconds expire. When the filmmaker, Alan Berliner, and his father argue (and this is frequent), we hear the bell from a boxing ring.

The sound design of Alan Berliner's at once comic and sad portrait of his father is generally consistent: one track, either the sound or image, continues when the other changes. And some changes, frequently when both sound and image change, are signaled by sound effects. Over the image of the numbers mentioned earlier, we hear Oscar Berliner's "testing, one, two, three, testing, one, two, three," then, "How long do you think this is going to take, Alan?" and Alan's reply, "About an hour." At the sound of the bing of the kitchen timer, the image changes to a still photo of Oscar as a young man standing behind a microphone.

Alan Berliner, who worked for several years as a sound editor and archivist, constructs intricate sound and image relationships in *Nobody's Business*. There is a certain amount of disassociation between them, with sounds frequently overlapping images that might not, at first, seem related. But we become accustomed to hearing a sound that we recognize, be it Mr. Berliner's voice, Alan's, ticking, or the "bing" of the kitchen timer, over an image that does not generate that sound. In the sequence when Alan is trying to interest his father in his forebears, Alan reads (in voiceover) a letter his great-grandfather had written to his son, Oscar's father. The images are different scenes from archival footage of turn-of-the-century Eastern European children, then footage of water. At the end of the letter, Alan reads, "You, son of mine, who had been destined to be a great rabbi, was now about to seek his fate in America." Just before he pronounces the word "now," we hear a gong and the image changes from a muted shot of water to a close, low angle shot of the Statue of Liberty in vivid color. The transitions in *Nobody's Business* are smooth, precisely because there is so little synchronization of sound and image.

In contrast, the four opening sequences of Jean-Marie Teno's 1992 *Africa, I Will Fleece You/Afrique, je te plumerai* employ four entirely different sound designs with shocking sound juxtapositions as transitions. The film uses speech, ambient sounds, and music to establish the narrative voice of the documentary and to characterize three different time periods. It opens with a long shot, panning over the rooftops of Yaoundé, the capital of Cameroon. The voiceover commentary, spoken softly, almost nostalgically, in Teno's voice, begins practically immediately, "Yaoundé, cruel city! You stuffed our heads with your official lies. . . . You respond with machine gun fire at your children who shout 'liberty'!" "Yaoundé, cruel city, you inspire shame." The film then changes to a drastically new sequence, and drastically new sounds, the sounds of the violent clash of civilians and the military.

The voiceover stops for a moment. Instead, we hear synchronous sounds, sounds emanating from the visuals, the ambient sound of brutal bloodshed. There is half a minute of grainy color images of fighting taken with a handheld camera and sync sound, and then the voiceover returns, reciting the names of young people killed. Then, again, a new sequence, and once again a dramatic change in historical black-and-white footage of celebrations of the so-called independence of Cameroon in 1960, with upbeat and cheerful pop music from the period, the first music we have heard so far. Children march; adults applaud. "They believed things were changing for the better." But this euphoria is short lived: the commentary, no longer spoken so softly and certainly not nostalgically, introduces Ahmadou Ahidjo, "Father of the Nation," and his long rule of darkness. The fourth segment has no music at all: turmoil again, and again synchronous sounds from the narrative world of violence. We watch color images of more fighting, taken with a handheld camera, and hear the sounds of gunfire, as the voiceover tells us about the reign of Paul Biya, Ahidjo's prime minister for fifteen years: "The apprentice was to surpass the mentor." Then we see and hear a press conference with Biya pronouncing democracy inappropriate for Cameroon, followed by shots of a man killed in a street skirmish. Fade to black. The dedication, "For all those who have died for freedom." And finally the title: *Africa, I Will Fleece You.*

By opening his film with such jarringly different sounds, the filmmaker calls attention to not only the different epochs in Cameroon's history but also to his own interpretation, his own understanding, of that history. His subjective voiceover commentary (far from the "nondescript professional quality" we heard in *Night Mail*) and the ambient sounds of the explosions of social unrest let us know how Jean-Marie Teno feels about the way the people of his country have been exploited, and, as he puts it, about "the soldier's uniform [that] is soiled with children's blood."

From these seven examples you can see that documentaries use a variety of soundscapes, mingling ambient sounds, words, sound effects, music—and often silences. Sometimes documentaries "speak" most eloquently by exploring moments of silence. We have already considered Trinh T. Minh-hà's use of silence as a sound in *Reassemblage.* And we have already considered *Lonely Boy*'s reflexive descent into silence. We have also discussed socially imposed silences, the silence of those who have been excluded, denied a voice. And we can imagine silence as a willing refusal to speak. But sometimes silence is more than the absence of sounds. It can be an anxious moment, or quiet moment, not an omission, but an active space, a space for feeling. In *Four Little Girls*, Denise McNair's father relates a painful incident when his young daughter, while shopping at Kress's department store, wanted a sandwich at their lunch counter. He had to explain to her that she could not eat there because she was black. When asked how the child reacted, Christopher McNair replies firmly, in an extreme close-up, "As if the whole world of betrayal had fallen on her. . . ." The soft background music fades and the camera holds on the father's face for four seconds of unbroken silence. The film does not query Mr. McNair about how he felt about having to make this clear to Denise. What is not said might be, at times, more expressive than what is.

10.1. Christopher McNair silently remembering his daughter Denise. From *4 Little Girls* (Spike Lee, 1997).

Speech

No matter how ingeniously documentaries use silence, ambient sounds, effects, and music, speech is generally the most important way they get their message across. A documentary's words, in interviews and voiceover commentary, can in fact be stronger than the images. In these cases, the images seem to illustrate the verbal argument. Voiceovers, such as those in *The River, Night Mail, Africa, I Will Fleece You,* or *Sweat and Felt,* commonly serve didactic purposes. They communicate information, introduce new concepts, and explain the nature of particular events. But more than simply descriptive or explanatory, voiceover commentaries are assertive. They are formal devices that allow documentary makers to exert authority over the material represented and, concomitantly, over their audiences too.

But how can we describe that authority? Various documentaries use different types of voiceover commentary, different modes of control over information, and have differing relations with the images. Magnus Bärtås and Agence TOPO chose young girls to read the biographical commentary in *Who Is . . . ?,* implicitly calling our attention to the "normal," detached, adult male voice, and the authority, superior knowledge, and dominance that we generally attribute to it. Some documentaries take a more explicitly reflexive approach, acknowledging the fact that the narration is presenting information to the audience. Mindy Faber's first-person voiceover in *Delirium* is an example. It is self-consciously authored, exposing its own constructed nature. By commenting on her own struggles and her own choices, Faber helps us to see that, for her, there can be no real separation between the private, the political, and the historical. The audience is aware that they are getting a well-researched yet personal point of view. Some voiceovers speak with authority about the story's telling, seeming to share inside information. Take Tony Buba's commentary in *Lightning Over Braddock: A Rust Bowl Fantasy*. Highly communicative, friendly, and folksy, it enlightens the spectators about the motivations of the filmmaker and about the progress of the story, every once in a while even seeming to give away secrets. At one point, Buba's voiceover questions the morality of paying $15,000 (three times the average per capita income of a Braddock resident) for the rights to one of the songs he had wanted to include in the film.

Other voiceover commentaries are more omniscient—and often very authoritative. The voiceover in *Prelude to War*, for example, is a disembodied voice, an anonymous third-person voice that appears knowledgeable about the information it presents. Audience members are supposed to take it as instructive commentary, unquestionably reliable and trustworthy. And some voiceovers promulgate authority and subjectify the disembodied voice with the use of a narrator who is a recognized and identifiable authority. Stella Bruzzi points out that the decision to use Harvey Fierstein, a well-known gay writer and actor, with his distinctive gravelly voice, to narrate *The Times of Harvey Milk* (Robert Epstein, 1984), a documentary about the murder of San Francisco's first openly gay man to be voted into office, "immediately makes the film into a statement about gay politics" (53).

If we ponder a variety of documentaries and the way that the voiceover commentary controls the transmission and flow of information in relation to both the story and the audience, it is clear that these approaches are not mutually exclusive. A voiceover can be reflexive about its information, forthcoming about sharing it with the audience, and also seemingly very knowledgeable about what it is commenting on. Sometimes the commentary changes, being tentative at the outset, for instance, and becoming less so as the documentary continues. But most voiceovers, whether personal or impersonal, are written speech, recorded in the studio, closely miked in order to reduce reverberations, intelligible and clear.

In most fiction films, the sound seems to be produced by—and is usually synchronized with—the image. This hierarchy is normally reversed in documentaries with voiceover commentary. The image is frequently subservient to the sound. Sometimes it seems merely a visual accompaniment to the information on the sound track. And sometimes a voiceover is all we have to explain the meaning of the images. We saw it in Chantal Akerman's *News from Home*, that series of nameless images of New York City streets, sidewalks, storefronts, and subways recorded in long takes. On the sound track over the ambient sounds, Akerman reads letters she received from her mother in Belgium describing the family's daily events, along with how much they miss her and regret not hearing from her. The voiceover commentary imposes a certain amount of significance to seemingly uneventful visual material. The intimacy of the letters from home ("My dearest little girl, I am very surprised not to have had any news from you. Your last letter was ten days ago. . . . My darling we think of you a lot and know that all's going well. We only ask one thing, that you don't forget us. Write. Your loving mother.") and Akerman's delivery, blandly read in a detached tone with accented English, or, in the French version, racing through the reading, in near monotone, sometimes drowned out by traffic noises, help us associate the unidentified shots of the streets and subways with the filmmaker's experience as a stranger in New York City. The sentiments of the letters combined with the anonymous images produce a tension between the ardent closeness of family life and the aloof observation.

From time to time, a voiceover vies with the images or contradicts them. Halfway through *My Mother's Place*, Richard Fung's 1990 documentary video, we see a home movie shot a few decades earlier. The grainy 8mm footage shows a prepubescent boy (the video maker himself) hopping from one side of the frame to the other, agitating his arms and legs, and sticking his tongue out at the camera. At first sight, it looks like any other home movie—unpretentious and amateurish. But the way it is presented adds a provocative note to the video maker's reminiscences. As we watch the images of Fung's boyhood, we hear a voiceover commentary that states: "Well, you can see from these pictures mom took of me that I was just an ordinary boy doing ordinary boy things." Fung, of course, was not

10.2. Richard Fung as a child. "I was just an ordinary boy doing ordinary boy things." From *My Mother's Place* (Richard Fung, 1990).

an ordinary boy. His self-conscious attitude toward the camera, the flamboyance of his gestures, and his openly girlish behavior say otherwise. Against what we see on the screen, Fung's commentary comes through as implausible and ironic. While *My Mother's Place* focuses mostly on his family's experiences as Chinese immigrants in Trinidad, this sequence "speaks" about Fung himself precisely by creating an incongruous relation between the visual record and the voiceover. This "disalignment" of image and sound is, as José Muñoz notes, "a deviation from traditional documentary, which is chiefly concerned with sound and image marching together as a tool of authorization" (92–93).

More common, as Muñoz reminds us, is a voiceover that reinforces—or even augments—the information in the image, a "marching together" of sounds and images. This is true in most third-person omniscient commentary. Even first-person voiceovers, such as Danae Elon's in *Another Road Home*, frequently enhance the image track by giving us the filmmaker's perspective, her inner thoughts, and by explaining what we are seeing, guiding our interpretation. Take, for instance, the scene after Elon meets up with one of Moussa's sons. Her voice, over images of the entrance to his home, admits, "I realized that I knew so little about Khalid and his family. Yet through all of the years growing up, our lives ran parallel." Similarly, in *Joyce at 34*, Chopra muses in voiceover as she picks up her bags at the airport, takes a cab into town, and enters the Block School where she is making a film: "It's too hard taking Sarah with me. I . . . I just got to take this job seriously. And as long as she is with me, all I'll think about is her. And if I don't have her with me, then I can be a person again."

Alberto Cavalcanti, the sound director of *Night Mail*, lamented this hand-in-glove correlation of sound and image, preferring instead a more confrontational or contrapuntal relation (37–38). Interestingly, *Night Mail* has both forms, the voice of omniscience, control, and certainty of the conventional, professional-sounding voiceover, and the more contrapuntal power of Auden's poem. Richard Fung's voiceover is more destabilizing, reveling in inconsistencies and ambiguities. The distance between the ostensible subject and the ironic tone of Fung's words is pronounced, the potential for secondary, connotative meanings unbound.

In addition to voiceovers, speech in interviews plays a crucial role in communicating information to the audience. And in many nonfictional works, it can be the fundamental driving force. *The Bombing of Osage Avenue* (Louis Massiah, 1987) is a good example. The commentary, by Toni Cade Bambara, provides some fresh information. But while television documentaries are often led by the voice-over commentary, in *The Bombing of Osage Avenue* the commentary frequently expands upon what has already been said by people in the neighborhood, a riff on the words of community members, bouncing off the interviews and spinning back around them again.

The precredit sequence begins, after a brief visual overview of the vicinity, with people from the Cobbs Creek community speaking about their West Philadelphia neighborhood. "We may not run in and out of everyone's house, but we all neighbors and we know each other," says Eddie Herring, who lives in the 6200 block of Pine Street. A teenage boy, Baba Renfrow, exclaims, "Like you would come past 58th and Walnut and you come past Sayre Junior High and you say, 'I know where I'm at now!'" Later, Marian C. Morris tells us, "When I moved out here in this neighborhood where I am at, it was mostly black, so I was more involved with my own people than I was where I was living before. Because I was with my own people. And I got to know so many people."

From these interviews, along with images of police in the streets, barricades, packing cars, then smoke, fire, and the sounds of rifles and machine guns, we learn of the tragedy that began on Mother's Day in 1985, when the Philadelphia police department tried to evict the organization known as MOVE from a residential neighborhood. And we learn how individuals felt about MOVE and their collective home nearby. Streetwise, sensible, poignant, and complex renditions of recent history, these interviews are the heart of the documentary. The interviewees, clearly intelligent and sensitive, speak in the vernacular and display their smiles when they talk about what Cobbs Creek means to them. They show their rage when they talk of the police invasion. And their vocal inflections alter as their feelings change. "Sunday morning we knew something was going to happen because they said we were going to have to vacate," one woman retrospectively remembers. The documentary also uses archival footage. "Why you gotta hurt 'em? There's kids in there. You're talking about children in there, all day, all night. Why you gotta hurt the kids? Think about the children! Think about the children!" shouts a woman on the street to news personnel the day of the attack.

The apparent spontaneity of the interviewees' speech contrasts sharply with Bambara's soft-spoken and clearly enunciated narration. "When you are part of a community, at home in the rhythms and rituals of a place, you don't imagine you are living on the edge of hell." Obviously written in advance with care and registered under optimal conditions in the studio, her speech was not recorded in the same space or time as the pictures; it is asynchronous. The voices from the community are direct speech, recorded on location, presumably unrehearsed, with background noise, regional accents, and variable velocity and pronunciation. There are stumbles, "you knows," "uhms," and "ahs," pauses and hesitations that can indicate an attitude toward the situation, now and then an attitude that the speaker might not have been able (or willing) to express otherwise. This can be an unconscious way of making a point—or avoiding an issue. It is a form of delivery that one seldom hears in the standard English of broadcasters or voiceover commentaries. It is the sound of community members speaking for themselves, in their own vibrant voices. These voices are not only the expression of creative power, but also, in the words of bell hooks, "a political gesture that challenges the politics of domination that would render us nameless and voiceless"—an act of resistance (126).

Shortly after the first interviews, Bambara's commentary elaborates on the testimonies: "What industry is this, your home a blazing smokestack belching up your prize possessions, neighborhood a free-fire zone and people killed?" Bambara's commentary—poetic, sharp, yet tender—never claims to be from that community. But neither is it entirely separate. Bambara's is another voice passing on stories, a sensuous, studied voice, in a timbre more often associated with bedtime stories than with voiceover commentary. "The dismemberment of a community, the relation of a people to a place, ruptured." Later we see TV news footage and still photos of an earlier attack on MOVE: "August 8th, 1978, the assault. An officer is killed. The building is bulldozed. Massive arrests. Nine members draw 30 to 100 year sentences." By minimizing subjects and verbs, and by employing the passive voice, Bambara cajoles language into a mode that is authoritative without appearing either personal or omniscient.

Six and a half minutes into the documentary, the title appears over footage of the blaze and the sound of Joe Zawinul's synthesizer: *The Bombing of Osage Avenue.*

10.3. "So I told them, 'Wait one minute. This is Mother's Day and I'm not going anyplace.'" From *The Bombing of Osage Avenue* (Louis Massiah, 1987).

Backlit by the raging fire, a helmeted official crosses the frame. Although ostensibly about Philadelphia's police department's bombing of the MOVE family's house and the 6200 block surrounding Osage Avenue, the documentary, more importantly, tells us what the catastrophe of eleven individuals dead and sixty-one homes burned down meant to the people of the West Philly neighborhood: "And the whole building was on fire.... It burned; it burned. Nobody did anything." "My heart is very heavy. I feel for those people." "You think you are just so helpless. . . . It was . . . [pause] like war." Because it also tells us of what the neighborhood meant to the people, the video forges commonalities and connections between those witnesses and the audience. Built on circles and recurrence, the story gets told again and again: the bomb drops and explodes another time, more gunfire, more people screaming, shouting, and reacting to what they see, spiraling around and around, until the agony seeps deep.

When experience is related to us through the interviewees' oral testimonies, sound is privileged and the visual is often put to its service, more illustration than new information, sometimes only supporting the sound with generic images. The reproduction, transmission, and communication of knowledge are gained mainly through the aural experience. In a way, the multiplicity of meanings inherent in those images and in the photographic image in general (its polysemy) are, to use Roland Barthes's term, "anchored" by the verbal specificity in the interviews, by the language and the passion of those voices. Linguistic elements can serve to clarify—perhaps even constrain—the multivalence of the visuals. This applies, as we have seen, to voiceovers as well. In Chris Marker's *Letter from Siberia* the same footage of a street scene is played four times, over each a different commentary, each time conferring different associations to the images. The images themselves are open to interpretation. But Marker's commentaries guide us to different understandings.

The power of the verbal in documentaries suggests that we should pay attention to word choice. This could fill a textbook in itself. For now, think of the different connotations in the following terminology: illegal aliens and undocumented workers; immigrants and settlers; emigrating and relocating; riots and uprisings; mob and crowd; global warming and climate change. . . . The term "illegal aliens," for instance, implies that these people are not valuable members of society. Criminals. The term "undocumented workers" implies that they are important to the workforce, productive members of society who do not have the proper documentation to enjoy all the fruits of our social order. Although two terms might turn up in a thesaurus as interchangeable, different nuances can change what is implied. Think of Toni Cade Bambara's (and our) repeated use of the word "community" and its connotations of communalism and kinship that words such as "population" or "public" or "society" do not have.

Music

But it is not only speech that can anchor the meaning of polysemic images. Michael Chanan writes insightfully about Santiago Álvarez's 1966 film *Cerro Pelado* (the name of the boat that brought Cuban athletes to the Central American and Caribbean Games in Puerto Rico). In the film, footage of a training camp of counterrevolutionaries is accompanied by a band arrangement of Rossini's

"William Tell Overture," familiar to Cuban and American audiences as the theme music of the television series *The Lone Ranger* (1949–1957). By adding well-known music from the western show, Álvarez presents the counterrevolutionaries as "imitation cowboys." The music, in this case, "both satiric and deflating," offers explicit commentary, like speech, conveying meaning to the images (197).

Most of the time, though, music is used in more subtle ways, as a means of creating or enhancing a certain atmosphere—or as an aesthetic device aimed at provoking a specific emotion. We are often aware of the way music helps set up the mood for a scene in a fiction film but tend to overlook its importance as a resource for documentary makers. In addition to creating atmosphere, a particular piece of music can be associated with a person or event. Or it may help designate the feeling of a time period, an era. *The Life and Times of Rosie the Riveter*, for example, uses a catchy 1942 swing tune sung by the Four Sergeants, both to bring to mind the epoch and as a signature theme playing over the introduction of the five participants and the title, reoccurring at a couple of points during the film, and returning for the closing credits. As the theme, the song has become emblematic of the film itself.

Film scholars commonly differentiate between diegetic and nondiegetic music. (The word "diegesis" means narrative in Greek.) We call it diegetic when the music is part of the world within the film, music that the people on the screen can potentially hear. Nondiegetic music, by contrast, is added to the sound track as a stylistic feature. While it has impact on the audience, it does not belong in the world represented in the film. In documentaries, diegetic music is likely to be related to the actual events and situations depicted, whereas nondiegetic music tends to provide commentary, atmosphere, or information that is not contained in the material documented. The music Chanan describes in *Cerro Pelado* is nondiegetic. He suggests it has been grafted on to conjure up the associations he mentions. But a documentary's music can also be the natural sound coming from the world that appears in the film. There might be music playing on the jukebox while someone is being interviewed in a bar, for example. Or, more widely, music or performers are the subjects of documentaries.

We have already come upon this in *Don't Look Back*, D. A. Pennebaker's film about Bob Dylan's 1965 concert tour of the United Kingdom, and in Roman Kroitor and Wolf Koenig's film about Paul Anka, *Lonely Boy*. There are also concert documentaries, such as Julian Schnabel's multiple-camera film of Lou Reed's 2006 performance of "Berlin" at St. Ann's Warehouse in Brooklyn (*Berlin*, 2007). And there are documentaries about music: Mani Kaul's *Dhrupad* (1982) on an ancient style of Hindustani classical music, for instance, or Tony Gatlif's *Latcho Drom* (1993) on Romani music.

There is, as well, at least one documentary about a single song. Humphrey Jennings's *The True Story of Lili Marlene* (1944), a British Crown film unit wartime documentary, parses the journey of "Lili Marlene," a tune about a sentry and a girl waiting under the lamplight. It documents the composition of the poem in 1923 Hamburg, its setting to music by Norbert Schultze in 1938, the song's recording by Lale Andersen, the record being played over Radio Belgrade in Nazi-occupied Yugoslavia, its enormous popularity with soldiers in the North African desert, and its eventual appropriation and transformation by British forces, who sent the song back to Germany, the same tune with different lyrics ("Oh, could we only meet once more / Our country free of shame and war . . .").

"Lili Marlene" is the sole music on the sound track. The film includes many different renditions of the song, such as an opera solo and a men's chorus, culminating in a projection into the future with it being played with no words at all on a player piano on the docks of London on a Saturday night, "when the blackout is lifted." The voiceover tells us that "the famous tune of 'Lili Marlene' will linger in the hearts of the Eighth Army as a trophy of victory and memory of the last war, to remind us all to sweep fascism off the face of the earth and make it *really* the last war." The final image is a tombstone for a warrior of unknown name and rank.

The True Story of Lili Marlene begins with an onscreen narrator explaining that "Lili Marlene" is the name of a song and "a modern fairy story." That voiceover seems to generate the images: of soldiers marching, soldiers listening, soldiers singing. . . . The music itself runs parallel to the images, with frequent points of rhythmic coincidence, so that the sound track helps establish the pace of the film. It is the melody, a fairly simple march-like rhythm that dominates the lyrics and the film.

From the very beginning of documentary during the "silent" years, music, besides drowning out the noise of the projector, was used to set emotional tones, to establish a mood or affective associations. And this has continued with music that is on the sound track, whether composed for the documentary or taken from existing sources. This type of music plays a role different from what we have in *The True Story of Lili Marlene*. Nondiegetic music, sometimes called "mood music" or "background music," is often less noticeable, more implicit. But it can subtly aid in constructing a more specific social environment, contributing to the argument and/or political concerns of the documentary. In Leni Riefenstahl's *Olympia* (1938), for instance, Herbert Windt's score is influential in conveying the political thrust of the film. The bulk of the documentary shows athletes performing in competition. But before we see any of the Olympic games, there is a striking sequence in which Riefenstahl introduces and prepares the audience for her ennobling and worshipful view of physical excellence: the prologue to the "Festival of Nations."

The ritual of the Olympic torch relay was introduced in the 1936 games in Berlin. Riefenstahl restaged it for the film, and it is German music that accompanies the torch's journey. This sequence begins with imagery from ancient Greece, accented by fog, clouds, chiaroscuro lighting, dramatic compositions, and acute camera angles. The human form is introduced as Myron's classical marble *Diskobolos* magically transforms into a silhouette of a live action discus thrower. Later the Olympic torch is passed onward by graceful, lithe, well-muscled, and near-naked runners from the archaeological site in Olympia to Bulgaria, Yugoslavia, Hungary, Austria, Czechoslovakia, and then to Germany.

Throughout this sequence, however, we never hear sounds reminiscent of music that might be found in any of these other countries, nothing that might suggest, for instance, a local folk idiom. The score is firmly grounded in the sprawling orchestral sounds of nineteenth-century German romanticism. In the beginning, a deep and earthy string sound, performed by cello and bass, plays under images of Greek ruins absent of human activity, evoking a long-buried tradition that will now be awakened from an extended sleep. The camera mostly pans slowly, and shots are connected by languid dissolves. The music too gives the impression of slow, archaic movement. Audience members versed in Western classical music can immediately recognize the strong influence of Richard Wagner, and perhaps Anton Bruckner and Johannes Brahms, as the sequence progresses. Although the film does not emphasize German athletes (indeed, it is the American track star Jesse Owens who draws the most attention), the music heard with its broad gestures, exalted emotions, and heavy orchestrations is in the German romantic style, and, one might argue, by connecting all the countries in the torch's journey, puts forth the idea of a pan-Germanic Eastern Europe (anticipating the Third Reich's expansion into that territory in their quest for "*Lebensraum*").

The lushly romantic music is an important part of *Olympia*'s rapturous idealization of the grace, poise, and vigor of the athletic physique. The music in Werner Herzog's *Lessons of Darkness*, a film discussed in chapter 8, also contributes to the veneration of its subject matter, in this case the landscape of postwar Kuwait. But here the filmmaker has chosen existing music—selections from the works of Edvard Grieg, Gustav Mahler, Arvo Pärt, Sergei Prokofiev, Franz Schubert,

Giuseppe Verdi, and Richard Wagner—and matched it to the atmosphere of stateliness and horror he is trying to evoke with his cinematography and voice-over narration.

A closer consideration of the film's opening illustrates how Herzog creates this synchronicity. As the brief credits run, *Lessons of Darkness* begins with a deep, attenuated bass tone, then a tone one-fifth higher joins the first, slowly repeating itself. These are the only sounds heard as the credits end and the disquieting prediction about the collapse of the universe appears. The tones continue as the narrator (Herzog himself in the English-language version), slowly and with little feeling, practically incants, "A planet in our solar system . . ." and we see a static shot of what looks like an otherworldly set of modern smokestacks or alien landing pads against an orange background. Then, as the image changes, we hear individual instruments (bass, wind, and brass) begin to fix the contours of the sounding major chord. These tones are repeated slowly, gracefully, neither deviating nor introducing any note that might alter the pure harmonic structure of that chord. There are no dissonances to be heard, no passing tones, only the repetitive description of this one open-sounding chord that allows nothing but its own perfection. Before long we have a new image, the view being described by the voiceover narration: "white mountain ranges, clouds, the land shrouded in mist." Accommodating the expanse of wide vistas and majestic topography, the camera here is distanced while panning

10.4. Deep, elongated tones of wind and brass over an image of "alien landing pads." From *Lessons of Darkness/Lektionen in Finsternis* (Werner Herzog, 1992).

to the right, taking in the grandeur of a mountainous landscape, and the extended string and brass notes in the music emphasize the imposing nature of what the camera is capturing. The camera pan is deliberate and unhurried, as is the music, and both image and sound seem to urge us to look and react without haste, and also perhaps to honor what we are seeing. Shortly, there is a cut to a man in a fireproof suit, silhouetted in front of a structure that is not immediately identifiable, backlit by what seems to be smoke, not mist. As the camera pans left, we eventually realize that the background is a rampant inferno. The man signals, stamps, and gestures at the camera as the music continues and the narrator informs us that "the first creature we encountered tried to communicate something to us." The music drowns out the noise of the fire and any sounds the "creature" may have been making, in a sense, muting the image. Already by the third shot, the viewer begins to feel the dislocation associated with postwar trauma. We are given little opportunity to orient ourselves in this cryptic and shadowy environment.

Soon we are seeing an unidentified "Capital City" from an aerial view as the aircraft from which the footage was taken moves forward, and the voice on the sound track tells us of the war that this city would soon undergo. Nothing in image or sound readily lets us know which city this is or where it is (it is actually Kuwait City, but it is possible to see the entire film without knowing this), and our dislocation increases. As the camera continues to track the city from above, moving steadily over the expanse of urban life, we hear a piece of what might be described as music of mourning, a simple, sad, insistent tune, sumptuously but quietly and simply orchestrated for strings. It seems to stretch out in our ears, as the city stretches out before our eyes, and again the feeling that seems intended is one of leisurely, perhaps elegiac, contemplation, observation, and remembrance. The music continues as we begin to watch low definition black-and-white archival footage of an air attack and an emergency warning siren abrasively sounds. This sequence ends in the middle of a musical phrase, almost a sonic question mark. The voiceover commentary is sparse. Throughout the film, there is barely any dialogue, and little ambient sound that is anything other than loud, crushing noise. Herzog lets the music carry the emotion.

Time and again in *Lessons of Darkness*, the music selected and excerpted contributes to a sense of disconnection, in large part because much of it insists on its own aural beauty while we are looking at exquisitely composed and austerely photographed images of devastation. We see parched land, oil-drenched terrain, dead vegetation, burning oil fields, scorched buildings, fields of bones, all to the accompaniment of precise, deliberate, grand, and lugubrious music. Herzog gives us the ideals of beauty, grandiosity, and excellence to listen to, and ugliness, destruction, and death to see. In addition to selecting acknowledged Western masterworks for his sound track, he excerpts pieces that are either explicitly sacred in nature, such as Verdi's *Requiem*, Mahler's *Resurrection*, and Pärt's *Stabat Mater*, or are taken from work where the mythological, supernatural, or godlike is part of the composer's chosen subject, such as the orchestral selections from Wagner's operas *Das Rheingold*, *Götterdämmerung*, and *Parsifal*. From *Das Rheingold*, we hear the music of the gods' triumphant entrance into Valhalla as we view a burnt landscape that will likely never again support life. The *Götterdämmerung* excerpt, which in the opera signifies the oncoming of either a terrible vengeance or the just retribution of a former goddess against ultimate evil, is heard here over

images of flames, smoke, manmade disaster, chaos, and darkness. Herzog has effectively created his own post-apocalyptic science fiction film by associating unidentified images from the trauma of what is now referred to as the First Gulf War
and its aftermath with European classical compositions that at least some of his
viewers will knowingly link to preexisting ideas of war and peace, good and evil,
mythology and religiosity, and creation and destruction. Together they create
what Herzog has called "an epic, ecstatic truth," which he contrasts with "accoun-
tants' truth," the fifteen-second clips of fires in Kuwait seen hundreds of times on
television news (Basoli 35).

Whereas much of the visual material in *Olympia* and *Lessons of Darkness* are cut
to the rhythm of the music, in *Rembrandt, Painter of Mankind/Rembrandt, Schil-
der van de Mens* (Bert Haanstra, 1957) music often provides continuity, easing
changes of images by bridging transitions. The film consists entirely of images of
Rembrandt's paintings, primarily portraits and groups of figures. It is structured
by a linear chronology. A voiceover tells us about his life and his artistic vision.
The music smoothes over transitions to reinforce chronology; it continues as the
images change, even when the voice stops. It starts up again after a fade, awaiting
the next image and the next segment of Rembrandt's story.

The score for *Rembrandt, Painter of Mankind*, composed especially for the film
by Jan Mul, strongly supports and enhances the images. Firmly entrenched in
Western classical tradition, although not at all in the style of Rembrandt's time,
the score is identifiable as generically "Western," "classical," and "cultured" music.
We have seen in *Africa, I Will Fleece You* and *The Life and Times of Rosie the Riveter* how music can be used to designate an era. Here, however, the music befits
a reverent film about the paintings of one of the world's most famous exponents
of Western culture, a figure who has transcended his time. And in keeping with a
more focused and intimate view of one person, the score is written for a chamber
ensemble, employing a smaller group of instruments and leaner sound than *Olympia's* symphony orchestra. In *Rembrandt, Painter of Mankind*, it is possible to pick
out the individual instruments in possession of a melodic fragment, and listeners
can discern them when heard in the group. We can also track the use of motifs, a
musical trope long embedded in Western classical music. For example, we hear the
combination of harp and flute whenever the voiceover refers to Rembrandt's wife.
This instrumental combination also appears at points when the narrator is telling
about religious subjects in Rembrandt's painting, thereby equating marital love
and religious devotion with the same open, airy and somewhat reverential sound.

In *Lessons of Darkness*, music frequently replaced the natural sound, rendering the images "silent." In *Rembrandt, Painter of Mankind* the music provides the

sounds for the naturally silent images. When we see the painting of the marching company of burghers, *The Night Watch*, for example, we hear twenty seconds of a military march, a rolling drum that keeps precision time with a piping piccolo. The music mimics the painting's imagined action, bringing the burghers and the drummer in the foreground to life.

The music also facilitates transitions by anticipating changes. Upon the announcement of Rembrandt's marriage to Saskia, the voiceover says, "They marry. He is successful! [Now louder and quite excited] Life is gay!" The flutes take a more prominent role, sounding florid arpeggios, continuing after the voice stops, as a brass fanfare joins in. After Saskia dies, even before the voiceover tells us that Rembrandt and his son Titus were not alone for long, the music predicts the happy news of a new wife by reintroducing the harp and flute combination, now with an added cello, in a three-quarter meter with an accelerated tempo. Like the other background music we have been considering, the use of music—harmonies, melodies, rhythm, orchestration, and construction—is both thematic and formal.

In *F for Fake/Vérités et mensonges* (Orson Welles, 1974), music takes a more aggressive role, contributing to the trickery of the documentary. The score, by Michel Legrand, is playful, at times deliberately commanding our attention when a phrase or musical quote is inserted to purposefully attract the ear (a recurring violin at "dramatic" moments in the story being told); at other times enhancing a mood already implied by images and/or narration (a jazzy waltz pattern with vibes first heard during a "girl-watching" sequence); and still at other times, being used as one of the many tricks that are in the arsenal of the filmmaker—and are part of the subject of the documentary.

The film begins with Orson Welles's easily recognizable voice over black leader, then over an image of a train in a European station. (In contrast to filmmaker Herzog's flatly spoken commentary, Welles's presentation is self-consciously theatrical.) His image finally appears, mid-body in flowing black cape and white gloves; he calls a small child "sir," suggests he hold a key ten feet over his head, and warns the boy to watch out for the slightest hint of hanky-panky. We see a shot of a film crew in the station. But we cannot see what they are shooting. There is a cut to a woman in furs in the train window watching. But we do not know who she is. "Before our very eyes," a key is transformed into a coin. Finally the camera tilts up and we see Orson Welles's face, trim gray beard, and huge black hat. And the little boy finds his key back in his pocket. Welles boasts of being "a charlatan." But he insists that the key was not symbolic of anything. "This isn't that kind of movie."

What kind of movie *is* it? The ostensible subject is the art forger Elmyr de Hory, who, over many years, painted in the styles of several well-known artists and successfully passed off his work as original to dealers, connoisseurs, and world-class art museums. We get the story of de Hory and his forgeries as well as the story of his eventual exposure and celebrity in the book *Fake!* by another figure, who later turned out to be a different sort of forger, Clifford Irving. But the film itself is also in the business of perpetrating some conscious tricks of its own. "Plotlines" aren't always relayed sequentially; new narratives appear at points in the film where the already present ones have not yet been resolved; frames freeze in mid-action; editing constructs time and space that may not be real; and the music confuses viewers about its purpose and source. These elements of trickery, like a pack of cards, are frequently shuffled and redealt in different configurations and it's very possible that, in this particular deck, the cards may be stacked. The film employs a battery of techniques to seduce the viewer into its story (or stories): quick cutting, shattered chronology, visual chaos, the truncation and redirection of narrative threads, and aural confusion.

That beginning is a few minutes of hocus-pocus. Welles performs magic tricks for the small boy, who is trying to follow his motions. But, unlike the child, the film spectators know that that magic can be performed with a simple edit. And the camera is so close to some of the tricks that there is no hiding where the coins come from. The boy and the audience are presented to Welles's "partner" François Reichenbach, who peers out from behind the camera and chirps, "Hello." (Reichenbach, who was the co-producer of this film, but not credited with camerawork, shot earlier footage for a documentary about de Hory, much of which was incorporated by Welles into *F for Fake.*) On the sound track we hear what we might call "tune-up" music, suggesting a sort of pre-performance period, the disordered sounds a group of musicians makes before a conductor appears to unite them into a single orchestral entity. And this is appropriate, because this sequence is actually a prelude to the body of the film. The filmmaker tells us that some sort of possible reality-bending is either going to be explored or exploited in this film: "Now it's time for an introduction. . . . this is a film about trickery—and fraud— about [dramatic pause] lies. . . . Almost any story is almost certainly some kind of lie. But not this time. No; this is a promise. During the next hour, everything you hear from us is really true and based on solid facts." This statement contains not only the filmmaker's proclamation of the subject of *F for Fake* but also a declaration of a commitment to both veracity and the aforementioned trickery. The running time of the film, however, is eighty-five minutes, not an hour. Are the last twenty-some minutes "really true"? Based on available facts? "Fake! Fake! Fake!" fills the screen while cascading violin music carries us away.

F for Fake plays tricks on the audience, both as an entertainment device and to enhance its observations on the moral ironies of illusionism, inducing us to think further about the subject. One of the tricks is the music itself. It is not always apparent whether the music is diegetic or nondiegetic, and this vagary contributes to the teasing nature in which the narrative unfolds. An example is a fragment of music, a violin played at breakneck speed, used several times in the film, first appearing as the "Fake! Fake! Fake!" covers the screen, just before Elmyr de Hory is introduced. The notes are many and quick. There is a rather jovial quality to the melody line, enhanced by the speed of the phrasing, but also an uncomfortable, grating, aural quality as the bow scrapes against two or more of the violin's strings, creating dissonance, like nails on a blackboard. It is highly kinetic music, and it matches in tone much of the similarly kinetic feel of the film's editing. It is heard at various moments in the film, usually when some aspect of a "character's" narration, or the film's narrative, may be questionable, or when a "character" in the film is straightforwardly espousing general or specific thoughts on the nature of forgery, authenticity, revelation or concealment, the music reminding us that some form of deception may be in play. One example of this is when Welles, commenting on the sound track, says that "Elmyr himself is a fake faker"; the fiddling reappears and jumps into action, and this time the split-second speed and tempo are coupled with a short sequence of fast-motion that depicts "the true Paganini of the palette" creating a painting. The shakes and screeches created by the music correspond with the rapid movements of Elmyr's brushwork.

Part of the deceptive feeling of the music is that we can't immediately tell if the "characters" in the film hear it or not. Pieces of filmed interviews with various subjects are sometimes quickly cut together as the music continues over the shots, or over freeze frames, giving the impression that this music was added to the sound track after the film was edited. But at other moments, some of these cuts seem to take place in a space (perhaps de Hory's home?) with many people present, drinking and laughing, as if at a party where music is playing in the background. In these sequences, it is possible to conclude that the music originates from within the film space.

Welles's film confounds the notion that trustworthy information can be gleaned from a documentary. And in doing so, the film explores many of the questions that have occupied us throughout the book, questions about authenticity, authority, evidence, ethics, and the creative tools that documentary film and video makers use to reshape reality into something worthy of notice. The story of a few fakers is wrought into an amusingly jaded, and wry, meditation about art and forgery, the factual and the confabulated, aesthetic value and commerce, sleight of hand, expertise, and the alternately revealing or concealing ways in which cine-matic stories are told, including the apparently "true" stories we expect to find in documentaries.

F for Fake is consistent with the contract it sets up with its audience in the first few minutes of the film. The sounds and images in this film, and, indeed, the sounds and images in most documentaries, are attempts to impose order on the discontinuity and otherness of the sociohistorical world. But the order Welles imposes is clearly not meant to provide easy answers or reassuring affirmations, as much as to provoke new disquieting questions. Whether they are extensively researched and lavishly photographed and scored historical epics, such as Ken Burns's documentaries, or more intimate and personal ruminations, such as *F for Fake*, these creative treatments of actuality, to evoke Grierson once again, take complex ideas and express them in visual and aural form, fashioning the docu-mentary's reality and crafting its truths.

Additional Filmography

The Song of Ceylon (Basil Wright, 1934)

A Stravinsky Portrait (Richard Leacock, 1966)

Gimme Shelter (Albert and David Maysles, 1970)

Gotta Make This Journey: Sweet Honey in the Rock (Michelle Parkinson, 1985)

Buena Vista Social Club (Wim Wenders, 1999)

Crossing the Bridge: The Sounds of Istanbul/İstanbul Hatırası (Fatih Akin, 2005)

Shine a Light (Martin Scorsese, 2008)

Works Cited and Further Reading

Anthony, Scott. *Night Mail: BFI Film Classics.* London: British Film Institute, 2007.

Barthes, Roland. "Rhetoric of the Image." In *Image, Music, Text*, ed. and trans. Stephen Heath. New York: Hill and Wang, 1977.

Basoli, A. G. "The Wrath of Klaus Kinski: An Interview with Werner Herzog." *Cineaste* 33 (1999).

Bruzzi, Stella. *New Documentary.* 2nd ed. New York: Routledge, 2006.

Bukatman, Scott, "Incompletion, Simulation and the Refusal of the Real: The Last Films of Orson Welles." *Persistence of Vision* 7 (1989).

Cavalcanti, Alberto. "Sound in Film." *Films: A Quarterly of Discussion and Analy-sis* 1.1 (November 1939).

Chanan, Michael. *The Politics of Documentary.* London: British Film Institute, 2007.

Corner, John. "Sounds Real: Music and Documentary." In *New Challenges for Documentary*, 2nd ed., ed. Alan Rosenthal and John Corner. Manchester: Manchester University Press, 2005.

Doane, Mary Ann. "The Voice in the Cinema: Articulation of the Body and the Space." *Yale French Studies* 60 (1980).

Gaines, Jane M. "*Lonely Boy* and the *Vérité* of Sexuality." *Canadian Journal of Film Studies* 8.1 (Spring 1999).

hooks, bell. "Talking Back." *Discourse* 8 (Fall/Winter 1986/87).

Leacock, Richard. "The Deep Well: Richard Leacock, Interviewed by Louis Marcorelles." *Contrast* 3 (Autumn 1964).

Muñoz, José, "The Autoethnographic Performance: Reading Richard Fung's Queer Hybridity." *Screen* 36.2 (Summer 1995).

Winston, Brian. *Claiming the Real II: Documentary: Grierson and Beyond.* London: British Film Institute; New York: Palgrave Macmillan, 2008.

INDEX

ABOUT THE AUTHORS

Louise Spence, professor of cinema studies at Kadir Has University in Istanbul, has published more than twenty articles in various journals and anthologies. She is also the author of *Watching Daytime Soap Operas: The Power of Pleasure* and coauthor (with Pearl Bowser) of the award-winning *Writing Himself into History: Oscar Micheaux, His Silent Films, and His Audiences.*

Vinicius Navarro is assistant professor of film studies at the Georgia Institute of Technology. He has written on documentary and experimental cinemas and on global television formats. He is currently working on an anthology on recent Latin American documentaries.